Photographs from the
Gerry Cranham Library

Contributions from
JOHN FRANCOME
GRAHAM GOODE
JOHN McCRIRICK
JIM McGRATH
JOHN OAKSEY
DEREK THOMPSON
JOHN TYRREL

The Channel Four
Book of
RACING

Sean Magee

With an introduction by
BROUGH SCOTT

Sidgwick & Jackson
LONDON
in association with
Channel Four Television Company

First published in hardback in Great Britain in October 1989 by Sidgwick & Jackson Limited

First published in paperback in a revised and updated edition October 1990

ISBN 0–283–06061–1

Designed by Ray Addicott

Phototypeset by Opus, Oxford
Printed in Great Britain by
Butler and Tanner Ltd,
Frome and London
for Sidgwick & Jackson Limited,
1 Tavistock Chambers,
Bloomsbury Way,
London WC1A 2SG

Cover, front
Mr Frisk leading in the 1990 Whitbread Gold Cup at Sandown Park.

Cover, back
Brough Scott interviews Pat Eddery, Newmarket, April 1990.

Half-title
Willie Carson and Salsabil after winning the General Accident One Thousand Guineas at Newmarket, May 1990.

Title spread
Quest For Fame (Pat Eddery) wins the Ever Ready Derby at Epsom, June 1990.

CONTENTS

PREFACE

Some years ago a friend of mine with at least one PhD decided that she would like to enlarge her education with a day at the races, so I took her to a National Hunt meeting at Newbury. On the way to the paddock for the first race she perused the racecard and asked me what '11 10' meant in a column of numbers against a horse's name. 'That's his weight,' I answered, but my friend was still perplexed. 'Sean,' she asked, 'how can a horse weigh 11 stone 10 pounds?'

Not everyone with a genuine interest in horse racing is quite as familiar with the niceties of the sport as they might wish to be, and the aim of *The Channel Four Book of Racing* is to supply some basic information about the nature of horse racing in Britain – its structure, rules, procedures and personalities – both for those with very little knowledge of it and for others who regularly enjoy racing through television or the occasional day at the races and are seeking more enjoyment through a greater appreciation of what is going on. Racing – as Brough Scott stresses in his introduction – is fun: and the more you know about it, the more fun you will find.

The book includes chapters on form and on betting, for these are integral parts of the sport, but it can provide no magical formula for flawless interpretation of form or a way to beat the bookies. Yet the appeal of racing goes far beyond the attempt to find winners, and just as the Channel Four transmission aims to convey an overall picture of the Turf, so the book, as a companion to that coverage, intends to provide a general introduction to the many aspects of this fascinating world – to the racehorse and its breeding, to administration and control, to the racecourse and to the owners, trainers, jockeys, officials and others who people it, to the excitement and lingering memories of the race itself. The book cannot tell you everything you might want to know, yet we hope that it will give you at least a flavour of the extraordinary sport of racing.

The Channel Four Book of Racing was first published in hardback in October 1989, and is now offered in paperback in a thoroughly revised and updated form. The overall structure of the book and much of the original text have been preserved, though the details of rules, procedures and personalities have been amended where appropriate, so that the book is as accurate as we can make it at the end of July 1990. This has meant altering where necessary the names of some of the major races to take account of changes in sponsorship, but as in the earlier edition it has proved impractical to signal every change of a race's name over the years: the major races at Channel Four courses listed on pages 45–55 have been given their 1990 names as far as is possible, and into that section has been introduced Uttoxeter, a course which will be covered by Channel Four for the first time in 1991.

But change has not been introduced for its own sake, and the text has not been arbitrarily tampered with where the original example serves to illustrate a general point. Thus the glorious figure of Nashwan, who strode through the pages of the first edition as he strode through the summer of 1989, still looms large.

ILLUSTRATIONS

The majority of the photographs in this book are from the Gerry Cranham Library. Though most of these were taken by Gerry Cranham himself, several – including the famous shot of the Queen Mother and admirer on page 201 – are by his son Mark.

Photographs in the book which are not from the Gerry Cranham Library come from the following sources: Flyingbolt and Fort Leney (page 29), the author; the point-to-pointers on page 76, Mike Roberts; Derek Thompson with Larry Hagman and Linda Gray (page 87), Tony Edenden; Dorothy Paget (page 89) and Gordon Richards (page 131), Hulton-Deutsch Collection; the photo-finish pictures (pages 100 and 185), Racecourse Technical Services; racegoers (page 203), Richard Schofield. Reproductions of the *Vanity Fair* caricatures of Fred Archer and Tod Sloan (pages 126 and 127) are supplied by the author. The photographs of the Channel Four team in action on Derby Day 1990 (pages 192–7) were taken by Mel Fordham.

Graham Goode's Derby racecard (page 110) is reproduced with Graham's permission. The map of courses in the British Isles (page 44), the owners' colours (page 97) and the drawings of equipment (page 173) are by Jackie Hunt.

The racecourse plans of the Channel Four courses (pages 45–55) are reproduced by kind permission of the *Racing Post*. The designs for owners' colours (page 96) are printed by permission of Weatherbys, and the form on page 142 by permission of the *Sporting Life* and the *Racing Post*. The spread from the Sandown Park racecard (page 204) is included by kind permission of the Clerk of the Course.

As the necessary revising of this book has shown, racing is a sport which is constantly changing – not only in its equine and human heroes and heroines and in its records, but in its very structure. The introduction of all-weather racing, for instance, has caused the Jockey Club to revise the definition of the Flat season, which officially now runs from 1 January to 31 December – though most followers of the sport consider that the season still goes from March to November as before. But the aim of *The Channel Four Book of Racing* is unchanged: to add to the enjoyment of those under the spell of this fascinating but complex sport by explaining how it all works.

Acknowledgments

The considerable list of people whose help with the first edition of this book is gratefully acknowledged therein has been augmented with this paperback, and a few fresh expressions of thanks are in order: to Hilary Davies and Ingrid Connell at Sidgwick and Jackson for their profound understanding of how the later an updated edition is delivered, the more up-to-date will it be; to Nick Withers at Opus; and to Peter O'Sullevan.

Several who had assisted with the first edition renewed the favour, and I am grateful for continued support to Andrew Franklin and all the Channel Four Racing team; to Norman Millward at Racecourse Technical Services; to Susanna Yager at Channel Four; to Gerry Cranham; to Mel Fordham; to Susie and Simon Finch and Andrea Findlay; to Charlie Webster; to Robert Cooper; and to Richard Beadle. I am especially grateful to Michael and Louise Wigley (without whom . . .) and to Gillian Bromley (ditto).

S.M.

INTRODUCTION

The attractions of racing are as simple or as complicated as you care to make them. Let's hope you can say the same for our programmes on Channel Four.

We should never lose the thrill of the simple things: the Thoroughbred racehorse at full gallop, the thunder of hooves as the runners swing round the final turn, the crash of the birch as steeplechasers reach for the sky, and the shouting, possessive excitement as the horse you have backed – 'your' horse – stretches for the line. On that level we can all enjoy the vivid, instant excitement of the race itself, and make a pin-sticking attempt at the galloping jigsaw of selecting a horse and having a bet.

But the real fun of this game is that the deeper you go the better it gets. There's no sporting activity that can involve you so completely, in which you follow the participants (both two-legged and four-legged) from the cradle to the grave: in fact, if you become a complete racing boffin the cradle is only second base, for long and serious discussions go on about exactly which stallion should dally with which mare to produce the horse which wins the prizes and lands the bets.

We are not really into breeding on Channel Four, although we do have Lord Oaksey – and if you got a pound every time John McCririck mentioned that 'My Noble Lord' went to Eton and he to Harrow you would have become a millionaire long ago. What we are trying to do is open the door into racing's absurd and glorious world and invite you in.

Come and meet the jockeys and trainers, men (and nowadays a few very talented women) who spend their whole working lives pondering the mental and physical problems of making one horse run faster than another.

Come and hear all the buzz of the betting ring, that frenetic little island of hope from which, before each race, McCririck desperately semaphores out how the money seems to be going.

Come and watch and re-watch the split-second decisions that need to be taken at the gallop. Analyse the potential of young horses as they develop like young plants through the Flat racing season. Assess the bravery of horse and man as they tackle the fences when the jumpers clash.

The beauty of Channel Four Racing is that we now have the chance to show you the best of all these bandy-legged worlds. In Britain we have the Derby, all the home Classics and top jumping. We have the big events from Ireland and from France, including the Prix de l'Arc de Triomphe, that autumn showdown in Paris. We have been to Australia, America and even – heaven help us – shown racing on the ice in St Moritz. In 1988 we flew to Woodbine racecourse in Toronto on a Friday night and got back on Sunday morning. The wife of one of the presenters was in bed when the team left and still there when he returned on the Sabbath: he never did discover about the interval.

Sometimes, disgracefully, some of us whinge about the hassle of it all. The truth is that we are almost ashamed of having the best fun in the firmament. Our only justification, on the screen or in these pages, is that we share some of the fun with you.

Brough Scott joined *The Independent on Sunday* in 1990 after writing on racing for the *Sunday Times* since 1974, and has presented the sport on television since 1981. The rider of over 100 winners as an amateur and professional National Hunt jockey between 1963 and 1971, he is the author of *The World of Flat Racing* and *On and Off the Rails*, and was voted Sports Journalist of the Year in 1984. In 1988 he also became Editorial Director of the *Racing Post*.

HORSES

John Francome was champion National Hunt jockey on seven occasions during a notable riding career described on page 132. He is the author of several successful books, notably his autobiography *Born Lucky*.

Racing is about horses, and the physical appearance of a horse before its race will tell you much about its chances. It is more than just coincidence that the horse judged to be the best turned-out in the paddock often transpires to be the winner, for most of the time the way that a horse appears mirrors the way that it feels – although it is easy to confuse a horse that is very relaxed with one that is tired, just as it is easy to confuse a horse that is on its toes with one that is fretting: in both cases it's a question of experience and of getting to know horses as individuals. It is certainly as interesting to study horses in the paddock as it is to see how they perform on the course, and equally as important if you want to improve your chances of backing a winner.

Sometimes I can look at horses before a race and one or two will immediately stand out from the others. It may be because they are more physically imposing, or that they look healthier in their condition, or often a combination. Sometimes they will all look about the same no matter how closely you consider them. Never force yourself to like a horse: there's always another race.

There is no doubt that observing horses in the paddock is most rewarding in the early part of the season when fitness is at a premium, and it is obvious even to the fairly novice observer which horses have being doing the most work at home. As the season progresses I tend to take more notice of the way horses are developing. Some big backward types will often begin to lose condition after just a couple of runs as the extra effort of racing compared with working at home takes its toll, whereas a smaller, stockier sort of animal that has all but stopped growing will suddenly begin to thrive.

Like human athletes, the general shape of racehorses reflects the type of distance they are best suited to running. Sprinters, built for power, are nearly all muscle, while long-distance runners tend to be lean, relying on stamina. If there are two horses in a race that I like the look of, I choose the one who seems better built to do the job.

Once you've made up your mind about a horse, watch how it moves to the start. If you're on the course, it's well worth running down to the one-furlong marker to observe it at close quarters as it canters down: you will be able to see whether it likes the ground or not and whether it is enjoying striding out, whatever the going happens to be. But a word of warning: don't do what I did on my first visit to Ripon and run the wrong way, or you'll miss it!

Previous pages:
The stallion Rainbow Quest.

THE THOROUGHBRED

A glorious compound of power and elegance, of strength and beauty, of stamina and speed, the English Thoroughbred racehorse is a highly specialized animal whose evolution has been skilfully contrived by breeders over the three hundred years since the importation of Arabian stallions at the end of the seventeenth century. Its influence has been huge: all the major racing nations of the world (and most of the minor) have imported English Thoroughbreds and based their own breeds of racehorse on the English model.

All modern Thoroughbreds trace their ancestry in the male line to just three founding stallions brought to England from the Near East. The Byerley Turk, foaled around 1680, had seen action at the Battle of the Boyne before being sent to stud in County Durham: among his distinguished descendants in more recent times is The Tetrarch, 'The

Typical of the modern late-maturing horse, five-year-old Mtoto (right), ridden by Michael Roberts, gets up to land the 1988 Coral–Eclipse Stakes at Sandown Park from Shady Heights.

Spotted Wonder' who was unbeaten in seven races in 1913 and was probably one of the fastest horses of all time. The Godolphin Arabian, foaled in 1724 and (according to some accounts) discovered in Paris pulling a water cart, is the direct ancestor of 1964 Derby winner Santa Claus. But the most influential of the three was the Darley Arabian, foaled in 1700 and sent to England as a four-year-old. He is the progenitor of the vast majority of modern Thoroughbreds, and many of the most powerful bloodlines of the twentieth century are offshoots of his, notably that of Northern Dancer, sire of Nijinsky and The Minstrel and grandsire of Dancing Brave.

Apparently none of the three founding sires ever raced, but it was not long before their influence on the racing scene became very marked. The Darley Arabian's son Flying Childers, foaled in 1714, is held to be the first truly great English racehorse despite running in only two races, and Flying Childers's full brother Bartlett's Childers was the great-grandsire of the legendary Eclipse.

Eclipse, foaled in 1764, was bred by the Duke of Cumberland, and sold on the Duke's death in 1765 to William Wildman, a Smithfield meat salesman, for 75 guineas. Wildman allowed Eclipse plenty of time to mature and did not put the horse into serious training until he was five years old. In April 1769 he held a secret trial on Banstead Downs, near Epsom, which touts tried to witness. According to a contemporary report, the touts arrived late: 'But they found an old woman who gave them all the information they wanted. On inquiring whether she had seen a race, she replied she could not tell whether it was a race or not, but she had just seen a horse with a white leg running away at a monstrous rate, and another horse a great way behind, trying to run after him; but she was sure he never would catch the white-legged horse if he ran to the world's end.' Eclipse – the 'horse with a white leg' – first ran in public the following month, in a race of four-mile heats at Epsom. Favourite at 4–1 on following rumours of the trial, he won the first heat with ease, at which point an Irish gambler named Dennis O'Kelly bet that he could predict the placings of the runners in the next heat in their correct finishing order. When challenged to do so he pronounced the phrase which was to become part of racing language: 'Eclipse first, the rest nowhere.' His prediction – that all the other runners would be 'distanced' by Eclipse (that is, finish over 240 yards behind him) – proved triumphantly correct, and O'Kelly went on to purchase a half share in the horse for 650 guineas, and later the other half for 1,100 guineas. In eighteen races Eclipse was never headed, let alone beaten, and never whipped or spurred. Retiring to stud in 1771, he sired three of the first five Derby winners.

Eclipse's skeleton is now in the National Horseracing Museum in Newmarket: even in that condition he'd probably be a good bet most years in the great Sandown Park race which bears his name.

Two other famous horses of the Eclipse era ensured the perpetuation of the lines of the Byerley Turk and the Godolphin Arabian. Herod, a great-great-grandson of the Byerley Turk, was bred like Eclipse by William, Duke of Cumberland, and foaled in 1758. After a fine racing career his achievements at stud included siring the winners of 1,042 races, among them three of the first five runnings of the Oaks, but as a racehorse he had been prone to break blood vessels, and is thought to

Kincsem, an Austro-Hungarian filly foaled in 1874, was unbeaten in fifty-four races, including the Goodwood Cup in 1878.

be the source of this tendency in many modern Thoroughbreds. Matchem (born 1748) combined in his pedigree strains from both the Godolphin Arabian and the Byerley Turk, and was one of the few racehorses in history to have been much more successful as a stallion than as a racer: blessed with exceptional longevity and virility, he covered a mare at the extreme age of thirty-three (and got her in foal) a few days before his death.

The Eclipse, Herod and Matchem lines are the only direct sire lines which have lasted to modern times, but mention should also be made of two other famous eighteenth-century racehorses. Highflyer, a son of Herod enjoying almost equal proportions of the blood of the three founding sires, was never beaten in races and proved a highly successful stallion. And Gimcrack, the tiny grey commemorated in the famous two-year-old race at the York August meeting, has the distinction of being the first English horse to make a raid on France, winning a match by covering twenty-two and a half miles in one hour in 1766. Ironically, on the two occasions when he raced at York, he was beaten.

The late eighteenth century was also a time of great change in the pattern of racing in England, with the exceptionally long races (usually around four miles) run in heats gradually giving way to different sorts of race and rendering obsolete the practice of waiting until horses reached the age of four or five before starting their racing careers. Two-year-old races were instituted late in the century; the introduction of handicaps, aiming to level out the chances of the field, made horse racing a more entertaining betting medium; and, most significantly, what became the Classic races were first staged – the St Leger in 1776, the Oaks in 1779 and the Derby in 1780, with the Guineas races following early in the next century (see pages 70–6).

As these developments became established in the nineteenth century, racehorses were bred to run faster and to mature earlier, and they were bigger. The Darley Arabian had stood 15 hands, and Eclipse was considered tall at 15 hands 3 inches. By the middle of the nineteenth century the average Thoroughbred was about six inches taller than his forebear of a century and a half earlier, and decades of selective and judicious breeding in conditions of better feeding and care had brought about major improvements in speed and scope, if not in constitution. Now the major aim was precocity, a trend which continued well into the twentieth century, as the status of staying races continued to decline and breeders concentrated on producing animals capable of winning over five and six furlongs as two-year-olds, even though the accepted ideal of the English Thoroughbred was the horse capable of staying one and a half miles as a three-year-old – the conditions of the Derby. The imposition of the Pattern (see page 69) has encouraged a move away from extreme precocity: there is no Group 1 race for two-year-olds in Britain before October, and it is very significant that many of the top Classic horses of recent years have not been raced at all at the highest level as juveniles: Nashwan ran in two fairly minor races as a two-year-old (the first in August), as did Dancing Brave; and Kahyasi and Quest For Fame ran only once at two.

And like most Thoroughbred racehorses, Quest For Fame has an ancestry that can be traced back, through Eclipse, to the Darley Arabian.

HOW THE DARLEY ARABIAN BRED QUEST FOR FAME

THE DARLEY ARABIAN
|
Bartlett's Childers
|
Squirt
|
Marske
|
ECLIPSE
|
Pot-8-os
|
Waxy
|
Whalebone
|
Sir Hercules
|
Birdcatcher
|
The Baron
|
Stockwell
|
Doncaster
|
Bend Or
|
Bona Vista
|
Cyllene
|
Polymelus
|
Phalaris
|
Pharos
|
Nearco
|
Nasrullah
|
Red God
|
Blushing Groom
|
Rainbow Quest
|
QUEST FOR FAME

EIGHT FAVOURITES

Everyone with the slightest interest in racing has favourite horses, and the criteria for attracting such affection vary: it may be that the horse did you a particularly good turn at 'double carpet', or it may be an old campaigner whose continued participation year after year brought continuity to the experience of following the sport; or a horse who was simply so good that its every appearance was a great racing occasion, or a horse who triggers special memories – the grounds are numerous, but to take a horse to your heart is one of the best experiences of racing. The following eight memorable racehorses cover the whole span of the sport, and each has a particular place in the affections of one of the Channel Four Racing team.

Desert Orchid

I've never met anyone – equine or human – who enjoys racing more than Desert Orchid. There's no need to worry about whether he'll win or not – all you've got to do is watch and enjoy a truly great racehorse.

DEREK THOMPSON

Desert Orchid's summer break in 1990 at Richard Burridge's Yorkshire stud was interrupted by a very special appointment – indeed, a royal appointment – when on 27 June he took part in the parade in London to mark the ninetieth birthday of the Queen Mother, joining two of Her Majesty's own great favourites Special Cargo and The Argonaut to offer National Hunt racing's own tribute to its greatest patron. His presence in the parade was entirely fitting, for over the past few seasons he had won an unshakeable place in the affections of the British public, who had taken to their hearts this dashing grey with the cavalier style of jumping and the indomitable spirit who by the end of the 1989–90 season had won thirty-two of his

Desert Orchid (Simon Sherwood) jumps the last fence to win the King George VI Rank Chase at Kempton Park in December 1988.

sixty-two starts, brought his owners half a million pounds in prize money, and been raised to the status of a national hero, complete with fan club.

There was little evidence of the rapture to come when on 21 January 1983 Desert Orchid ran his first race in the Walton Novices' Hurdle at Kempton Park: he fell. His first season consisted of four runs, with a second at Sandown Park his best placing, but the following season he won six of his eight starts, though he was unplaced behind Dawn Run in the Champion Hurdle. In the 1984–85 term he won only once from eight starts, and was tailed off in the Sagaro Stakes at Ascot on his only outing on the Flat. But when he switched to steeplechasing in the winter of 1985 he was an immediate success, winning four chases, including three of the top novice events of the season. By the 1986–87 season Desert Orchid was one of the most popular jumpers in training, his superbly bold jumping and attacking, front-running style endearing him to all who saw him. But he was thought to be very much a two-mile chaser, and when he lined up for the King George VI Rank Chase at Kempton Park on Boxing Day 1986 he seemed to stand little chance against such top-notch staying chasers as Wayward Lad, Forgive 'N Forget, and Combs Ditch – the last of which David Elsworth's stable jockey Colin Brown chose to ride instead of the grey. Ridden for the first time by Simon Sherwood, Desert Orchid started at 16–1, but announced his extraordinary versatility in the most emphatic style by running the rest of the field into the ground, building up a sizeable lead in the early stages which he maintained to the line. He won twice more that season before being returned to two miles for the Queen Mother Champion Chase at the Cheltenham National Hunt Festival, where he finished a highly honourable third behind Pearlyman and Very Promising. The following year he was second to Nupsala in the King George after setting an unsustainable pace with Beau Ranger, and second to Pearlyman in the Queen Mother Chase at Cheltenham; but reunited with Simon Sherwood he won at the Liverpool Grand National meeting and then raised the roof at Sandown Park when holding off Kildimo to take the 1988 Whitbread Gold Cup.

By the end of 1988 Desert Orchid had won three more chases (including a second King George), and two fine victories under large weights in handicaps paved the way for his first bid at the Cheltenham Gold Cup. Rain and snow had turned the Cheltenham going into a morass and the course was thought not to be to his liking: two fences out he seemed well held by Yahoo, who still held a narrow lead at the last (see page 108). But Desert Orchid clawed his way back up the hill to win by one and a half lengths and unleash scenes as emotional as any witnessed on a British racecourse. Partnered by Richard Dunwoody following Simon Sherwood's retirement, he was back for the Gold Cup a year later, having won a third King George and three other chases. But he could finish only third behind 100–1 winner Norton's Coin and Toby Tobias. Any suggestion that he was past his best was dispelled by a brilliant victory under twelve stone in the Jameson Irish Grand National at Fairyhouse, where he won by twelve lengths (despite making an almighty hash of the last fence) and was accorded a rousing ovation by the wildly enthusiastic Irish crowd – who, after all, know a great chaser when they see one.

Desert Orchid once ran in blinkers – in the Blue Circle Welsh Champion Hurdle at Chepstow on 8 April 1985. He was pulled up.

Freddie

But for the 1965 Grand National and Freddie I'm sure I would not now be working in racing. That great spectacle, his gallant second, and his subsequent races captured my imagination. I was hooked – completely!

JIM MCGRATH

Like many other famous horses – Crisp, Wyndburgh, Bustino – Freddie is best remembered for a race he did not win. But his heroic part in the memorable finish of the 1965 Grand National will always be remembered by anyone who saw it.

Freddie was reared and trained by his owners Reg and Betty Tweedie near Kelso in Scotland, where part of his training routine included rounding up sheep on the farm. He graduated to steeplechasing from hunting and point-to-points and soon became one of the finest and most popular hunter-chasers of the modern period, winning the Foxhunters' Chase at Cheltenham in 1964 and failing by only half a length to concede 22 pounds to Popham Down in the Scottish Grand National at Bogside. The next year saw his first attempt at the Liverpool National. Carrying 11 stone 10 pounds and starting favourite at 7–2, he engaged in a furious battle in the closing stages with Jay Trump, trained by Fred Winter and ridden by the American amateur Tommy Smith. At the last fence Jay Trump held a slight lead; Freddie battled back, and at the Elbow looked as if he would pass his rival, but Jay Trump would not be denied, and at the post had three quarters of a length to spare over his gallant rival. It had been one the greatest finishes in the history of the race.

After taking second behind Arkle in the 1965 Hennessy Gold Cup, Freddie made a fresh attempt at the Grand National the following spring. Once more favourite (at the absurd price of 11–4), once more he found a Fred Winter runner too good: this time it was the outsider Anglo who sploshed home twenty lengths in front. The next season Freddie won the Gallaher Gold Cup at Sandown and took part in his third Grand National. But this was 1967, and in the famous mayhem at the twenty-third fence Freddie, in company with most of the field, was brought to a halt. He eventually got over the obstacle but by then Foinavon was well on his way to one of the most notorious results in the history of the race; Freddie finished seventeenth. He continued to race the following season but had begun to show traces of a heart murmur and his career was halted in November 1967. Freddie returned to the Tweedies' farm to enjoy a long and deserved retirement; he died in 1985 at the age of twenty-eight.

Indian Skimmer

Blessed with an amazing turn of foot, courageous and hardy, Indian Skimmer was simply the ideal racehorse.

JOHN FRANCOME

The career of Indian Skimmer – owned by Sheikh Mohammed and trained by Henry Cecil – gives the lie to the notion that all great horses who run on the Flat are retired as soon as is decent. There is of course much less reason to retire a filly than a colt, as she will produce one foal a year at stud and he will sire many, but none the less the decision to keep Indian Skimmer in training as a four-year-old and again as a five-year-old has added much lustre to the Flat in recent years. Yet there was little hint of the achievements to come on her only outing as a two-year-old in October 1986, when she ran fourth to Tweeter in a maiden race at Newmarket. The following year she won a humble graduation race at Wolverhampton before moving into the big league with victories in some of the top races in Europe for three-year-old fillies – the Pretty Polly Stakes at Newmarket, the Tattersalls Musidora Stakes at York, and the Prix Saint-Alary at Longchamp. She had not been entered in the Oaks, but the ease of her victories at York and Longchamp suggested that she was among the very best fillies of her generation, and she confirmed this emphatically by showing a dazzling turn of foot to beat One Thousand Guineas winner Miesque in the Prix de Diane Hermes at Chantilly – the French equivalent of the Oaks. Absented with back trouble for the rest of the 1987 season, she returned in 1988 and showed herself to be an outstanding racehorse, winning the Phoenix Champion Stakes at Phoenix Park, the Sun Chariot Stakes at Newmarket, and the Dubai Champion Stakes at Newmarket, where she sprinted clear of a top-class field. She then went to Kentucky for the Breeders' Cup Turf over one and a half miles, the furthest she had raced, and put up a marvellous performance to finish a close third to Great Communicator and Sunshine Forever.

Back again for the 1989 season, she won the Gordon Richards EBF Stakes at Sandown Park and the Prix d'Ispahan at Longchamp before returning to Sandown for the Coral–Eclipse. But it had been impossible to give her a proper preparation on the sun-baked gallops, and she finished third: that she had no answer to Nashwan's raking stride that day in no way detracted from the delight she had given racing fans for several seasons.

Le Garçon d'Or

There are many ways in which a horse can grab the attention and the affections of the racing fan – by winning big races, by repeatedly showing resolution or spirit, or just by being around for so long that its participation is part of the scene. No horse since the war has so epitomized the last category as Le Garçon d'Or, the robust little bay gelding trained at Richmond in Yorkshire by Jack Ormston. He raced mainly over the sprint distances of five and six furlongs (though he stayed seven he never won at that distance), acted on any going, and was a particularly good mount for an apprentice jockey. But the extraordinary thing about Le Garçon d'Or was the length of time he was competing. He ran in his first race two days before Merryman II won the Grand National in March 1960; he was finally retired after running nine times as a fifteen-year-old (a remarkable age for a sprinter) in 1973. He gave *fourteen seasons* of honest endeavour, and became the first horse this century to register thirty-four wins in flat races on winning a selling plate at Edinburgh in June 1972.

After an inauspicious start in the Croxteth Plate at Liverpool on 24 March 1960 – he was tailed off – Le Garçon d'Or won his second race, at Thirsk the following month, though he had to survive an objection for crossing. Later that first season his wanderlust got him into more trouble and he was disqualified after winning at Redcar, though it was at the same course that he scored his second victory (ridden by Frankie Durr). In all he ran in 182 races, his most successful season being in 1968, when as a mere ten-year-old he won six times from sixteen outings. His final season in 1973 was the only one in which he did not mark up a victory.

Le Garçon d'Or was the sort of horse I would love to have owned. He had no pretensions to grandeur, but for year after year there he was, always giving his best.

GRAHAM GOODE

Merryman II

Merryman II was bred in Midlothian by Lady Joan Hope, daughter of a former Viceroy of India, and sold in 1955 to Winifred Wallace, a keen sportswoman who rode her new purchase to three victories in point-to-point races before he recorded his first success under National Hunt Rules in a hunter-chase at Kelso in April 1958. He won the Liverpool Foxhunters' Chase in March 1959 and put up a classy display to win the Scottish Grand National at Bogside the following month. By the beginning of his 1959–60 campaign Merryman II was in full training with Neville Crump at Middleham, the Grand National very much their target.

On the day he was up against twenty-five rivals for the Liverpool race. As well as being the first time that the Grand National was televised live, this was the last running of the race before the fences were sloped on the take-off side to prevent horses from getting too close before jumping. So Merryman II can claim to be the last of the 'old-style' National winners – and right well did he win it, Gerry Scott bringing him home an easy fifteen lengths ahead of Badanloch, with Clear Profit third. A year later Merryman II was back at Liverpool, an 8–1 chance in a field of thirty-five. Despite being kicked by another horse at the start and having an unfamiliar jockey on board (Derek Ancil had taken over from the injured Scott), he put up a superbly courageous performance to run Nicolaus Silver, who was carrying 25 pounds less, to five lengths. Neville Crump trained three Grand National winners, but considered Merryman II the best of them – 'One of the few greats'.

Mill Reef

Mill Reef was bred in the USA by his owner Paul Mellon, trained by Ian Balding at Kingsclere and ridden throughout his career by Geoff Lewis. His first race was at Salisbury on 13 May 1970 (by today's standards very early in the season for a horse with middle-distance Classic aspirations), when he won the Salisbury Stakes at 8–1. He followed up with an eight-length victory in the Coventry Stakes at Royal Ascot before going down by a short head to My Swallow at Maisons-Laffitte after a very bad journey from England, and resumed his winning ways with an easy triumph in the Gimcrack at York. There followed wins at Kempton and in the Dewhurst Stakes at Newmarket, and Mill Reef retired for the winter. The next season he took the Greenham Stakes *en route* to his famous showdown with Brigadier Gerard and My Swallow in the Two Thousand Guineas, and after his three-length defeat by 'The Brigadier' was never beaten again, winning the Derby from Linden Tree, the Eclipse Stakes from Caro, and the King George VI and Queen Elizabeth Stakes from Ortis, and ending his brilliant three-year-old career with a stunning victory three lengths ahead of Pistol Packer in the Prix de l'Arc de Triomphe.

In his first race as a four-year-old, the Prix Ganay at Longchamp, Mill Reef showed breathtaking acceleration to win by ten lengths, but his dour victory by a neck over Homeric in the Coronation Cup suggested that something was amiss with the horse. Whatever it was,

Mill Reef at the National Stud in Newmarket.

Mill Reef did not have the chance to dazzle the racegoing public again; on 30 August 1972 he fractured a foreleg on the gallops. A combination of veterinary brilliance and equine stoicism saved him for a highly successful stud career: among the offspring he sired at the National Stud were Shirley Heights, winner of the 1978 Derby (and himself sire of a Derby winner in Slip Anchor (1985)), Acamas (Prix du Jockey-Club, 1978), Fairy Footsteps (One Thousand Guineas, 1981), Wassl (Irish Two Thousand Guineas, 1983), and Reference Point (Derby and St Leger, 1987). He was put down early in 1986 at the age of eighteen on account of a deteriorating heart condition. Blessed with an almost flawless conformation and a temperament to match, winner of twelve of his fourteen races, Mill Reef was one of the greatest racehorses of the modern era.

Persian War

The period since the war has been rich in great hurdlers – Bula, Comedy Of Errors, Dawn Run, Hatton's Grace, Lanzarote, Monksfield, National Spirit, Night Nurse, Sea Pigeon, See You Then, Sir Ken – but for many people Persian War takes the honours. He won the Champion Hurdle in 1968, 1969 and 1970 and was second to Bula in 1971. He also won the Daily Express Triumph Hurdle, the Sweeps Hurdle in Ireland, the Schweppes Gold Trophy, and the Welsh Champion Hurdle, and in building up his remarkable record he showed himself as tough and resilient a horse as any that has raced under National Hunt rules.

Persian War was bred by Jakie Astor and trained on the Flat by Major Dick Hern, winning over two miles. He was sold to the Lewes trainer Tom Masson in the autumn of 1966 and early the following year was bought by Henry Alper, an insurance assessor who had been watching racing from Newbury on television and was smitten by the horse's performance when winning a small novice hurdle. In Alper's claret and blue colours – reflecting his other passion, West Ham United – and under the aegis of trainer Brian Swift at Epsom, Persian War won the Victor Ludorum Hurdle at Haydock and the Triumph Hurdle at Cheltenham. By the following spring the horse was being trained by

He was not only a champion on the track, he was a wonderfully kind and generous character off it. I once rode him in a gallop in France over a mile and three quarters with two good Flat horses. At a mile they were cantering over him but he just tried and tried and was actually going away from them at the finish. It was the bravest piece of work I ever experienced.

BROUGH SCOTT

Colin Davies at Chepstow, and he put up a superb performance to win the Schweppes Gold Trophy at Newbury under 11 stone 13 pounds, a crushing burden for a five-year-old. Then came the Champion Hurdle at Cheltenham, for which Persian War started 4–1 second favourite: he beat the favourite Chorus II by four lengths, and was the first hurdler to be voted Horse of the Year. The following season he was a heavily-backed 6–4 favourite for the Champion, run in heavy going (his first victory had been on firm); again he won by four lengths. Less than three weeks later he won the Welsh Champion Hurdle on rock-hard ground. For the 1970 Champion, run on yielding going, he was again a short-priced favourite at 5–4, despite not having won a race for eleven months, and he strode up the Cheltenham hill in majestic style to beat Major Rose by one and a half lengths.

Alper was a somewhat capricious owner, and by the time of the 1971 race Persian War had moved trainers once more – to Arthur Pitt – and had won the Irish Sweeps Hurdle at Fairyhouse. Despite a gallant effort, however, a fourth Champion Hurdle victory was not to be; he went under by four lengths to the king of the new generation, Bula. Poor Persian War was soon on the move yet again, and it was from Dennis Rayson's yard at Exning that he went to his last victory in a £374 hurdle at Stratford in June 1972. He was finally retired at the age of eleven and died in 1984, aged twenty-one.

Sea Bird II

Sea Bird II was quite simply the finest horse I have seen in forty years of racegoing. He won the 1965 Derby with contemptuous ease and went on to win an even better race for the Arc, beating Reliance six lengths with a very high-class field strung out behind.

JOHN TYRREL

Sea Bird II, trained in France by Etienne Pollet, is held by most racing experts to be the best horse to have competed in Europe since the war. A bright chestnut with a narrow white blaze and two white stockings on his hind legs, he was unbeaten as a three-year-old in 1965 after winning two of his three races as a juvenile. His *annus mirabilis* began with victories in the Prix Greffulhe and Prix Lupin, and he started the Epsom Derby (the only time he ever ran outside France) as 7–4 favourite. Ridden with great confidence by Australian jockey Pat Glennon, he achieved one of the easiest Derby victories ever, sweeping into the lead without coming off the bit and winning effortlessly from the subsequent King George winner Meadow Court. After a similarly facile win in the Grand Prix de Saint-Cloud he took on an exceptionally strong international field for the Prix de l'Arc de Triomphe, in which he was up against the winners of the Irish, Russian and American Derbys as well as the unbeaten Reliance, who had won the French Derby and the St Leger. It was Reliance who, with Sea Bird, drew away from the field early in the straight; but Sea Bird then showed a dazzling burst of acceleration which took him six lengths clear of his rival, despite veering towards the stands, for one of the most scintillating victories ever seen.

Sea Bird did not race again, but was retired to stud in the USA, where he stood for five years before returning to France. He died in 1973. Among his progeny were the brilliant mare Allez France, among whose triumphs was the 1974 Arc, and the remarkable Sea Pigeon, winner of the Champion Hurdle in 1980 and 1981 and the Ebor Handicap in 1979.

It is sad to recall that Sicalade, the dam of this superlative racehorse, was sold as butcher's meat for the equivalent of £100 before he ever ran.

BREEDING

'Rather a sweet little horse, actually. But unfortunately no bloody good.' Trainer John Dunlop's pronouncement on Snaafi Dancer illustrates the perils of the huge international operation that the bloodstock business today has become. Snaafi Dancer, a superbly bred son of the most prestigious stallion of the modern era, Northern Dancer, had caused a sensation in 1983 as the subject of a prolonged duel between Sheikh Mohammed and Robert Sangster at the yearling sales in Kentucky. He was knocked down to the Sheikh for a staggering $10.2 million (at the time by a long way the world record price for a yearling) and was put into training with Dunlop at Arundel, Sussex, but proved useless and never raced.

So money does not necessarily buy success; but it often will, and bloodstock acquisitions at the highest level seem to be virtually monopolized by a few very rich men, notably Sheikh Mohammed and other members of the Maktoum family from Dubai, Robert Sangster and his consortium (which includes Stavros Niarchos), Prince Khalid Abdullah, and the Aga Khan. They and a group of owner–breeders which includes the Queen, Lady Beaverbrook, Jim Joel, Louis Freedman (owner of Reference Point) and Lord Howard de Walden (owner of Slip Anchor) appear to dominate the world of breeding; but in reality it is much more than the exclusive domain of the super-rich. Desert Orchid may be a far cry from Nashwan in terms of pedigree, but that great horse was home-bred by James Burridge from a mare whose dam he had purchased for 175 guineas.

At any level, the real fascination of breeding is in the choice of mating, as enthralling and unpredictable in horses as it can be in humans. (The dancer Isadora Duncan suggested to George Bernard Shaw that they should have a child together: 'With my body and your brains, what a wonder it would be!' Shaw replied: 'Yes, but what if it had my body and your brains?') All sorts of theories have been tried out in the quest for the perfect racehorse, the crudest being the notion of mating the best with the best to produce the best. It is not that simple, of course, as the breeder John Hislop has written: 'All that the breeder can do is to try to arrange matters so that there is a reasonable chance of the right genetic shake-up emerging, and hope for the best.' That unassuming comment, though, belies the amount of thought and study that can go into choosing the right match, especially when the coffers are not bottomless. Hislop had acquired, for 400 guineas, a broodmare who traced back to the immortal Pretty Polly, winner of three Classics in 1904. From this mare he bred La Paiva, sending her to the unfashionable stallion Queen's Hussar. One of his attractions was that he was cheap, his fee at the time being £250; but he was also very well bred and had a particularly fine conformation. His offspring showed a preference for firm going, a trait balanced by the family of La Paiva, for the stock of

Fillies and mares often race when in foal: both The Princess (1844) and Glass Doll (1907) won the Oaks when pregnant.

GOOD COMPANIONS

Racehorses can be nervous creatures, and many find the constant companionship of another animal soothing. The most obvious companion, when turned out in a field, is another horse or a donkey, but some horses have had more unusual friends. That great French mare Allez France owed some of her equanimity to her stable relationship with a sheep, and goats are often a source of cameraderie: the 1933 Oaks winner Chatelaine had a goat as a live-in companion and more recently the Grand National winner Foinavon was accompanied by a goat on his travels. Sunnyhill, a gigantic Irish chaser of the late 1950s, had a goose for a pal, while Gregalach, winner of the 1929 Grand National, was almost inseparable from a rough-haired terrier.

her sire, Prince Chevalier, act well on soft going. Many other signs suggested that a mating between Queen's Hussar and La Paiva would produce a very good horse. It did. He was called Brigadier Gerard.

The aim in breeding is to produce a balance of both temperamental and physical attributes that will provide the ideal combination of speed, stamina, toughness, conformation and courage which is the perfect racehorse. Many breeders seek this through inbreeding (that is, choosing a mating in which a particular horse or a particular family of horses appears on both sides of the pedigree) in order to strengthen some chosen feature. The opposite of inbreeding is outcrossing, where the parents do not have ancestors in common in their recent pedigree: the stallion and the mare may each be closely inbred, but they are unrelated to each other. Queen's Hussar was inbred 3×3 to Fair Trial: that is, the famous stallion Fair Trial appears twice in the third generation of Queen's Hussar's pedigree, being both the grandsire of his sire and the grandsire of his dam. Her Majesty the Queen's mare Highlight was inbred to the legendary stallion and 1933 Derby winner Hyperion, who was Highlight's great-grandsire on the sire's side and grandsire on the dam's side. Thus Queen's Hussar and Highlight had no close common ancestors, but each had strong inbreeding in its pedigree. The Queen sent Highlight to Queen's Hussar, and the product was Highclere, who won the One Thousand Guineas and the Prix de Diane and foaled Height of Fashion, the dam of Unfuwain and Nashwan.

Breeding on an international scale is an immensely complex business, but the fundamental cycle of the breeding year in Britain is fairly straightforward. On the day after St Valentine's Day begins the unromantically named 'covering season', which lasts until 15 July. The owner of the mare will have decided, usually after much research, which stallion he wishes to mate her with. The stallion will normally be standing at a stud, and the mare is sent there during the covering season. If she is carrying a foal conceived the previous year she will arrive shortly before that foal is due, and after the foal is born will await the next covering. She will come into season ('on heat') about eight to ten days after foaling, and thereafter at three-weekly intervals.

If the mare appears to be in season she will then be subjected to the attentions of a 'teaser', a stallion kept by the stud simply for the purpose of gauging the mares' sexual response; it is not practical to allow the stallion who will actually cover to engage in this foreplay, for if the mare is not ready she may lash out and cause damage to millions of pounds' worth of horseflesh. The teaser flirts with the mare by nibbling her across the 'trying board' over which they meet, and if she reacts favourably he is led away to carry out his frustrating duties on another mare while the vet examines this one. (The teaser is sometimes, but not always, sterile, and just occasionally enjoys a slice of the action. In 1986 the broodmare Branitska was due to be covered by the stallion Wolver Heights at the Stetchworth Stud in Newmarket. 'Branitska just would not take to Wolver Heights at all,' according to stud owner Bill Gredley, 'and kicked him like mad. In the end we brought the teaser forward, and because she stood still for him we thought, "Why not?"' The offspring, Call To Arms, was just beaten in the 1989 Dewhurst.)

If the mare is ready, she is washed off in the appropriate area (to

---

COLOURS

A Thoroughbred horse's colour is registered at birth, though colouring can occasionally change with age. The basic colours are:

Bay   All shades of brown, with the 'points' (muzzle, mane, tail and extremities of the legs) black.

Brown   Distinctly brown all over.

Black   Distinctly black all over.

Chestnut   A range of shades from a light golden colour to a dark 'liver' chestnut.

Grey   A range from pure white to dark grey. Grey horses tend to get whiter as they get older. (About three per cent of racehorses are greys.)

Roan   A combination of red, white and yellow or black, white and yellow hairs which gives a washy appearance. The colour is unusual in racehorses, but not unknown: Roan Rocket won the Sussex Stakes in 1964.

Colour is sometimes held to be an indication of a horse's temperament. A 'flashy' chestnut (in particular a filly) is often thought to be unreliable, but many of the old wives' tales about not trusting a horse with white legs were demolished by the dour courage of The Minstrel's performances in the Derby, the Irish Sweeps Derby, and the King George VI and Queen Elizabeth Diamond Stakes in 1977. And of course, there was Eclipse . . .

prevent the spread of infection), her tail is bandaged and she is fitted with felt shoes on her hind feet in case she should lash out at the stallion, who is then led into the covering barn to meet his mate. One groom holds the mare's upper lip in a twitch (a loop of rope attached to a stick) to keep her still while another lifts one of her forelegs to prevent her kicking out. He releases it as she is mounted, when the stallion man, who looks after the stallion and supervises the mating, helps his charge achieve efficient penetration. The whole covering operation should take a minute or two.

Since a mare will not be got in foal at every covering, the procedure is repeated when she is again in season, and a stallion will sometimes cover the same mare several times. (He will often need to cover several mares in a day, as it cannot be accurately predicted well in advance exactly when any mare will be receptive.) She will return to her owner until the process is repeated the following year. (Although a pregnancy can be detected as early as 14 days after covering, the mare will not normally return to her owner until the pregnancy has become properly established, around two months after covering.)

It is common for the best male racehorses to be 'syndicated' for stud duties, which means that ownership is divided into shares (normally forty), each worth an equal proportion of the total sum agreed among the members of the syndicate. Dancing Brave, valued at £14 million after his brilliant racing career, was syndicated in shares costing £350,000 each: sixteen of these shares were sold off to breeders, who were thereby each entitled to send one mare to him each covering season, and the rest were divided between his owner Khalid Abdullah and members of the Maktoum family, to whose Dalham Hall Stud in Newmarket he was retired. If the shareholder does not choose to send a mare to the stallion for one season he may sell the privilege of being served by that stallion (a 'nomination') to another breeder. Each mating for a breeder not belonging to the syndicate is charged at an agreed rate depending on the ability of the horse and the probable potential of its offspring: to have a mare served by Nashwan (whose syndication valued him at £18 million) in 1990 would cost a breeder £100,000 per go, with a 'no foal, no fee' condition which allows for the payment of the fee only if the mare is certified in foal on 1 October of the year in which the covering took place. Alternative conditions which sometimes apply provide for the breeder to pay half the fee at covering and half when conception is confirmed, or for part of the fee to be held back until a live foal is born.

The stallion: the brilliant miler Kris at the Thornton Stud, Yorkshire, in 1988. Note the difference in physique between a stallion and a horse in training: the stallion has a thicker neck, is less 'light' behind the saddle, and is generally more muscled up.

Stallions are normally restricted by their owners in the numbers of mares they may cover in a season to around forty or fifty: forty would be for the shareholders, the remaining number possibly being kept by the stud to offset running costs (as stipulated in the share agreement). Too many offspring would undermine the value of the stock. But others have had to be more vigorous. Spread Eagle, who won the Derby in 1795, was reported to have covered 234 mares in Virginia in 1801, and much more recently the dual Ascot Gold Cup winner Le Moss, breeding mainly for National Hunt racing, is said to have covered 210 in 1986.

The gestation period of a Thoroughbred is about eleven months (320 to 360 days), so a horse resulting from a covering in March should

NAMES

The naming of racehorses is controlled by Weatherbys, and names are restricted in length to eighteen characters (including spaces), which causes conflations such as Shewhomustbeobeyed, Thethingaboutitis and – contracted to the regulation length at the expense of an 'h' – Letsbeonestaboutit. (Until 1946 a horse could run unnamed.) No longer can a horse's name consist solely of initial letters (such as ESB), though these can be spelt out phonetically (such as Jay-Dee-Jay). The list of *Registered Names* contains nearly a quarter of a million protected names which cannot be used: they include those of any racehorse up to ten years after its death, broodmares up to fifteen years after death and stallions up to twenty-five years after death or being taken out of stud, and in perpetuity the names of all Classic winners and the winners of the Ascot Gold Cup, the King George VI and Queen Elizabeth Diamond Stakes, and the Grand National.

Royal Mail won the 1937 Grand National and another Royal Mail won the Whitbread Gold Cup in 1980, but the Whitbread winner had '(NZ)' after his name to indicate that he was bred in New Zealand; a horse bred outside the British Isles carries a suffix to its name to indicate its country of foaling: thus Musical Bliss (USA) or Nijinsky (CAN).

The names of other celebrated horses (such as Arkle) are protected by dispensation of the *International List of Protected Names*. Nonetheless, familiar names do recur, and in the last few years horses called Crisp, Dunkirk, Predominate and Lanzarote have revived memories of the much greater animals which bore those names in the past.

Weatherbys, who receive about 10,000 applications for registration of new names every year, can always turn down a proposed name on the grounds of good taste, though whoever allowed Paul Cole's colt Snurge to be so named clearly did not have access to Eric Partridge's *Dictionary of Slang and Unconventional English*. Woodrow Wyatt had a two-year old in 1959 which, it being election year, he wanted to name Vote Labour. Permission was withheld. But anyone who witnessed Margaret Thatcher with her new grandson on the steps of 10 Downing Street in spring 1989 would appreciate the political undertones to the naming of a horse owned by Clement Freud MP – Weareagrandmother.

A horse's name is often a creative compound of the names of its sire and dam (for instance, Warning, by Known Fact out of Slightly Dangerous), and an increasing number of companies own horses which bear the company name: so Cronk Garages Ltd had Cronk's Quality and Cronk's Courage in Geoff Lewis's yard in 1990. And sometimes the name has a particular personal meaning for the horse's owner. The spelling of the name Kybo, that good hurdler and chaser owned by Isidore Kerman, recalled the advice which always concluded the letters Kerman's mother sent him when he was at school: 'KYBO' exhorted, 'Keep Your Bowels Open'.

be foaled the following February. It can be difficult to decide upon the ideal timing: an early foal may be mature sooner than others of its generation, but a later foal will have the benefit of better grass and climate when it is very young. A commercial breeder may sell it as a foal later that year, but is more likely to wait until the following year, when it will be sold as a yearling and go into training with a view to racing on the Flat the year after as a two-year-old. (The business of buying foals and then selling them on as yearlings the next year is known as 'pin-hooking', and can be very profitable, as it cuts out the costs of breeding and of keeping the pregnant mare.)

The great international circus of yearling sales, when trainers, owners and bloodstock agents compete for the best young horses, starts at the Keeneland Sales in Kentucky in July, moves on to Deauville in France and the Goffs' sales in Ireland and culminates in the October sales held at Newmarket by the famous firm of Tattersalls, founded in 1766 and the most renowned bloodstock auctioneers in the world. In the catalogue at any of these sales the name of a horse which has won a Group race or a Listed race (see page 70) is given in bold type to advertise its eminence: hence the importance of a horse getting its 'black type'. The record paid for Snaafi Dancer in 1983 was passed in Kentucky in 1985 when Seattle Dancer was sold to the Robert Sangster group of breeders for $13.1 million: he at least turned out to be a pretty good racehorse, winning two Group 2 races in Ireland. But after the crazy prices being paid in the mid-1980s the market has settled down again, with breeders having come to realize that yearling prices were bearing little relation to possible return through either racing or breeding.

And what of poor Snaafi Dancer himself? He was sent to a small stud in Canada, where disappointment continued to dog him: he got only two of his mares in foal during his first covering season.

A **'breeze-up' sale** is a bloodstock sale at which the lots are actually put through their paces in front of the would-be purchasers, cantering over about three furlongs of the course at which the sale is being held.

Yearling sales at Tattersalls in Newmarket.

THE HORSE

A horse at birth is a **foal**, a **colt** if male and a **filly** if female. Its father is its **sire** and its mother its **dam**. (A horse is 'by' its sire and 'out of' its dam.) The foal will stand for the first time normally within an hour of being born and will suck from its dam within two hours; it has a close bond with its dam but shows increasing independence before being weaned at about five months old. The official birthday of every racehorse in the Northern Hemisphere is 1 January, and at the start of the year after its birth the foal becomes a **yearling**. At the age of five a colt becomes a **horse**, and a filly a **mare**.

Another horse sharing the same dam is its **half-brother** (or **half-sister**). Another horse sharing the same sire and dam is its **full brother** (or **full sister**). Another horse sharing the same sire but not the same dam is *not* described as its half-brother (or half-sister). Twins are rare, for while as many as 30 per cent of conceptions result in twins, in most cases one of the eggs is 'popped' by a vet to ensure that only one foal is born: twin foals would probably be too weak, though there are instances of successful racing twins.

A **gelding** is a horse that has been castrated ('cut'). The operation usually takes place in the autumn of the horse's second year; although it can be done later it is unwise to delay too long. The operation is performed under local anaesthetic and is quite painless. It comes as a surprise to some non-racing people to learn that the likes of Arkle, Red Rum and Desert Orchid cannot procreate, but had they not been gelded they would not have achieved what they did in steeplechasing. Although the common explanation for gelding a potential chaser –

The National Stud

Some of the best stallions in British bloodstock have stood at the National Stud. Those on duty for the 1990 season were the 1969 Derby winner Blakeney (at twenty-four years old approaching the end of his stud career); the good sprinter Chilibang; Jalmood, one of the best three-year-olds of 1982; Petoski, winner of the 1985 King George VI and Queen Elizabeth Diamond Stakes; the brilliant miler Rousillon; and the newcomer Reprimand, winner of the Gimcrack in 1987 and the Trusthouse Forte Mile in 1989. Their services are supplemented by those of Town and Country, who stands in Shropshire as a National Hunt stallion, while Weld will commence covering as the Stud's other jumping stallion in 1991.

The National Stud was born in 1916, when Colonel Hall Walker (later Lord Wavertree) presented his bloodstock and sold his stud in Ireland to the nation. The bloodstock included forty-three broodmares representing some of the best bloodlines in the British Isles, and the stud had produced the Derby winner Minoru. One of the early aims of the National Stud was to breed high-quality light horses for the Army, but when the use of horses for military purposes diminished after the First World War it concentrated more on the production of high-class

Not all Classic winners retire to a life of permanent luxury at stud. Aurelius, who won the St Leger in 1961, proved a failure at stud, was gelded and turned to jump racing. He won over hurdles and fences and was second past the post in the 1967 Champion Hurdle, only to be disqualified for hanging on the run-in.

that only an exceptionally dry-eyed 'full' horse would willingly launch itself over four and a half feet of packed birch – is plausible enough, there is more to it than that, for the ungelded horse is likely to have his mind on other things as he matures and will find it difficult to stand up to the wintry rigours of the jumping game. An ungelded horse is an **entire**, and there have been few chasing entires of note – Fortina won the Cheltenham Gold Cup in 1947, and the last entire to win the Grand National was Battleship in 1938. Hurdlers tend to be younger than chasers and the obstacles they have to face are easier to negotiate; consequently several horses enjoyed notable hurdling careers without being gelded: Monksfield, for instance, won two Champion Hurdles before starting a stud career tragically abbreviated by his death in 1989. Of course, geldings do not only run under National Hunt Rules, and though they may not compete in the Classics (on the argument that it does no good for the breed were a Classic race to be won by a horse which cannot pass on his excellence), most of the big flat races are now open to them, and old geldings such as Teleprompter (see page 98) or Bedtime or Chaplins Club had a hold on the affections of the racing public which few here-today-gone-tomorrow Classic winners could match.

A **rig** is a horse imperfectly gelded, or in whom only one testicle has descended: not surprisingly, such horses are often rather difficult.

A entire at stud is a **stallion**, and a mare used for breeding is a **broodmare**.

Thoroughbreds. Its policy was to sell most of its produce at public auction, keeping the best fillies for future breeding purposes while leasing them for their racing careers: in 1942 four of the five Classics were won by two horses leased from the Stud to King George VI (the colt Big Game won the Two Thousand Guineas, and the brilliant filly Sun Chariot the fillies' Triple Crown), and in 1957 Carrozza, leased to the Queen, won the Oaks under Lester Piggott. In 1943 the Stud's bloodstock was moved to Gillingham in Dorset, and a second location at West Grinstead in Sussex was used after the Second World War: it was here that the famous Italian horse Ribot was born. But in the early 1960s it was decided to concentrate exclusively on standing high-class stallions, and a new stud was built for this purpose on the present 500-acre site in Newmarket, close to the July Course: the first stallions to stand there were Never Say Die and Tudor Melody, who moved in during 1966.

The National Stud has exerted a considerable influence on world racing through great stallions such as Blandford, Big Game, Never Say Die – and Mill Reef, who covered over twenty mares in his first season at the Stud only a few months after breaking his leg, and whose influence on world bloodstock will be felt for a long time to come. John Skeaping's statue of this wonderful horse adorns the Stud's spacious grounds.

Stallions take their early-morning stroll at the National Stud in Newmarket: the horse leading is Petoski.

AGE, HEIGHT, WEIGHT AND SPEED

A top-class racehorse on the Flat is unlikely to race beyond four – many do not race beyond three – as the sums they can command for covering duties at stud outstrip what they might earn on a racecourse. Nowadays it is unusual for the Derby winner to stay in training as a four-year-old: Teenoso won the King George but both Slip Anchor and Henbit were retired early in their four-year-old season when it was realized that they had not trained on. Any age over six is fairly old for a horse on the Flat, though a steeplechaser will normally carry on until he is at least twelve, being thought to be in his prime at nine. No horse has won a race at over eighteen, and only Wild Aster, foaled in 1901, won three times at that age, taking three hurdle races within a week in March 1919. Fresher in the memory are Sonny Somers, Fred Winter's marvellous old chaser who gained his last two victories in 1980 at eighteen, and Le Garçon d'Or (see page 17), who raced to an exceptionally old age for a Flat performer. The oldest horse to have taken part in a race is Creggmore Boy, who ended his career in the Furness Selling Handicap Chase at Cartmel in June 1962 at the age of twenty-two. A Thoroughbred normally lives to around thirty; the Australian gelding Tango Duke is reported to have been forty-two on his death in 1978.

A horse is measured, at the shoulder, in 'hands', a hand being four inches. The normal height for a mature Thoroughbred is around 16 hands (5 feet 4 inches).

A mature racehorse in training will weigh around 1,100 pounds. (A foal weighs 80–120 pounds at birth.) Most trainers keep a very careful eye on the weight of their horses, being aware that each horse has an ideal 'racing weight' when it is fit, and they make regular use of equine weighbridges to keep the weight monitored. A horse may lose around forty pounds on a single day through the stress of travel and racing, and when little weight is lost through racing that is a sign that the horse has come out of the race well (Nashwan shed only 4 pounds when winning the Coral–Eclipse Stakes in July 1989). Similarly, the loss of a great deal of weight indicates that something was amiss. When Nijinsky won the St Leger he was suffering from a ringworm virus, and though he took the race with apparent ease he had lost almost more weight on that one trip from the stable of Vincent O'Brien in Ireland than on all his other overseas trips put together. Clearly he was a sick horse when winning at Doncaster – yet it was not his performance which indicated this, but his weight loss.

The speed at which races are run is often exaggerated. In the fastest modern British race on record, the Tadworth Handicap over five furlongs at Epsom on 2 June 1960, the winning horse averaged under 42 miles per hour. Nashwan averaged 37.33 miles per hour when winning the Two Thousand Guineas over one mile on good to firm going in May 1989, and Desert Orchid's average when winning the Cheltenham Gold Cup in appallingly heavy going in March 1989 was a little short of 27 miles per hour. Of course, horses usually (though not always) speed up towards the end of a race, and the runners at the end of a five-furlong sprint downhill on firm ground are probably clocking around 44 miles per hour.

Dayjur knocked more than a second off the five-furlong record at York, when winning the Keeneland Nunthorpe Stakes on 23 August 1990. His average speed throughout the race was just over 40 miles per hour, and nearly 45 through the penultimate furlong.

Retirement and Death

Only a very small proportion of racehorses retire to stud after their racing days are over. For the rest there are few alternative careers. The 1983 Grand National winner Corbiere had an honourable go at show jumping, and it is not unknown (though somewhat rare) for an ex-racehorse to find employment as a polo pony. The Thoroughbred is a highly strung and highly specialized animal and few make suitable riding-school hacks, though it is common for ex-chasers to enjoy a stint following hounds in their twilight years: Crisp, Birds Nest, Frenchman's Cove, Grand Canyon, Midnight Court, Titus Oates and Uncle Bing are just a few of the familiar National Hunt performers who have graced the hunting field in recent decades. Others find a retirement job as a trainer's hack. Devon Loch, whose sensational slide on the run-in of the 1956 Grand National is described on page 93, became hack to Noel Murless, Tingle Creek to Tom Jones, Comedy Of Errors to Mercy Rimell. Red Rum, a celebrity on the racetrack, became a bigger celebrity off it, his services much in demand for personal appearances opening supermarkets and betting shops.

Those who are able to reproduce the species do not always get the opportunity to do so in the sylvan glades of Newmarket. Scottish Rifle, winner of the Eclipse Stakes in 1973, became champion sire in Czechoslovakia, and the brilliant two-year-old Provideo took up stud duties in Tasmania.

Most racehorses end their days at grass, but some have more dramatic ends. Whatever happened to Shergar after he was kidnapped from the Ballmany Stud in County Kildare on the night of 8 February 1983, he is generally assumed to have been killed by his abductors, though his body was never recovered. Less sensational but no less distressing are the deaths in action, for it is a sad fact that the sport of racing is dangerous and stressful for its participants and will always claim its equine victims. The death of any horse during or as a direct result of a race is always a matter for deep regret and often the stimulus to change the conditions under which that race is run (as when Bechers Brook on the Grand National course was amended after the deaths of two horses in the 1989 running). Inevitably it is the famous horses whose loss is most keenly felt, and it is painful to recall some of the notable chasers and hurdlers of recent times who have lost their lives on the racetrack, among them Alverton, Brownes Gazette, Celtic Ryde, Dawn Run, Ekbalco, Forgive 'N Forget, Golden Cygnet, Killiney, Lanzarote, Noddy's Ryde and Ten Plus. But it is not only in National Hunt racing that deaths in action occur: Dovekie and Serenader, both owned by Sheikh Mohammed, were put down after accidents on successive days of the Royal Ascot meeting in 1990. About thirty horses are killed each year on the Flat, and around 175 over jumps.

At grass: two famous racehorses enjoying retirement in an Oxfordshire field in 1980. On the left is Flyingbolt (then twenty-one years old), winner of the Two Mile Champion Chase at Cheltenham in 1966 and the following day third in the Champion Hurdle, beaten less than four lengths: he was one of the very best Irish jumpers of the post-war era, winning the Irish Grand National and at his prime being handicapped within two pounds of Arkle. His companion is 1968 Cheltenham Gold Cup hero Fort Leney, twenty-two when this photograph was taken. Flyingbolt died in 1983 at the age of twenty-four, being put down after suffering a stroke (an event very rare in horses). Fort Leney did not survive him long, dying in 1984 at the age of twenty-six.

AILMENTS AND INJURIES

The racehorse is a strong and powerful creature, but its life subjects it to a great deal of stress and strain – imagine the pressure put on the forelegs of a steeplechaser as it lands over a jump at 30 miles per hour. Horses are susceptible to all sorts of disease and injury; the following are some of the problems that crop up most often in racing stables.

The Virus

'The virus' is common racing parlance for a variety of respiratory conditions. Virus infections can spread rapidly in stable yards and on racecourses, and often the first sign of the presence of the virus is a lacklustre performance on course. Equine flu is a severe viral respiratory infection: its major symptom is a dry cough – hence the horror of coughing in a racing stable – accompanied by high temperature and a nasal discharge. It usually takes a horse two to three weeks to recover, after which it will need a period of convalescence.

Soft Palate Disease

When a horse has a soft palate complaint it 'swallows its tongue', usually when under pressure at the end of a race: the horse gurgles and suddenly slows right up, then gets its breath back. What has happened is that the junction between the larynx and the soft palate has become unsealed, causing the passage of air to be obstructed. Once the horse can swallow and reseal the junction, it recovers.

Whistling and Roaring

Conditions of the larynx affecting the horse's capacity to breathe, these respiratory disorders can be cured or eased by 'tubing' – making a hole in the horse's neck and inserting a tube, so that the obstruction in the larynx is by-passed – or by Hobdaying (after Sir Frederick Hobday, former principal of the Royal College of Veterinary Surgeons), which involves removing the offending ventricle in the larynx.

Tendon Strain

The tendons are the ligaments which, in the foreleg, attach the muscles above the knee to the pastern (the bone above the hoof) and to the pedal bone within the hoof. Tendons are obviously subjected to great strain when a horse is galloping, and are placed under particular stress by jumping. Uneven going, tired muscles and jolts to the leg all increase the likelihood of tendon strain, which in severe cases causes the tendons to give way completely, commonly known as 'breaking down'. The best treatment for tendon strain is several months of rest before a period of gentle walking, then ridden walking, before the horse can get back into serious training.

A common method of treating recurrent tendon strain is 'firing', the application of red-hot irons to the skin around the affected area, on the principle that the scar tissue is stronger than the damaged tissue. In bar or line firing the iron is drawn across the skin in lines about an inch apart; in pin firing the iron is inserted through the skin to the tissue or to the tendon; acid firing involves the application of concentrated sulphuric acid to the skin. Unpleasant as such treatments sound, they are held by many to be very effective. But veterinary opinion is nowadays against firing, and a new method of treating damaged forelegs is the implantation of carbon fibres to strengthen the tendons: the Queen Mother's fine chaser Special Cargo underwent such treatment and after an absence of two years advertised its benefits through the revival of his racing career in the spring of 1984, culminating in his memorable victory in the Whitbread Gold Cup (see page 185).

Splints

Splint bones are small bones between the knee and the fetlock, and a 'splint' is the common name for a bony enlargement of one of these, caused by a kick or by stress on the bones and ligaments.

Sore Shins

Common among young racehorses, inflammation of the shins results from the stress placed on the legs by fast work or racing on hard ground.

Fractures of the Knee

A horse's knee joint consists of at least seven bones, and repeated stress on the front aspect of those bones can result in 'chip' fractures, causing swelling and lameness. These can be healed by drugs or surgery, but most of all by rest: premature resumption of work will cause the condition to deteriorate.

Overreaching

An overreach is a cut on the back of a front foot just above the heel, caused by the front of the hind shoe striking the front heel, often when the horse is stretching towards the end of a race.

Breaking Blood Vessels

To see a horse pull up with blood coming out of its nostrils is a distressing sight. This indicates a haemorrhage in the lungs caused by strenuous exertion, and can be treated by drugs and by a period of rest which can take from a few days to several months. The horse will be 'scoped' – subjected to endoscopic examination of its airways – and while the condition will not necessarily recur each time the horse races, a tendency to break blood vessels is worrying in any horse.

Cast in Box

A horse is said to have been 'cast in its box' if it lies down in its box in such a way that it is trapped – often against a wall or under the manger – and cannot get up without assistance. The experience will probably leave it stiff and distressed.

COURSES

John Tyrrel was racing presenter and adviser for Southern Television from 1976 until 1981, and joined ITV's *World of Sport* in August 1977. His announcing of the results and betting shows has been a feature of Channel Four Racing since its inception.

It is one of the beauties of British racing that most of the racecourses evolved by accident rather than design. When the Romans, led by their ageing and terminally ill emperor Severus, laid out a course at York in 208 AD on the land we know now as the Knavesmire, they naturally followed the pattern of the flat, oval Circus Maximus in Rome. Chester likewise reflects the style of the Roman racetracks, whereas the wide sweep of Newmarket recalls the passion of James I for hare coursing and all country sports. Goodwood, with its spectacular setting on the Sussex Downs, began as an amusement for the county militia; Edinburgh, Redcar and Yarmouth all started as seaside events on the local beaches. Henry VIII raced horses at Windsor, and if Queen Anne hadn't had an eye for a line of country there wouldn't have been a Royal Ascot.

But perhaps the greatest curiosity is Epsom. Were the famous dinner party hosted by the Earl of Derby in 1779 to reassemble in ghostly form today to decide on a race for the three-year-old championship of Europe, Epsom, with its ups and downs, its left-hand and right-hand bends, would be an unlikely choice of venue – though to be fair to the Earl and his friends, the Derby was first run over a dog-leg 'straight' mile, not today's switchback mile and a half.

It was not until the late nineteenth century that a degree of conformity was introduced as courses were founded on a more commercial basis. Sandown Park, opened in 1875, was the original 'drawing-room' course – so called because a novel enclosure system enabled women to go racing in comfort for the first time – and with the opening of Kempton Park, Hurst Park, Newbury, Lingfield Park and Haydock Park during the following decades the concept of the park course was firmly established. These courses may have lacked the rugged rough-and-tumble of the older country tracks, but they allowed spectators a real close-up of spectacular equine sport.

So the wheel came full circle – from the Roman amphitheatre, via the bleak straights of Newmarket, the loops of Goodwood, Salisbury and Hamilton, the undulations of Epsom and Catterick and the sausage shape of Taunton, back to tracks designed to get enthusiasts closer to the action, in the best Roman style. And enthusiasts didn't come any keener than the boys back at the Circus Maximus.

Previous pages:
The July Course at Newmarket.

'An American friend who was over here to see Epsom, Ascot, Goodwood, Newmarket and other places of historical interest,' wrote the former jockey Jack Leach in his *Sods I Have Cut on the Turf*, 'remarked to me once that it was curious that they did not have a band playing some appropriate tune during the parade for the Derby. He said, "As far as I can make out, Epsom has everything; all the fun of the fair, gypsies, tipsters, millions of people, everything, but no band." I pointed out the Salvation Army Band which was playing some mournful dirge and had banners displaying "Prepare to meet thy God," but that was not quite what he meant.' That was some decades ago, but were Leach's American friend to return today he would almost certainly find music – a steel band or a jazz band at Sandown Park or Goodwood, a military band at Ascot – and much else besides. For British racecourses have twigged that they are in the business of entertaining the public, and the gradual modernizing of buildings is being accompanied by a modernizing of attitudes. Courses advertise themselves more actively, and some undertake initiatives designed to bring in a steady flow of racegoers: Sandown Park and Kempton Park, for instance, have recently admitted female racegoers free to some evening meetings.

There are fifty-nine racecourses in Great Britain, offering around a thousand days' sport annually. Excluding all-weather courses, of these fifty-nine (sixty if you count Newmarket's two courses – the Rowley Mile and the July Course – separately) fifteen stage flat racing only, twenty-five jumping only, and the remaining nineteen put on both. From Perth in the north to Brighton in the south, from Yarmouth in the east to Chepstow in the west, the diversity of terrain they offer to horse and jockey and the range of facilities they provide for the spectator form one of the abiding attractions of the British racing scene. On Newmarket's Rowley Mile course a ten-furlong race is straight but undulating; a horse running over the same distance at Chester negotiates an almost constant left-hand turn over ground which is dead flat. At Ascot spectators are well served by escalators in the grandstand; at Bangor-on-Dee there is no stand at all.

Since the end of the Second World War many courses have closed, most recently Teesside Park (formerly Stockton), which held its last meeting in 1981, Lanark in 1977, and Wye in 1974. Alexandra Park was the only racecourse in London when it shut in 1970 at the end of a particularly grim decade which had seen the loss of such venues as Buckfastleigh (1960), Hurst Park (1962), Manchester and Woore (both 1963), Lewes and Lincoln (both 1964) and Birmingham, Bogside and Rothbury (all 1965). Gatwick, where the Grand National was run during the First World War, staged its last official meeting in 1940.

It is unlikely that this list of casualties will lengthen significantly in the foreseeable future: the number of meetings required to sustain the programme of fixtures in Britain and generate a high level of betting turnover demands the regular use of a large number of courses, for

On 1 August 1898 the sporting press carried a full programme of runners and riders for a meeting at Trodmore, and the following day printed the results. But no such course existed: the scheme was an ingenious fraud, the perpetrators of which were never found. Whoever they were, their ingenuity was not rewarded, for most bookmakers refused to pay out.

The first evening meeting in Great Britain was held at Hamilton Park (near Glasgow) on 18 July 1947.

grass needs time to recover from racing (unlike America's dirt tracks, where racing can take place over a single circuit for weeks on end). With all-weather tracks now established in Britain at Lingfield Park and Southwell (see page 43), the nature of the sport is bound to change in some ways, but the wonderful variety in British racecourses remains.

This variety manifests itself both in the more obvious aspects of a racecourse, such as turf, layout, size, shape or landscape, and in the less tangible but no less marked matters of atmosphere and style, contrasts which come across even on television. At Sandown Park, where the horses emerge out of the parade ring on to the Rhododendron Walk and return along it and then through the crowd to the unsaddling enclosure, the proximity of the spectators to the action heightens the excitement for both racegoers and television viewers, whereas the vast open spaces of Newmarket make for a less hectic atmosphere: many Newmarket racegoers find the time spent waiting in the stands as the runners for the Cesarewitch in mid-October make their way to the two and a quarter mile start the best opportunity all year for quiet contemplation or for the first draft of the Christmas card list.

The difference between Newmarket and Sandown Park reflects an important moment in the history of racecourses. Newmarket racing grew out of a Royal enthusiasm for coursing and hunting on the heath in the early seventeenth century; at other places race meetings evolved as part of civic celebrations such as festivals and fairs, or as the town became popular for other reasons – Epsom, for instance, became a spa town in the seventeenth century on account of the medicinal properties of its waters (Pepys recorded in 1667 that 'I did drink four pints and had some very good stools by it'), and horse racing became an established part of its social fabric. Races which had developed in this way were usually held on common land. But Sandown Park was the first of the 'park' courses – that is, the first course to charge entrance fees to all who wanted to watch the racing. Until Sandown opened, a little over a century ago, money was charged at courses only for entrance into the stands and enclosures; access to the rest of the course was open and free to all. The Sandown experiment of enclosing the whole course with a fence was a great success, and soon led to the founding of other courses close to London, such as Kempton Park, Hurst Park and Newbury, which held its first meeting in 1905.

The variety extends further: to ownership – Ascot is owned by the Crown, while Epsom, Kempton Park and Sandown Park are controlled by United Racecourses Ltd, a subsidiary of the Betting Levy Board, and some courses are limited companies in their own right – and finance, which may come from money taken at the gate, grants and subsidies from the Betting Levy Board, sale of hospitality facilities, television rights, rights to Satellite Information Services (SIS) to beam pictures into betting shops, and so on; and through putting the racecourse to alternative uses when racing is not taking place.

On 4 July 1981 Paul Cook rode a winner on each of three different courses: Princes Gate in the 2:15 at Sandown Park, Ramannolie in the 5:00 at Bath, and Pavilion in the 7:50 at Nottingham.

Sandown Park has been especially innovative in this last respect, with its golf course and driving range and artificial ski slope, and other courses too have joined the search for ways to use their grounds on the very many days each year when there is no racing. Several now have caravan parks and golf courses, and many offer the use of their buildings for non-racing activities such as conferences, exhibitions and banquets. The urge to mix banquet and sport on race-days themselves is increasingly evident in the entertainment and hospitality facilities which courses offer to businesses; sometimes, sadly, to the detriment of facilities for other racegoers. (It is now impossible, for instance, to reach a position high enough in the Members' stand at Chepstow to see the first two fences in the straight, for the higher reaches of the stand are entirely given over to boxes for entertaining.) Most new racecourse grandstands are designed with an eye to the need for corporate hospitality, which is an increasingly important source of income for the courses: some such boxes at Goodwood have no view of the course at all, a shortcoming however probably not noticed by many of the people being entertained.

Horses have simpler tastes and no need of banqueting facilities, but many display a distinct predilection for a certain sort of racecourse or indeed for one specific course, and the 'horses for courses' theory is one which the punter ignores at his peril, particularly at tracks with unusual terrain, such as the switchbacks of Epsom and Brighton or the tight bends of Plumpton and Fontwell. Horses have general preferences – despite his memorable win in the 1989 Tote Cheltenham Gold Cup, Desert Orchid is widely held to be better right-hand than left-hand – and preferences for certain sorts of track. The latter usually relate to physique or action: an exceptionally long-striding horse such as Assert would be seen to best effect at a 'galloping' course (that is, a course without tight bends to slow him down) like York, where he won the Benson and Hedges Gold Cup in 1982, while a more compactly built animal will be at an advantage on a sharp track: the wiry little chaser Gambling Prince, for example, won seven times around the bends of Stratford. And at the more idiosyncratic courses an older horse who has won there already is always worthy of consideration. 'Horses for courses' can be a useful maxim, then, but nevertheless a good horse should be able to act anywhere.

And a good racegoer should be able to act anywhere, from the atmospheric but less than ideally angled grandstand at Kelso which was built in 1822 to the modern comforts of York. Spectator numbers have risen steadily in recent years. Paid attendance for the 1,005 fixtures held in 1989 amounted to over 4.9 million, at an average of nearly 6,000 per Flat day and nearly 4,000 per jumping day. The best attended race is of course the Derby, for which several hundred thousand people crowd on to Epsom Downs; 73,501 attended Royal Ascot on Gold Cup day 1990; 56,884 went to Cheltenham on 15 March 1990 and saw Norton's Coin win the Gold Cup, while 22,750 had been at Kempton Park on Boxing Day 1989 to see the same horse finish last behind Desert Orchid in the King George VI Rank Chase.

But although thousands may flock to a great event, for large numbers of racegoers the variety in British courses is the spice of the sport. And that variety is well represented in the courses covered by Channel Four Racing, even more so with the addition of Uttoxeter in March 1991. The ten Channel Four courses are described on pages 45–55.

Racecourses are sometimes used as location shoots for films and commercials. The interior of the Sandown Park grandstand masqueraded as an airport terminal in the famous British Caledonian television advert in which businessmen 'wish they all could be Caledonian girls'.

By the end of 1989 Rapid Lad had won twelve times at Beverley. He had not won elsewhere since 1982.

Sedgefield is the only jumping track in the country where the final fence is an open ditch.

DRAW

The numbered position in the starting stalls which a horse must take up in relation to the other horses at the start of a flat race.

Facing from the start towards the finish, draw number 1 is always on the left-hand side. The draw is made the day before the race and on some courses and over some distances has an extreme effect on a horse's chance; the contours or shape of a course can mean that certain draws are much more advantageous than others. A draw is not made for National Hunt races as the minimum distance for jumping races is two miles and difference in starting position would have no effect over these longer distances.

FURLONG

One eighth of a mile (220 yards). ('The distance' is 240 yards from the winning post.)

THE GOING

The condition of the ground, a crucial factor in any horse race.

The Clerk of the Course announces the probable state of the going for a meeting some time in advance to advise trainers about the likely conditions, and will announce alterations until on the day of the meeting he declares the official state (which can alter during the course of an afternoon's racing, say in the case of torrential rain). The seven official states of the going in Britain for turf races are:

> hard;
> firm;
> good to firm;
> good;
> good to soft;
> soft;
> heavy.

THE STEWARDS

Time was when Stewards were not necessarily the models of probity that they are today. The tale is often told of the callow young Steward in the 1920s who, with an older and more experienced colleague, witnessed a piece of patent non-trying in a race. 'Did you see that?', he asked his senior. 'Yes, I saw it.' 'What are you going to do?' 'Do?', replied the old Steward: 'Do? Back it next time out, of course!'

It is the duty of the course Stewards at any race meeting to see that the Jockey Club's Rules of Racing are adhered to. Appointments are made by the racecourse and approved by the Stewards of the Jockey Club, and there must be at least four Stewards for every meeting. A Stewards' Secretary (the Stipendiary Steward) provides the Stewards with advice relating to the conduct of the meeting and to the Rules.

The responsibilities and powers of the Stewards, as laid down in the Rules, are wide-ranging. They include the power to abandon the meeting or to abandon certain races within the meeting (usually on account of the weather), and control over all the stands and enclosures; they can 'enquire into, regulate, control, take cognisance of, and adjudicate upon, the conduct of all officials, and of all owners, nominators, trainers, riders, grooms, persons attendant upon horses, and of all persons frequenting the Stands or other places used for the purpose of the Meeting' (Rule 14(viii)).

The Stewards' most public function is to identify and rule upon possible breaches of the Rules during the race itself. To this end they are assisted by the technology of the camera patrol (see pages 41–2) and by having some of their number stationed in a raised position looking straight down the course, from which vantage point it will be possible to see interference, misuse of the whip, and so on. They will be on the look-out for horses apparently not being asked to run on their merits, for extraordinary changes in form (which might suggest that a horse's ability has deliberately been concealed), and for other signs that any race might not be truly run and fairly contested. They can instigate investigations of their own (a Stewards' Enquiry) or respond to an objection from a jockey or, more unusually, an official – for example, the Clerk of the Scales (see page 180), who has to object if a rider does not weigh in at the correct weight. They can impose a hefty fine and, in the case of riding offences, suspend a jockey from competing for up to fourteen days.

If the Stewards of the meeting require a possible breach of the Rules to be investigated at a higher level (or want to suspend a rider for more than fourteen days) they report the matter to the Stewards of the Jockey Club in London, popularly known as 'referring the case to Portman Square'.

THE CLERK OF THE COURSE

The Clerk of the Course bears sole responsibility to the Stewards for the general arrangements of a race meeting. The role has an importance far beyond that of oiling the wheels: Clerks such as the late John Hughes, of Liverpool and Chepstow, and Bill McHarg, of Ayr and other Scottish courses, exerted a tremendous influence on the very nature and quality of the sport at their courses.

The formal duties of a Clerk of the Course are: to conduct the racing at meetings authorized by the Jockey Club, including responsibility for the condition of course and fences, for the correct measurement of distances and adequate marking of the course; to provide a parade ring and ensure that all horses are paraded therein having been saddled in the appointed place; to see that each horse carries a clean number-cloth; and to make sure that horses owned by disqualified persons are not started for any race.

In practice, of course, his (or her) duties are much wider. The Clerk will declare the condition of the going, and will be responsible for making any changes to that description. He (or she) will arrange for the compilation and printing of the racecard. He will negotiate with sponsors about particular races or meetings, and with the Jockey Club about the programme of racing on his course, which will be formulated on his initiative in accordance with regulations laid down by the Jockey Club.

FENCES AND HURDLES

Steeplechase fences (except water jumps) must not be lower than 4 feet 6 inches in height. Plain fences are usually constructed of birch packed together and held in place by a wooden frame on the ground; on the take-off side an apron of gorse is sloped to the fence to encourage horses to jump, and painted rails along the ground provide a 'ground-line' by which the horse will judge when to take off. An open ditch incorporates a ditch protected by a low rail on the take-off side, forcing the horse to make a bigger jump than it would at a plain fence. In the first two miles of a race there must be at least twelve fences and in each succeeding mile at least six. For each mile there must be at least one open ditch. (The fences on the Grand National course at Liverpool are of an unorthodox build – thorn dressed with gorse, fir and spruce.)

Hurdles are constructed like sheep hurdles, with gorse and birch woven into a wooden frame which is driven into the ground: they give if clouted. They must be not less than 3 feet 6 inches from the top bar to the bottom bar. In the first two miles of a hurdle race there must be at least eight flights of hurdles, with an additional flight for every completed quarter mile beyond that.

Hurdles may be lower and easier to clear than steeplechase fences, but speed, accuracy and fluency when jumping are nevertheless vital components in the make-up of a top hurdler, as Celtic Shot (ridden by Peter Scudamore) demonstrates when winning the Allinson Bread Handicap Hurdle at Cheltenham in November 1987.

TECHNICALITIES

Technology is of vital importance to modern racing. Not only do the millions of pounds involved in the betting and breeding sides of the Turf demand that results are as fair and as unequivocal as possible, but the lure of racing as a spectator sport necessitates the use of the best available technology for enhancing the enjoyment of those who follow it – both on the track and off it.

The technological support for a race meeting is provided by Racecourse Technical Services (RTS), a subsidiary of the Betting Levy Board, which provides the starting stalls and the teams which man them, the photo-finish equipment, the camera patrol which films each race, official electrical timing facilities, the racecourse public address and race commentary system (first used on a British racecourse at Goodwood in 1952) and the radio links whereby officials on the course can communicate with one another.

Starting Stalls

Starting stalls were first used to start a race in Britain in the Chesterfield Stakes at Newmarket on 8 July 1965 (they had been in use in France since 1962). Experiments continued throughout the 1966 season and in 1967 they were first used in the Classics. Today they are used for all races on the Flat, unless special reasons (such as location, high wind or very heavy going) make them impractical or unsafe.

Loading up the starting stalls at Chester. The horse drawn 7 (that is, seventh from the left looking from behind the stalls) has been withdrawn: that stall is left open. When the race has started the stalls will be towed out of the way before the runners come round again.

Starting stalls are mobile, and are moved from meeting to meeting, towed by Land Rover, from the depot in Newmarket. RTS (whose main base is in South London) maintains over twenty sets of ten-bay stalls and can cover up to six race meetings per day: the number of sets of stalls needed for a course varies depending on how many horses can be accommodated in line across the track. At each meeting there is a team of nine professional horse-handlers, under the direction of a leader, whose role is to load the horses into the stalls as efficiently and speedily as possible. This can be a hazardous occupation, and injuries to handlers from kicks or from being pushed against the stalls are not uncommon.

The stalls are so designed that the horse is led in by the handler, who then gets out by ducking under the front gate. It is dangerous for the jockey to let the horse get its head down to that gap under the gate as it may try to wriggle out. Within the stall there is a small shelf on each side on which a jockey whose mount is loaded in early may rest his feet in order to take the weight off the horse's back while the other runners are being loaded.

Electrical Timing

Electrical timing on all major courses is controlled by RTS and involves the breaking of an electrical circuit when the Starter presses the button which opens the front gates of the stalls: that instant is the start of the race. The timing is plotted on the photo-finish strip so that an accurate time can be read off for each horse finishing.

The Camera Patrol

RTS provides complete video coverage of each race for post-race scrutiny by the Stewards (and, where appropriate, by television viewers: the head-on pictures which you will often see immediately after a race are taken from the official camera patrol). Nowadays cameras pick up every part of the race, and can illuminate an incident by supplying pictures taken from different angles: much of the most telling evidence in the controversial disqualification of Royal Gait from the 1988 Ascot Gold Cup, when jockey Cash Asmussen was judged to have ridden recklessly in bumping El Conquistador just after the turn into the straight, came from a film patrol camera *behind* the runners. The cameras are directed from a scanner van in much the same way as television coverage is controlled, and the number of cameras covering a course has recently been increased with the advent of Satellite Information Services. The pictures that SIS beams into betting shops are mainly supplied by RTS, as is the commentary.

An RTS race patrol camera at Sandown Park.

Coverage by the camera patrol is a major innovation in racing: by scrutinizing every moment of a race it reduces the possibility of foul riding and by providing head-on pictures of the finish it ensures that a horse not keeping a straight course will be spotted (this can be very difficult to notice from the stands). Those who backed Brook in the Queen Anne Stakes at Ascot in 1974 had special reason to be grateful for the presence of the film patrol: he finished fourth behind Confusion, Gloss and Royal Prerogative, but those of his backers who

COLOUR PHOTO FINISH

A major technical breakthrough came to British racecourses at the beginning of 1990 with the provision of colour photo-finish equipment, which allows for greater accuracy than the black-and-white method previously used. Racecourse Technical Services have facilities for colour on racedays at all courses except Cartmel, Fakenham, Perth and Sedgefield, where permanent darkrooms are not available.

The system uses high-speed chemicals (exclusive to RTS) to produce a colour negative, which is transmitted to the Judge by means of a negative video converter: he can then study the photo of the finish on a colour television monitor and has the facility to enlarge the picture by up to six times if necessary. If he needs to consult a colour print before making his decision, one is produced by means of a computerized colour enlarger and a paper-carrier, in which the cat-gut used to superimpose the winning line on the print is movable to facilitate the making of adjustments.

The negative video converter can be connected with the racecourse closed-circuit television system to transmit the colour photo-finish to the public enclosures, and the same signal can be sent to the Channel Four scanner van for incorporation into the televised coverage.

A colour photo-finish print is reproduced on page 100.

tore up their tickets should have heeded the advice never to do this before 'weighed in' is declared, for the camera patrol revealed that the first three home had all been engaged in a sustained bout of scrimmaging; all three were disqualified and the race was awarded to the fourth past the post: Brook.

The Photo Finish

The photo-finish camera was introduced to British racecourses at Epsom on 22 April 1947. The first Classic to be decided by photo finish was the 1949 Two Thousand Guineas, which Nimbus won by a short head from Abernant; and Nimbus was again the victor later that year in the first Derby to be decided by photo.

On the racecourse, the photo-finish camera is usually situated directly above the Judge's box. Normally two cameras are used, one to cover the whole width of the track and the other to concentrate on that part of the track by the winning post furthest away from the stands in order to make the maximum use of the strip of mirror (six inches wide and six feet tall) which is attached to the far winning post and which enables the Judge to see what is happening from the far side if the finish is so close that the view from the stands side does not give him enough information. The camera has a vertical adjustable slit aperture the size of which varies according to the light: the most common setting is 0.008 inches: whatever passes through this aperture when the camera is operating is recorded on a strip of moving film, so that a photo-finish picture is essentially one of time rather than of area. The camera operator adjusts the speed of the film moving through the camera according to the speed at which the runners are likely to pass the post: thus a horse which comes through much more slowly than anticipated will appear elongated on the photo-finish strip. The camera is left running until the last horse crosses the finishing line, and the Judge will name the distances between the horses from the evidence of the photo-finish strip. A 'spinner' attached to the base of the far winning post names the course, the date, and the race number, and records this information constantly on to the strip.

As soon as the last runner has passed the post the photo-finish booth is blacked out and the film developed: this takes less than a minute. If the Judge cannot place the leading horses without recourse to the camera he announces 'photograph' (which he should do when the distance in question seems to be less than half a length) and consults the evidence of the television monitor on to which the finish is transmitted. If the finish is so close that he cannot pronounce on that evidence, he will ask for a print, from which it is easier to distinguish small distances. Identical prints will then be produced for public display: the white line superimposed on the print displayed is produced by stretching a length of cat-gut across the paper-carrier in which it is made.

ALL-WEATHER RACING

'I used to get sand kicked in my face as a kid, and now I'm getting paid for it,' said jockey Richard Fox at Lingfield Park on 30 October 1989. It was a historic date in the history of British racing, for that Lingfield meeting heralded a revolution in the sport with the advent of all-weather racing. Britain's second all-weather track, at Southwell, held the first hurdles meeting two days later on 1 November.

Lingfield's all-weather course is made of Equitrack and Southwell's of Fibresand: in both the actual racing surface consists of specially graded sand, stabilized with synthetic fibres. Their installation followed many years of concern about the number of racing fixtures lost to the weather, and matters were brought to a head after the sacrifice of seventy-two days in January and February 1985. The Jockey Club investigated the feasibility and desirability of all-weather racing, and in November 1985 approved the go-ahead 'to minimise the effect on racing and betting of adverse weather conditions during the winter months'. Several courses investigated the possibility of staging such racing, and eventually the pioneering rôle went to Lingfield and Southwell.

It was Niklas Angel, a three-year-old colt trained by Conrad Allen and ridden by Richard Quinn, who went into the history books as the first winner of an all-weather race in Britain, and the first impressions of the opening meetings were favourable. But soon the novelty wore off and the problems started. At Southwell on 8 November none of the few bookmakers who had not packed up and gone home on a foul day would form a market for the sixth race, refusing to bet as they were wary of an early move for one of the runners. Although one bookie offered prices right on the off-time, it was not enough for starting prices to be returned, and the notion of all-weather racing producing betting turnover took an ironic blow. A harder one followed on 14 November, when the meeting at Southwell had to be abandoned – because of the weather. Fog had restricted visibility to eighty yards. And two days later the plastic hurdles used on all-weather tracks claimed a victim in the filly Batu Pahat, who had to be put down at Lingfield after injuring her fetlock.

But racing on artificial surfaces has gradually come to be accepted as part of the scene. Although some of the traditional notions of the shape of the racing year will have to be altered, it is here to stay.

There are three categories of going for all-weather racing: fast, standard, and slow.

With the coming of all-weather racing the official Flat season now runs from 1 January to 31 December.

Horses which race on all-weather surfaces are given, for handicapping purposes, a Jockey Club rating separate from their turf rating.

The Lingfield Park all-weather course is the first track in Britain to have installed a permanent system of sectional timing.

All-weather racing at Lingfield Park, November 1989.

RACECOURSES OF THE
BRITISH ISLES

Flat
National Hunt
Flat and National Hunt

The courses covered by Channel Four
Racing in 1990 are shown in boxes, as
is Uttoxeter, covered for the first time
in 1991.

CHANNEL FOUR COURSES

Ayr

There are five racecourses in Scotland – Ayr, Edinburgh, Hamilton Park, Kelso and Perth – and though they all have their charms Ayr is indisputably the finest. The Western Meeting in September is the best Scottish fixture of the year, and the William Hill Scottish National is one of the highlights of the jumping season throughout the UK.

Although horses were raced at Ayr as long ago as the sixteenth century, the present course has been in use only since 1907. Under the inspired direction of Clerk of the Course Bill McHarg, who retired in 1988, it has become one of the most popular tracks in Great Britain. A left-handed oval circuit of just over one and a half miles, the course has gradual bends and long, easy gradients which favour the long-striding, galloping type of horse with plenty of stamina.

And stamina is the quality especially required for Ayr's most spectacular event, the Scottish National in April. Run from 1867 until 1965 at the now defunct course at Bogside, this famous race takes up nearly three circuits of today's course (on which, incidentally, there is no longer a water jump) for its 4 miles 120 yards. Winners since the war include three horses who also won the Grand National itself: Merryman II and Little Polveir won the Scottish race before their Aintree triumphs, while Red Rum skated home at Ayr in 1974 just three weeks after his second National victory, four lengths ahead of Proud Tarquin and Lord Oaksey.

Ayr's other great race puts the emphasis on speed. The Ayr Gold Cup, first run in 1804, is a six-furlong handicap with a huge field which invariably proves one of the trickiest betting challenges of the entire year. It is no place for faint-hearted horses, and is occasionally won by a very good horse indeed. Peter O'Sullevan's wonderfully tough sprinter Be Friendly beat thirty-two opponents in 1967, but the greatest performance in the race in recent memory was when the giant Roman Warrior humped 10 stone to victory in 1975, ahead of such high-class horses as Import and Lochnager.

It is a tribute to the excellence of Ayr that it was to this course that the St Leger was transferred in 1989 after the cancellation of the race at Doncaster.

MAJOR RACES

Scottish Champion Hurdle
William Hill Scottish National
Scottish Classic (Group 3)
Doonside Cup
Harry Rosebery Challenge Trophy
Ladbrokes Ayr Gold Cup

An endearing feature of Ayr fixtures on televison is the habit of the people who live in the houses skirting the far side of the course of coming to their back doors during a race and waving tea towels at the camera: are they craning their necks round towards the television set indoors to see whether they're actually on the telly?

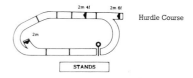
Hurdle Course

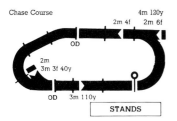

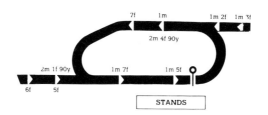

Chester: the field for the Ladbroke Chester Cup in 1989 making its way to the start alongside the Roman wall.

Chester

Scenically placed on the banks of the River Dee and hard up against the Roman city walls, Chester is the tightest and roundest Flat racecourse in the country, with a left-handed circuit of a few yards over one mile and a home straight of hardly more than a furlong. It thus favours a medium-sized, nimble type of horse, sharp-actioned enough to break quickly from the stalls and keep a handy position without getting dizzy. It is dead flat.

Chester racecourse (popularly known as the Roodee) is notable for its history as well as for its remarkable size and shape. The silver bell first run for at the request of the Mayor in 1540 was the earliest recorded regular prize in racing history, and Chester is the most ancient meeting still run at its original location. But it is also a highly modern course now, with a new stand opened in 1988 after the destruction by fire of the old County Stand three years previously.

And the modern standard of racing here is high. Despite its oddities, Chester is a useful preparation for a Derby horse, encouraging an adaptability to unusual conditions which will come in handy when tackling the even odder contours of Epsom. The Chester Vase has long been one of the established Derby trials, with several horses taking the Blue Riband at Epsom after winning here – Papyrus, Windsor Lad and Hyperion before the war and, in more recent times, Henbit and Shergar; Quest For Fame was second to Belmez in 1990. Old Vic won the 1989 running as a prelude to his victories in the French and Irish Derbys. Parthia won the Dee Stakes, another of the big three-year-old races at the May meeting, prior to victory in the Derby in 1959, and Sir Harry Lewis took the same race before winning the Irish Derby in 1987. The Ormonde Stakes for older horses also has some high-class recent winners (Crow in 1978, Niniski in 1980 and Teenoso in 1984), while the Chester Cup over two and a quarter miles is a race with a very long tradition: at one time it was second only to the Derby in the volume of ante-post betting it attracted. Among its winners are such old favourites as Trelawny (1960), Peter O'Sullevan's Attivo, who won the race in 1974 after taking the Daily Express Triumph Hurdle at Cheltenham, John Cherry, who won in 1976 and then went on to win the Cesarewitch, and Sea Pigeon, winner in 1977 and 1978.

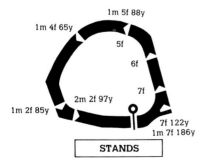

1m 5f 88y
1m 4f 65y
5f
6f
2m 2f 97y
7f
1m 2f 85y
7f 122y
1m 7f 186y
STANDS

Doncaster: the spacious parade ring in front of the grandstand.

Doncaster

Home of the St Leger, Doncaster is regarded as one of the fairest and best racecourses in the country. A pear-shaped track of nearly two miles round, it has a long, sweeping turn into the four and a half furlong straight, and generally favours the long-striding, staying type of horse. It is wide and flat, except for a slight rise and fall on the far side.

Horses were already being raced at Doncaster in the late sixteenth century, though today's course on Town Moor was not established until 1778. The present grandstand was opened in 1969, and the siting of the paddock right in front of the stand is a very popular feature with racegoers. (Less popular was the indoor betting hall, which allowed bookmakers to conduct their business protected from inclement weather: somehow it didn't feel right to bet with a course bookie indoors.)

The pinnacle of the Doncaster year is the St Leger (which is described in detail on pages 75–6), though the St Leger meeting in mid-September is no longer the massive popular celebration it once was; certainly not in 1989, when the Classic was removed to Ayr following the discovery of subsidence in the Doncaster straight. Doncaster also usually provides the book-ends of the Flat racing season by staging the opening meeting and the closing meeting, both featuring races inherited from other courses: the Lincoln Handicap is the first major race of the season, and has been run at Doncaster since

MAJOR RACES

William Hill Golden Spurs Handicap Chase

William Hill Lincoln Handicap

Laurent Perrier Champagne Stakes (Group 2)

A.F. Budge Park Hill Stakes (Group 2)

May Hill Stakes (Group 3)

Tote Portland Handicap

Doncaster Cup (Group 3)

Kiveton Park Stakes (Group 3)

Flying Childers Stakes (Group 2)

St Leger Stakes (Group 1)

Racing Post Trophy (Group 1)

William Hill November Handicap

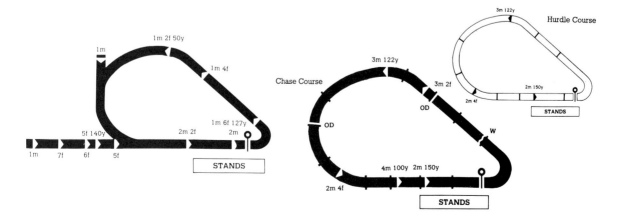

Lincoln racecourse was closed in 1964, while the November Handicap moved to Doncaster after the demise of Manchester in 1963. Doncaster also stages the last Group 1 race of the British season, the one mile race for two-year-olds run variously as the Timeform Gold Cup, then the Observer Gold Cup, the William Hill Futurity and now the Racing Post Trophy. Reference Point was the first horse to win the Derby after taking this race, and it has been won by several other notable performers, including Noblesse, Ribocco and Vaguely Noble; Shergar was runner-up to Beldale Flutter here in 1980.

Jump racing at Doncaster was revived after the war, having been discontinued in 1911, but is not today of the quality it enjoyed when races such as the Great Yorkshire Chase were among the top events of the calendar. That race has now been replaced by the William Hill Golden Spurs Handicap Chase, the conditions of which are framed to attract a big field of only moderate horses, thus effecting hefty betting. Never mind: Doncaster remains one of the top courses in Britain.

Epsom

Epsom, home of the Derby (see pages 72–4), is one of the strangest courses in any major racing country. Take the Derby itself: the runners race uphill immediately after the start and round a right-hand bend before tacking over to the opposite rail in order to negotiate the left-hand bend into the steep descent down Tattenham Hill to Tattenham Corner. They reach the straight just under four furlongs from the winning post and continue downhill until the ground rises very slightly inside the final furlong. As if all these changes of gradient were not enough, the course slopes in towards the far rail in the straight, so that tired horses tend to lean to the left. To win the Derby a horse needs the speed to keep a good position in the early stages of the race, the stamina to last out up the wide home straight, and, most important, the balance and agility to be able to gallop both uphill and downhill – in short, to be the complete middle-distance racehorse, and it will need riding by the complete jockey.

Epsom also stages the Oaks (see page 75) and the Coronation Cup, the first Group 1 race of the season for four-year-olds and upwards: this invariably attracts small but high-class fields, and has been won by many of the great racehorses of the century, including, in recent memory, Mill Reef, Roberto, Bustino, Time Charter, Rainbow Quest and Triptych, who won it twice – as did another famous mare, Petite Etoile.

Races over five, six and seven furlongs start on different chutes which run on to the main horseshoe-shaped course, and sprint races at Epsom are exceptionally fast. The five-furlong course, which starts sharply downhill, saw the fastest time ever recorded in British racing when Indigenous (carrying 9 stone 5 pounds) won the Tadworth Handicap on 2 June 1960 in a time of 53.6 seconds – an average of 41.98 miles per hour. That race was timed by hand; the fastest time ever recorded by the more reliable electrical mechanism was also over the Epsom five furlongs, 53.7 seconds by Spark Chief on 30 August 1983.

MAJOR RACES

Racal–Vodafone Blue Riband Trial Stakes

Westminster–Motor (Taxi) Insurance City and Suburban Handicap

Princess Elizabeth Stakes

Woodcote Stakes

Ever Ready Derby Stakes (Group 1)

Diomed Stakes (Group 3)

Hanson Coronation Cup (Group 1)

Gold Seal Oaks Stakes (Group 1)

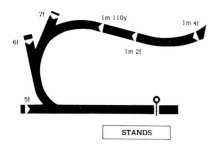

Racing has taken place on Epsom Downs for well over 300 years. In 1648 a group of Royalists staged races there as a diversion for Charles I during the Civil War, and Samuel Pepys mentions coming across horsemen at Epsom 'upon the Hill, where they were making of matches to run' in 1663. The original Epsom grandstand, which was opened in 1830 and survived for nearly a century, was for a time the home of a young girl named Isabella Mayson, whose stepfather was Clerk of the Course. She was to achieve lasting fame as Mrs Beeton.

Kempton Park

Kempton Park, opened in 1878 near Sunbury-on-Thames in Middlesex, has made very significant improvements to its facilities in recent years. The new arrangement for parade ring and unsaddling enclosure works very well indeed, and the general atmosphere at the course is now buoyant after years in the doldrums.

But the standard of jump racing here has always been high, with the King George VI Rank Chase on Boxing Day one of the most eagerly awaited events of the whole year. The recent exploits of Desert Orchid in the race are fresh in the memory, particularly his spectacular and widely unexpected victory when running the rest of the field into the ground in 1986 at a starting price of 16–1. For the few years before that the race had been largely dominated by the Dickinson family, who sent out Gay Spartan to win in 1978, Silver Buck in 1979 and 1980, and Wayward Lad in 1982, 1983 and – after Burrough Hill Lad had interrupted the sequence for Jenny Pitman in 1984 – in 1985. Most of the great steeplechasers since the war have won the race; among them Cottage Rake, Halloween (twice), Limber Hill, Mandarin (twice), Saffron Tartan, Mill House, The Dikler, Pendil (twice), Captain Christy (twice) and, of course, the immortal Arkle. His victory in 1965, though, was marred by the fatal accident to the brilliant two-miler Dunkirk, who had set up a huge lead before his stamina gave out approaching the final open ditch, where he took a crashing fall. A year later the race produced even deeper gloom with an injury to Arkle

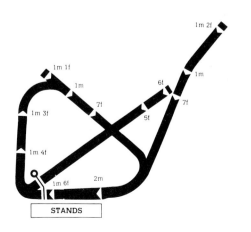

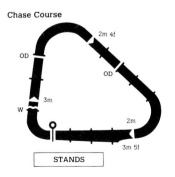

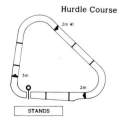

himself, who broke a pedal bone in his off fore hoof, apparently when striking the guard-rail of a fence on the second circuit. The great horse ran the last mile or so with the broken bone, and was overtaken just before the line by Dormant. He never ran again.

The King George is now complemented at the Christmas meeting by the Christmas Hurdle, the best hurdle race of the mid-season period, won in 1983 by Dawn Run *en route* to her Champion Hurdle victory; Kribensis repeated the double in 1989–90 (and had also won the Christmas Hurdle in 1988). The best known flat races at Kempton are long-established handicaps such as the Rosebery, the Queen's Prize and the Jubilee Handicap, though the September Stakes has Group 3 status and serves as a useful warm-up for the Arc.

A right-handed course of triangular shape and about thirteen furlongs round, Kempton is quite flat and can suit horses of doubtful stamina, as its fairly sharp bends deter the sustaining of a punishing pace. The ten-furlong Jubilee course joins the main course just before the straight (which is three and a half furlongs long); the sprint course cuts across the main course and has a separate winning post.

Newcastle

Although Newcastle's most famous race is still the Northumberland Plate, a two-mile handicap first run in 1833, the course nowadays attracts most attention for its National Hunt racing, notably the Eider Chase, a traditional trial for the Grand National, and the Fighting Fifth Hurdle, run in November over two miles. This race is often contested by the very best hurdlers: Comedy Of Errors, twice Champion Hurdler, won it three times; Night Nurse beat Comedy Of Errors and Sea Pigeon in 1975 and was beaten by Bird's Nest the following year; Sea Pigeon beat Bird's Nest in 1978; Gaye Brief won in 1983 and Browne's Gazette in 1984 (tragically, he collapsed and died in the same race a year later). That the Whitbread Gold Cup was run at Newcastle during the rebuilding of Sandown Park in 1973 is a tribute to the quality of its jumping track.

On the Flat, Newcastle's only Pattern race is the Beeswing Stakes, a seven-furlong Group 3 race for three-year-olds and upwards run in July. The race commemorates a famous mare who during her eight seasons in training won over fifty races, including the Ascot Gold Cup, the Doncaster Cup four times and the Newcastle Cup six times. The

---

MAJOR RACES

Tote Eider Handicap Chase

Newcastle 'Brown Ale' Northumberland Plate

Federation Brewery Beeswing Stakes (Group 3)

Bellway 'Fighting Fifth' Hurdle

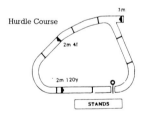

Hurdle Course

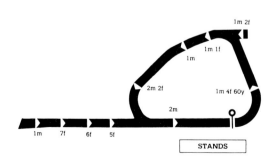

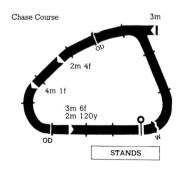

Chase Course

Northumberland Plate has lost much of its former status but has had some distinguished winners in its time: the 1952 winner Souepi won the Ascot Gold Cup the following year, and Piaco won in 1967 after taking the Doncaster Cup in 1966: a notoriously difficult horse (his mood was not improved by being gelded), he hated getting his head wet, so connections had to be careful of running him in the rain!

Newcastle races used to be held on the Town Moor but were moved in 1882 to the present site of Gosforth Park. The course is about one and three quarter miles in circumference, left-handed and mainly flat, though there is a slight climb from the turn into the straight. Both the straight course and the round course, with its easy bends, suit a big, long-striding horse. It provides one of the fairest tests in the country.

Newmarket

To racing folk, Newmarket is 'Headquarters' – the home of the Jockey Club, the largest centre for training racehorses in the country, the site of the principal bloodstock sales and of many famous studs, including the National Stud (see pages 26–7), and venue of two top-ranking racecourses.

Newmarket began developing as a sporting centre back in the early seventeenth century, when James I was drawn to the place by the excellent coursing and hunting to be had locally. He built a palace in the town, and Charles I kept up the Royal connection. But it was the second King Charles who really made Newmarket synonymous with horse racing, founding races and riding in some of them himself: the Rowley Mile course takes its name from Charles II, nicknamed 'Old Rowley' after his favourite hack. Another of his favourite mounts is commemorated in the Nell Gwyn Stakes, run at the Craven meeting in the spring. After the founding of the Jockey Club some time around 1750 the town gradually established itself as the administrative centre of the sport, and although the main business of the Jockey Club is today carried on in London, Newmarket remains the focal point of British racing.

> Charles II's palace in Newmarket – near where the Rutland Arms is today – was connected with Nell Gwyn's house across the road by means of an underground passage.

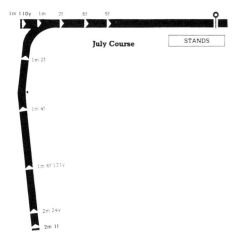

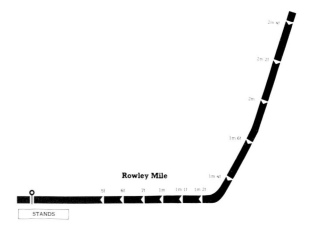

As a training centre Newmarket is unparalleled. About three thousand horses are in training here, and the town is home to many of racing's best-known trainers: Henry Cecil at Warren Place and Sefton Lodge, Michael Stoute at Freemason Lodge and Beech Hurst, Luca Cumani at Bedford House. The town is surrounded by miles of gallops, some of them – such as Warren Hill or The Limekilns – with names almost as famous as those of the great horses trained on them.

Newmarket's two courses are the Rowley Mile, where racing takes place in the spring and autumn, and the July Course, used in the height of summer. For about a mile from the point most distant from the stands they follow the same track (the Beacon Course), which then divides into two separate straights, about eleven furlongs long for the Rowley and about a mile for the July. The two straights are separated by the Devil's Dyke (or Devil's Ditch), an ancient earthwork which stretches for miles across the Heath: the Rowley Mile course cuts through the Dyke at the Running Gap. Both courses are exceptionally wide and offer a severe test of a horse's courage and stamina. Newmarket Heath can be the bleakest place imaginable, and for horse and racegoer alike is no place for the faint-hearted.

The Rowley Mile

Strictly speaking, the course for each distance up to ten furlongs bears a separate name: the Rous Course for five furlongs, the Bretby Stakes Course for six, the Dewhurst Stakes Course for seven, the Rowley Mile, the Cambridgeshire Course (nine furlongs) and Across the Flat (ten furlongs). Races run over distances above ten furlongs take in the Cesarewitch Course. All races up to ten furlongs are perfectly straight and the course is mainly flat until the Bushes, about two furlongs from the finish, where the runners experience a downhill gradient for about a furlong to the Dip, from where they have a stiff climb up to the winning post.

More Group 1 races are run on the Rowley Mile than on any other course in Britain, and the standard of sport here generally is very high indeed. Its first meeting of the year, the Craven meeting in April, is for most people the moment when the Flat season really starts, with the seven-furlong Nell Gwyn Stakes for fillies and the one-mile Craven Stakes for colts offering clues to the One Thousand and Two Thousand Guineas respectively; other highlights of this meeting are the European Free Handicap and the Earl of Sefton Stakes. The next meeting sees the first two Classics, the Guineas races themselves (see page 71), and the Jockey Club Stakes. When the action returns to the Rowley Mile course after moving across the Devil's Dyke for the summer two marvellous meetings in October dominate the closing stages of the season. The first is the Cambridgeshire meeting, where the famous nine-furlong handicap is supported by the Cheveley Park Stakes and the Middle Park Stakes, Group 1 two-year-old contests for fillies and colts respectively, by the Jockey Club Cup for stayers and by the ten-furlong Sun Chariot Stakes for fillies. Centrepiece of the second October meeting is the Cesarewitch, the two and a quarter mile handicap which, like the Cambridgeshire, attracts huge sums in betting; run on the same day is the ten-furlong Champion Stakes, the

---

ROWLEY MILE COURSE

Major Races

Nell Gwyn Stakes (Group 3)

EBF Earl of Sefton Stakes (Group 3)

Ladbroke European Free Handicap

Charles Heidsieck Champagne Craven Stakes (Group 3)

General Accident One Thousand Guineas Stakes (Group 1)

General Accident Jockey Club Stakes (Group 2)

General Accident Two Thousand Guineas Stakes (Group 1)

Palace House Stakes (Group 3)

Tattersalls Cheveley Park Stakes (Group 1)

Newgate Stud Middle Park Stakes (Group 1)

Jockey Club Cup (Group 3)

Cheveley Park Stud Sun Chariot Stakes (Group 2)

William Hill Cambridgeshire

Jameson Whiskey Challenge Stakes (Group 2)

Three Chimneys Dewhurst Stakes (Group 1)

Bottisham Heath Stud Rockfel Stakes (Group 3)

Dubai Champion Stakes (Group 1)

Tote Cesarewitch

Mail on Sunday 3-y-o Series Final

last of the big middle-distance races of the Flat season. Won over the years by many great horses, including Brigadier Gerard (twice), Triptych (twice), Sir Ivor, Petite Etoile and Pebbles, it was also the occasion of sensational defeats for Nijinsky in his last race, and Allez France. The Dewhurst Stakes, often the most informative two-year-old race of the season, is also run at this meeting.

The July Course

All Newmarket meetings in June, July and August are held on the July Course, and it was to this course that all the Classics were transferred during the Second World War. All races up to one mile are straight, with a downhill gradient until the ground rises through the final furlong.

Highlight of racing here is the July Meeting, three days of top-class sport including the Princess of Wales's Stakes over a mile and a half, the six-furlong July Stakes (the oldest two-year-old race still run), the one mile Child Stakes for fillies, and the six-furlong Cherry Hinton Stakes for two-year-old fillies. The top event of this meeting is the July Cup, a Group 1 six-furlong contest which is one of the key races of the year for sprinters. In the period after the war the famous Abernant won the race twice, as did Right Boy, and in the recent past it has gone to such familiar performers as Moorestyle, Marwell, Sharpo, Habibti, Chief Singer, Never So Bold and Ajdal – who had last run over twice the distance, in the Derby.

JULY COURSE

Major Races

Van Geest Criterion Stakes (Group 3)

Princess of Wales's Stakes (Group 2)

Hillsdown Cherry Hinton Stakes (Group 3)

Anglia Television July Stakes (Group 3)

Child Stakes (Group 2)

Carroll Foundation July Cup (Group 1)

Sandown Park

Sandown Park, at Esher in Surrey, is for many people the perfect racecourse, with excellent facilities for racegoers, a circuit seemingly custom-built for dramatic races, and sport of the highest order both on the flat and over jumps.

Its most exciting occasion, and for many enthusiasts the best day's racing of the year, is Whitbread Gold Cup Day in late April. The Whitbread itself, a handicap steeplechase run over three miles five furlongs towards the end of the jumping season, was the first sponsored race on its initial running in 1957, and since then has not only been won by most of the great chasers of the age (Taxidermist, Pas Seul, Arkle, What A Myth, Mill House, The Dikler, Diamond Edge (twice) and Desert Orchid) but has produced some of the greatest races, such as the unforgettable 1984 contest described on page 185. Whitbread day also features a marvellous programme of flat racing, including the

Mr Frisk in 1990 was the first horse to win the Grand National and the Whitbread Gold Cup.

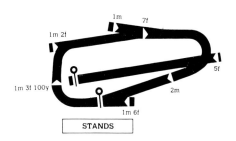

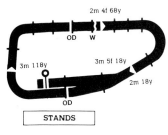

Chase Course

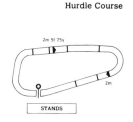

Hurdle Course

Gordon Richards EBF Stakes and the Classic Trial, the race which between 1979 and 1986 was won on four occasions by horses who went on to win the Derby – Troy, Henbit, Shergar and Shahrastani.

Sandown's other great race, the Eclipse Stakes over ten furlongs, was first run in 1886, and is the earliest race in the Flat season in which the cream of the middle-distance three-year-olds can take on their elders. It often attracts an overseas challenge and has seen some famous contests, including the stirring battle in 1968 between Royal Palace, Taj Dewan and Sir Ivor. The race was won by both Mill Reef (1971) and Brigadier Gerard (1972) as well as, in recent years, by the likes of Pebbles, Dancing Brave, Mtoto (twice) and Nashwan.

The track is oval in shape and about one mile five furlongs round, and the very testing five-furlong sprint course cuts through the main course and has its own winning post. The highest point of the main course is beyond the winning post, making the straight a gradual uphill climb. The chasing course is among the most exhilarating in the country, the three plain fences in quick succession before the turn towards the Pond Fence (three from home) forming an especially tricky sequence.

Sandown's opening in 1875 owed much to the energy and enterprise of Hwfa Williams, who was Clerk of the Course for fifty years and whose implementation of the 'park' course idea made such a difference to racegoing. Not least among the improvements which Sandown offered was that, according to a contemporary report, 'a man could take his ladies without any fear of their hearing coarse language or witnessing uncouth behaviour.'

Uttoxeter

The televising by Channel Four Racing of the Midlands Grand National (renamed the Ansells National to acknowledge sponsorship by the brewery) at Uttoxeter in March 1991 marks a significant moment in the fortunes of a course which typifies the appeal of the small jumping tracks.

If you tend to lose your place during the running of the Scottish National at Ayr you'd better concentrate during the Midlands. The four-and-a-half-mile trip (as long as the Grand National itself) starts on a chute at the end of the home straight, and the runners come up to the winning post and then make three complete circuits. Although the bend beyond the winning post is fairly tight, the far side (which includes a slight bend to the right before the water jump) has only minor undulations, and with the turn into the straight a gentle one, the course is well suited to a galloping sort of horse – and, naturally, one with plenty of stamina. Rag Trade won the Midlands Grand National in 1975 and the following spring took the Welsh Grand National on the way to beating Red Rum in the real thing at Liverpool, and another notable winner in recent years is The Thinker, who lifted the 1986 race and next season took the Cheltenham Gold Cup.

Uttoxeter (in Staffordshire, not far from Stoke-on-Trent) may not be Newmarket or York, but jump jockeys have long considered it one of the best and fairest of the small courses which make up the backbone of the National Hunt game, and its addition to the itinerary of Channel Four Racing's travelling circus adds a fascinating and engaging new element to the team's coverage.

Chase Course

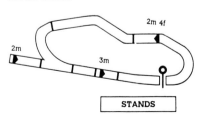

2m 4f

2m

3m

4m 4f

3m 2f

OD

W

STANDS

Hurdle Course

2m 4f

2m

3m

STANDS

York

As John Tyrrel notes in his preface to this chapter, there were horse races in York in Roman times, and properly regulated sport has taken place on the Knavesmire, a vast stretch of common land just outside the centre of the city and once the site of public executions, since 1731. Now among the very top racecourses in the world, this was the scene of one of the most famous races in history in 1851, when a crowd of 100,000 witnessed the match between Voltigeur and The Flying Dutchman. Both horses had won a Derby and a St Leger, and The Flying Dutchman, giving his younger rival 8½ pounds, was fractionally the favourite for the two-mile contest. He prevailed by a length.

Since then York has seen many great races, and the August meeting provides very high-class sport: not for nothing has York been called 'the Ascot of the North'. The International Stakes began life in 1972 as the Benson and Hedges Gold Cup, and this ten-furlong contest was launched in sensational style when Roberto inflicted upon the great Brigadier Gerard the only defeat of his eighteen-race career. Other notable winners of the race are Dahlia, who won it twice (beating Grundy into fourth place in 1975), Wollow, Troy, Commanche Run and Triptych. The two other Group 1 races of the August meeting are the Yorkshire Oaks and the Nunthorpe Stakes (recently the William Hill Sprint Championship), while the biggest betting race is the Ebor Handicap over a mile and three quarters, which is often won by a high-class horse in defiance of the handicapper – the outstanding Irish mare Gladness won carrying 9 stone 7 pounds in 1958, and other classy winners in recent years have been Sir Montagu (1976), Jupiter Island (1983) and Kneller (1988), while Sea Pigeon humped 9 stone 10 pounds to victory in 1979. The winning owner of the Gimcrack Stakes, the meeting's major two-year-old race, traditionally makes the principal speech at the annual dinner of the York Gimcrack Club in December.

York's other big meeting, in May, is a quieter affair but none the less fascinating; the Dante Stakes has recently regained its status as an important Derby trial, going to Shirley Heights (1978), Shahrastani (1986) and Reference Point (1987), all of whom went on to win at Epsom, and Sanglamore (1990), who won the Prix du Jockey-Club at Chantilly.

Wide and flat, York is as fair a test of the Thoroughbred racehorse as can be imagined, with easy left-handed bends encouraging the relentless galloper. For horse as for spectator, it's a hard place to fault.

MAJOR RACES

Tattersalls Musidora Stakes (Group 3)

William Hill Dante Stakes (Group 2)

Kosset Yorkshire Cup (Group 2)

Duke of York Stakes (Group 3)

William Hill Trophy

John Smith's Magnet Cup

Juddmonte International Stakes (Group 1)

Aston Upthorpe Stud Yorkshire Oaks (Group 1)

Great Voltigeur Stakes (Group 2)

Scottish Equitable Gimcrack Stakes (Group 2)

Tote Ebor Handicap

Pacemaker Update Lowther Stakes (Group 2)

Keeneland Nunthorpe Stakes (Group 1)

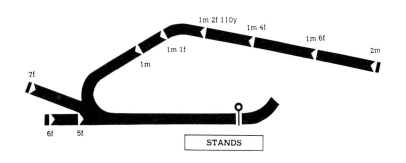

THE SHAPE
OF RACING

John Oaksey has been racing correspondent for the *Sunday Telegraph*, the *Daily Telegraph* and *Horse and Hound* and is the author or co-author of several books, including *The Story of Mill Reef*. For two decades he was a top amateur jockey (riding as John Lawrence before he succeeded to his father's title, Lord Oaksey), winning the 1958 Whitbread and Hennessy Gold Cups on Taxidermist and finishing a narrowly beaten runner-up on Carrickbeg in the 1963 Grand National. He was leading amateur under National Hunt Rules in the 1957–58 and 1970–71 seasons.

Horse racing is a spectator sport which also happens to be an extremely popular medium for gambling. Racing and betting are inextricably entwined and the sport's prosperity depends on the relationship between the two.

It took the Jockey Club, the self-electing social association which still governs horse racing, a long time to recognize this relationship and until this century the lofty official line was that the Club 'takes no cognisance of betting matters'. But since 1961, when the government legalized off-course betting in shops and set up the Levy Board to collect and distribute a 'subsidy' for racing, the crucial question has been how much should the bookmakers – or, to be more exact, their customers – pay for the 'betting medium' with which horse racing supplies them.

It is all very well to look enviously at the French (who have a Tote monopoly, with no bookmakers allowed) or the Australians (who have bookies on course with a Tote monopoly off it). The fact is that we are stuck with bookmakers and several thousand betting shops. No government would ever dare make them illegal now.

The basic problem is that racing has become top heavy. An influx of enthusiastic Arabs to whom money is, almost literally, no object, means that British flat-race horses are as good as – if not better than – any in the world, and the few top stables which house the best are prosperous affairs. Even in those, however, a stable lad's basic wage is not much over £100 a week – not nearly enough to finance a mortgage when he wants to marry and buy a house. So experienced lads are driven to look for better-paid jobs outside racing, and the result is a grave shortage of skilled labour, even at the top.

A massive increase in prize money seems to be the only way to justify higher training fees and better wages, and this is needed even more desperately in jumping than on the Flat. I have never been able to understand why the owner of a Derby winner, whose three-year-old colt becomes worth several millions the instant he passes the post, should get a prize of around £300,000. Desert Orchid, who is a gelding without stud value, was worth no more after galloping three and a quarter miles to win the Cheltenham Gold Cup than he had been that morning – yet his owner got only £68,000! At present, when the Levy Board doles out money it gives 60 per cent to the Flat (in a vain attempt to keep pace with richer countries) and only 40 per cent to jumping – something which we do better than any other nation. If there were any justice or common sense in the system it would be the other way round.

John Oaksey

CONTROL, ADMINISTRATION, FINANCE

The racing business employs many thousands of people, both directly and, through the betting and bloodstock industries, indirectly, and each year the destiny of billions of pounds is determined by the results of races. So it is of crucial importance that the sport is properly controlled, administered and financed. These roles belong, respectively, to the Jockey Club, Weatherbys and The Horserace Betting Levy Board.

The Jockey Club

By the middle of the eighteenth century racing was in a parlous state. Rules were practically non-existent, corruption and doping were widespread and criminality was rife. The Jockey Club came into being in Newmarket in an attempt to bring some sort of order to the sport. Originally it was more concerned with arranging matches and settling bets, but in due course it began to publish rules (its first recognizable order was issued in 1758) and generally establish authority over the running of races at Newmarket. A tendency developed for other racecourses to refer their disputes to the Jockey Club, and its influence grew steadily over the next century until it became (as it has remained) the ruling body of the sport.

Three figures dominated its early history:

Sir Charles Bunbury, who became Steward of the Jockey Club in 1768, was especially influential both in building up the authority of the Club and in improving the speed of the Thoroughbred by introducing shorter races for younger horses. During his regime the Classics were founded, and the first Derby was won by his own Diomed.

Lord George Bentinck was a zealous reformer in the early nineteenth century, at a time when the sport was still very ill-regulated. He outlawed the custom of the winner's owner giving a present to the Judge after a big race, and sought a more efficient way of starting races than the prevailing one whereby the Starter shouted 'Go!' as soon as the field had made a rough line: indeed, he can be credited with the organization of race meetings in roughly the form we know them. He achieved many great benefits for English racing, but never his own ambition of leading in a Derby winner. He sold his racing interests in 1846 to concentrate on politics, and in 1848 Surplice, one of the yearlings he had disposed of, triumphed at Epsom. Bentinck was desolated: Benjamin Disraeli, encountering him in the House of Commons Library the day after the Derby, described how Bentinck 'gave a sort of superb groan. "All my life I have been trying for this, and for what have I sacrificed it?" he murmured.'

┌─ **THE NATIONAL** ──────
HORSERACING MUSEUM

Opened by Her Majesty the
Queen on 30 April 1983, the
National Horseracing Museum
is situated, appropriately enough,
at the very heart of British racing,
next to the Jockey Club Rooms in
the High Street, Newmarket.
Over 25,000 visitors a year come
to the Museum, in whose five
galleries is displayed a wonderful
collection of works of art,
documents and memorabilia
illustrating the rich history of
racing over three centuries. Here
you can see the skeleton of
Eclipse and the stuffed head of
Persimmon (who won the 1896
Derby when owned by the Prince
of Wales, later Edward VII), as
well as offcuts from various other
famous horses. There is a
reconstruction of a weighing
room from the time of Fred
Archer, whips and saddles used
in big races, and even the
woollen headband worn by
Lester Piggott while he was
recuperating from his
horrendous accident when
dragged under the Epsom stalls
by Winsor Boy in 1981. Superbly
mounted displays of exhibits and
photographs illustrate all aspects
of the sport, historic and modern
– the great owners, the great
jockeys and trainers, racecourses,
betting, and the technical
wonders of the modern Turf.
But racing has not become
simply a 'museum piece': films of
famous races are played
continuously, conveying the
immediacy and excitement of the
race itself.

A spell in the National
Horseracing Museum is the
perfect complement to any visit
to Newmarket; don't under-
estimate the time you will want to
appreciate its riches to the full.

Admiral Henry John Rous, best remembered for working out the first weight-for-age scales (see page 148), was elected a Steward of the Jockey Club in 1838 and gained a huge reputation as a handicapper: it was he who handicapped the famous match at York between The Flying Dutchman and Voltigeur (see page 55). He became public handicapper in 1855 and pursued his duties energetically, watching races from the top of the stand with a large telescope (he was, after all, an admiral) and rushing down after the race to see which horses were blowing most. At Newmarket he would watch from the Bushes, and was in the habit of roaring at non-trying jockeys as they came by. Probably the most influential of all Turf administrators, Rous was instrumental in the transformation of racing from the ill-structured days of the early nineteenth century towards the organized sport that we know today.

The Jockey Club remains at the centre of this sophisticated organizational web, the ruling force, its responsibilities and functions extending to every area of racing. It formulates, enforces and administers the Rules of Racing. It investigates possible breaches of those Rules and hands out punishment to offenders. It licenses jockeys and trainers and ensures that they behave within the Rules, both on the racecourse and at training establishments. The Rules are extensive, and in order to ensure that they are all adhered to the Club has its own security service and a laboratory (funded by the Levy Board) to test horses for the use of drugs. Through Racecourse Technical Services (a subsidiary of the Levy Board) it provides racecourses with the technology of camera patrols, photo-finish equipment and starting stalls. It appoints Stewards to control individual race meetings and see that the Rules are observed, and supplies racecourse officials such as Judges, Starters, Clerks of the Scales, and Veterinary Officers. It stipulates minimum values of races and its handicappers lay down the weight which each horse will carry.

On a wider canvas, the Jockey Club determines the shape of British racing by authorizing fixtures and race programmes. It imposes the Pattern (see page 69), which ensures a highly structured programme of top-class racing, and generally keeps a very firm hand on the sport.

The Jockey Club was incorporated by Royal Charter in 1970 (and changes in its Charter can be authorized only by the Sovereign in Council). It consists of six Stewards (including the Senior Steward and the Deputy Senior Steward), who are elected from the members and who serve for a period of three years (four years for the Senior and Deputy Senior Stewards), and approximately 120 individual members (each elected by the existing members), in addition to many *ex officio* members such as the Stewards of overseas Jockey Clubs. From its present headquarters in Portman Square in London, its routine functions are carried out through four main standing committees: the Administration and Finance Committee, the Licensing Committee, the Race Planning Committee, and – most in the public eye – the Disciplinary Committee, each of which is chaired by one of the Stewards.

Until comparatively recently the Jockey Club was the epitome of the male bastion, but in 1966, after years of resistance, it agreed to grant training licences to women – the first being Florence Nagle, who had to go to the Court of Appeal in order to secure the right. Another breakthrough occurred in December 1977, when the Countess of Halifax, Mrs Priscilla Hastings and Mrs Helen Johnson Houghton became the first women to be elected to membership.

A tribute to the global influence of the Jockey Club is the number of foreign racing authorities which have taken its name: the Jockey Club de Buenos Aires, the Australian Jockey Club, the Jockey Club de Belgique, the Jockey Club Brasiliero, the Royal Jockey Club of Thailand, the Jockey Club de Uruguay . . .

Weatherbys

If the Jockey Club is the government of racing, Weatherbys is its civil service, implementing the rules and regulations and generally ensuring that the day-to-day running of the sport goes as smoothly as is feasible.

The company, which operates from the Jockey Club premises in Portman Square and from Wellingborough in Northamptonshire, is a family firm working under contract to the Jockey Club. Its history goes back over 200 years, to the time when one James Weatherby was appointed Keeper of the Match Book, Stakeholder and Secretary to the Jockey Club in 1771. Weatherby's nephew, also James, published in 1793 the first volume of the General Stud Book, the official genealogical record of the English Thoroughbred, which has been published by the company ever since. Weatherbys also produces the weekly *Racing Calendar*, the official organ of the Jockey Club, in which are listed all big-race entries and weights, accounts of Stewards' Enquiries and other official information relating to the organization of racing. The company maintains detailed statistical records of many aspects of the sport.

Among the particular functions for which Weatherbys is responsible are:

Entries

Big races apart, a horse is entered for a race five days before it takes place. Weights are allocated the following day, either according to the advertised conditions of the race or by the Jockey Club handicapper, depending on the nature of the race. The horse may be pulled out ('scratched') at any time up to the day before the race, when, if it is to take part, it must be declared to run. The entry for most big races closes many weeks in advance, and the potential field is thinned out through a series of forfeit stages, when each owner will incur a further fee unless he takes the horse out of the race. Classic races close long before the running – closing date for the 1990 Derby, run on 6 June, was 28 February 1990 – but for some very big races a later entry will be accepted on payment of a large supplementary entry fee. All entries must be recorded at Weatherbys, and though the company will now accept entries by fax, therein lies a danger: the connections of the French chaser Nupsala dialled the wrong fax number when trying to confirm the entry for the horse for the 1988 King George VI Rank Chase at Kempton Park on Boxing Day – the entry was not received at Weatherbys in time, and the horse could not run.

Sponsorship is a vital part of modern racing. Though some may lament the distortion that the attentions of commercial sponsors have brought about to the traditional nomenclature of the racing year – the Nunthorpe Stakes at York, for instance, became the William Hill Sprint Championship between 1976 and 1989 – few could dispute that sponsorship has done racing a massive amount of good, by putting a great deal of money into the sport (around £5 million per year into individual races at present) and by bringing to racecourses large numbers of people whose interest would otherwise not have been engaged.

The first commercially sponsored horse race was the Whitbread Gold Cup in 1957, won by Much Obliged; the John Smith's Magnet Cup at York, first run in 1960, is the longest running sponsored flat race. Most of the major races under both codes are now sponsored, though races at Royal Ascot are kept free from commercial links, and the Classics have been sponsored only since 1984.

A glance down the fixture list shows that alcohol and bookmaking loom large in racing sponsorship, but many companies whose business has little or no obvious connection with racing itself are finding sponsorship an effective advertising medium. Many sponsors will now underwrite a whole day's programme rather than just a single race, most supplement the prize money with an award to the stable lad or lass looking after the horse judged to be the best turned out in the parade ring, and some are even putting money towards improvement of the courses.

Accounts

Every registered owner must have an account with the Jockey Club, the stakeholder Pratt & Co., or Weatherbys: the great majority choose to have one with Weatherbys. From this will be deducted entry fees, and to it will be added prize money won, after mandatory deductions have been made – including percentages for the jockey, trainer, and so on. Jockeys and trainers may have their own accounts with Weatherbys, and riding fees will be transferred directly from the owner's to the rider's account. No prize money is released to owner, trainer or jockey until the winning horse's specimen (if one has been taken) has been cleared by the Horseracing Forensic Laboratory in Newmarket.

Names and Colours

All racehorses' names and all owners' colours must be registered with Weatherbys (see pages 24 and 88).

The Horserace Betting Levy Board

Founded in 1961 following the legalization of off-course betting, the Levy Board provides racing with its major source of finance by collecting part of the betting turnover from the bookmakers (including the Tote) and distributing it for the greater good of the sport. The first annual levy (1962–63) raised less than £1 million; the twenty-eighth (1989–90), the cause of a prolonged squabble between the racing authorities and the bookmakers which had to be sorted out by Home Secretary Douglas Hurd, was expected to yield around £34.5 million.

The original purpose of the Levy Board was that the proceeds it raised should be used for 'the improvement of breeds of horse, the advancement or encouragement of veterinary science or veterinary education, and the improvement of horseracing', and it is the last of these aims with which the Board is principally concerned. For with off-course betting severely depleting racecourse attendances and therefore takings at the gate, courses are in great need of financial support.

The Levy Board helps on several fronts. It provides grants and interest-free loans to racecourses, not only for the building of new stands and facilities but also for infrastructural improvements such as watering systems and drainage; it puts a large amount towards prize money, supplementing the contributions of owners, courses and sponsors; and it gives financial support in less visible areas, for example in providing more sophisticated technical equipment and subsidizing Jockey Club Security Services and the Horseracing Forensic Laboratory, with its highly elaborate techniques for detecting doping. It also puts money into the breeding industry and veterinary science.

Prize Money

The prize money for a race consists of

– the stakes put up by the owners of the entered horses, plus
– added money, from sources such as sponsors, the racecourse, and the Levy Board.

Sponsorship: no doubt about who supports the 1988 St Leger, as Willie Carson pushes Minster Son clear of Diminuendo in the Doncaster straight. But sponsorship does not necessarily last for ever: in spring 1989 Holsten announced that they would not be continuing to sponsor the final Classic after that year's running. In the event the 1989 St Leger was run without sponsorship, as it was not possible for Holsten Pils to support the race when it was rerouted to Ayr.

It is distributed to the connections of the placed horses according to regulations set down by the Jockey Club, the distribution varying according to the sort of race and the number of placed horses' connections to be rewarded. (Recently prizes in some big races have gone to horses placed as far down as sixth, rather than just to the customary first four places.) In Pattern races on the Flat and the top jumping races 60 per cent of the total prize money goes to the winner; in other races the percentage is higher.

The 1990 Jockey Club Rules laid down the distribution of the total prize money to the connections of the winner of a Pattern race (with prizes going to the first four) as follows:

46.44 per cent to the owner of the winner;
5.78 per cent to the trainer of the winner;
4.06 per cent to the jockey of the winner;
3.00 per cent to the stable from which the winner was trained.

Connections of each of the first four horses receive mandatory percentages (which are separate from any 'presents' which the owner may wish to give jockey or trainer), and the regulations also allow for percentages to apprentice training, to the Jockeys' Valets Attendance Fund, and to the Jockeys' Association Pension Fund: this explains why the percentages for the winning connections listed above add up to just short of 60 per cent. (The percentage for a winning jump jockey is higher than that for a Flat jockey, but if an amateur jockey qualifies for a percentage that sum goes to the Jockey Club.)

The prize money for the winning owner is expressed in terms of 'Penalty Value', which is the amount to be used for calculations should that winning horse be subject to a penalty under the conditions of a future race (and is the amount used for calculating prize money won by trainers, and so on). Penalty Value is the profit made by the winner's

THE EUROPEAN BREEDERS' FUND

The European Breeders' Fund (EBF), which has been in operation since 1984, is the largest individual sponsor in British racing. It takes the form of a scheme whereby stallion owners in the five major European racing countries (Great Britain, Ireland, France, Germany and Italy) each put up a sum of money equal to the average value of a nomination to each of their stallions in the year in question, thus qualifying the offspring conceived that year by each stallion to participate in the scheme. Allocations for 1990 in Britain came to about £730,000, and this money is distributed in a number of directions: to prize money for selected races, the names of which will include the 'EBF' abbreviation; to breeders' prizes (Flat and National Hunt); to owners' premiums (Flat); and to veterinary research.

Thus the 1990 Gordon Richards EBF Stakes, run on Whitbread Day at Sandown Park, included in its prize money £5,000 donated by the EBF. The fund also put up £3,000 for the breeder of the winner, with an extra £2,500 to go to the owner of the winner 'if it is a qualified progeny sired by a stallion whose name is included in the Consolidated Final List of stallions issued by the European Breeders' Fund or which are eligible under the terms of the Breeders' Cup (USA)'. Breeders' Cup Limited (BCL) is the American equivalent of the EBF, and the two sides have made a cross-registration agreement which allows horses nominated to one programme to participate in both.

connections – that is, their portion of the total prize money less the owner's original stake money. (The 1990 Pattern percentages were unchanged from 1989.)

As an example we can look at the Trusthouse Forte Mile run at Sandown Park on Friday 28 April 1989. This was a Group 2 race over one mile with an estimated total value of £50,000, with £40,000 added to the owners' stakes through the sponsorship of Trusthouse Forte. To enter a horse for this prestigious race cost the owner £210, to maintain its entry at the first forfeit stage (that is, the date by which the owner has to withdraw the horse or pay a further fee) cost another £240, and to confirm its entry with an intention to run cost a further £150 – a total of £600 to take part. It attracted an original entry of twenty-six, with sixteen standing their ground at the forfeit stage and six confirmed (though only five faced the Starter). Thus the total entry fees were:

26 at £210	£ 5,460	
16 at £240	£ 3,840	total fees £10,200
6 at £150	£ 900	

So the total prize money for the race was:

entry fees	£10,200	total £50,200
added money	£40,000	

The Penalty Value is calculated:

	£30,120 (60 per cent of total stakes)
less winner's entry fee	£ 600
Penalty Value	£29,520

The race was won by Sheikh Mohammed's Reprimand, and the Sheikh's take-home amount would have been

	£23,312 (46.44 per cent of total stakes)
less entry	£ 600
	£22,712

So £22,712 is given in the racecard as the owner's prize money; £9,048 went to the owner of the second, £4,199 to the owner of the third, and £1,709 to the owner of the fourth.

£22,712 better off, Sheikh Mohammed talks to Derek Thompson.

THE SHAPE OF THE RACING PROGRAMME

Underpinned as it is by the essential functions of control, adminis-tration and finance, horse racing is about races, and the shape of the competitive side of the sport is carefully designed and controlled. In flat racing the key element of this structure is the Pattern (page 69), which includes the Classics (pages 70–6).

But it is not only the top races which are subjected to strict control by the Jockey Club. Regulations constantly monitored by the Race Planning Committee govern all meetings and the conditions of individual races, not only to guarantee the sport's participants and followers a great variety of competition, but also to provide a wide array of tests for the Thoroughbred horse and thus keep the breed on its mettle. The capabilities of horses at particular stages of development are borne very much in mind in the race planning process, both to avoid putting unnecessary demands on a horse too early in its career and to ensure that the tests provided for it are carefully structured. Thus races for yearlings have been banned since 1859; two-year-olds may not run over more than six furlongs before June, more than seven furlongs before August, or more than one mile before September; a horse may not run in a hurdle race until 1 July of the year in which it is three years old, or four years old for a steeplechase. (In common racing parlance, a sprinter races at five or six furlongs, a miler at around a mile, a middle-distance horse at one and a quarter to one and a half miles, and a stayer at one and three quarter miles and over.)

There are conditions, too, for individual race meetings. For instance, at least one half of the prize money for a Flat meeting (other than an all-weather fixture) must be apportioned to races of a mile or over for three-year-olds and over; there can be no more than one selling race per day of the meeting; any course staging four or more days' racing annually must put on at least two apprentice races during the season; no single day may include more than four handicaps. In National Hunt racing at least 55 per cent of the prize money per meeting must go to steeplechases, and each day's programme must contain at least two chases, one of which must be of three miles or upwards.

The Principal Types of Race

Within this controlled programme are run many different sorts of race. The main categories of race are given below.

Weight-for-Age

According to the Jockey Club, a weight-for-age race is any race which is not a handicap; so the category includes a variety of races. The official

Fourteen runners went to post for the Ladbroke Chester Cup on 10 May 1989. It was a handicap for horses rated 0–115, and the race conditions demanded that the top weight carried in the race be not less than 9 stone 10 pounds, with a minimum weight of 7 stone 7 pounds. Top weight was carried by Travel Mystery. She had originally been allotted 8 stone 7 pounds but on the day actually carried 9 stone 13 pounds, because (a) she incurred a three-pound penalty for her win in the Insulpak Sagaro Stakes at Ascot, and (b) none of the horses above her in the original handicap had been declared to run. So the weights rose by the 17 pounds' difference between the stipulated minimum top weight of 9 stone 10 pounds and Travel Mystery's original 8 stone 7 pounds, and with her three-pound penalty she carried 20 pounds more than she had been allotted in the first place. *All* the weights of the runners in the race were raised by 17 pounds, but for three runners at the foot of the handicap – Mils Mij, Spring Forward and Suivez Moi – the rise of 17 pounds was not enough to bring them into the handicap proper, as they had originally been allotted 6 stone 3 pounds, 5 stone 5 pounds, and 4 stone 11 pounds respectively. When the weights were raised, those figures went up to 7 stone 6 pounds, 6 stone 8 pounds, and 6 stone, but as the minimum weight actually to be carried in the race was laid down as 7 stone 7 pounds they had to carry that weight (less apprentice allowances for two of them), putting them at varying degrees of disadvantage, according to the original handicap, with their rivals.

Simple, isn't it?

weight-for-age scale (see page 148) lays down the differences in weights to be carried by horses of different ages in order to compensate for the immaturity (and relative weakness) of younger horses. These differences vary according to the time of the year and the distance of the race: in late March a four-year-old would have to carry thirteen pounds more than a three-year-old over five furlongs, and one stone three pounds more over one mile; in early October, by which time the rapidly maturing three-year-old will almost have caught up his elder in terms of development, the difference over five furlongs will be just one pound, over a mile four pounds. An additional factor is that fillies and mares are officially deemed to be the weaker sex, and carry less weight than colts of the same age: a female Derby runner would carry five pounds less than a male runner.

A weight-for-age race is sometimes referred to as a 'conditions race', for the entrants must satisfy certain conditions relating to age, sex or previous performance (winners of Group 1 and Group 2 races, for instance, may not run in some Group 3 races). Sometimes the conditions are more unusual: the Washington Singer Stakes at Newbury is restricted to two-year-old colts and geldings whose sires won a race over one and a half miles or more, a fact which caused the disqualification of 1988 winner Prince Of Dance when it was realized that his sire Sadlers Wells had not met this requirement. Weights are stipulated in the race conditions, and may vary according to age, sex, and whether the horse has won certain sorts of race (in which case it will incur a 'penalty' of a certain number of pounds above the basic weight).

Handicap

A handicap is a race in which the weight each horse is to carry is individually allotted by the official handicapper, who adjusts the weights according to past performance – the theoretical goal being to give all horses in a race an equal chance of winning. The Jockey Club handicappers maintain a list of official ratings for every horse (from 0 to 140 for the Flat, 0 to 175 for National Hunt), so that handicaps can be framed very speedily. The ratings are revised on a weekly basis, but if a horse wins a race after the weights for a future race have been allotted he may incur a penalty for that later race in order to take account of the improvement in performance not yet reflected in his official rating.

Weights are allotted from the highest (which will be specified in the race conditions) down to the lowest in accordance with the handicapper's assessment of each horse's chance, the lowest-ranked horse being allotted a weight which reflects its perceived chance compared with the top-ranked (and top-weighted) horse, however low such a weight may be and even if it is below the lowest weight actually to be carried in the race. This is the 'long handicap'. Any horse whose weight is so low that it is below the minimum to be carried is said to be 'out of the handicap'. If at the five-day or overnight declaration stage the highest-weighted horse still left in the race has less than the originally stipulated top weight to be carried, that horse's weight is raised to the level of the original minimum top weight and all the other weights are raised by the same amount – so a horse originally out of the handicap may then be racing off a true weight in relation to the new top weight (see panel).

A **limited handicap** is one in which the range of weights which the horses will carry is kept narrow (probably one and a half stone). This encourages high-class horses to be entered, as they will not be asked to concede more than a comparatively small amount of weight to any other runner. Another kind of modified handicap stipulates that the abilities of the horses taking part shall all be within a set range: for example, a handicap designated '0–70' would be open only to horses rated no higher than 70 on the Jockey Club scale, and thus would afford an opportunity for a lower-class horse to chalk up a win.

A **nursery** is a handicap for two-year-olds.

By their very nature handicaps cannot be expected to sort out the very best horses, as the purest races can only be run on level terms. But by the same token they are excellent betting races: the big handicaps always attract large fields and the very notion of handicapping makes for open betting. Traditionally the major handicaps of the Flat season are the Lincoln at Doncaster, the Royal Hunt Cup (Royal Ascot), the Stewards' Cup (Goodwood), the Ebor (York), the Ayr Gold Cup, the Cambridgeshire and the Cesarewitch (both Newmarket) and the November Handicap (Doncaster). Many of the landmarks of the jumping season are handicaps, including the Mackeson Gold Cup (Cheltenham), the Hennessy Gold Cup and the Tote Gold Trophy (both Newbury), the Whitbread Gold Cup (Sandown Park) – and of course the Grand National at Liverpool.

Satisfaction for the handicapper, as less than a length separates the first four home in the Rous Memorial Handicap at Ascot in July 1986. The winner (in blinkers) was Cree Bay, ridden by Willie Carson.

Maiden Race

A maiden is a horse which has not won a race. Maiden races are for 'maidens at starting', which means that if a horse is entered for a maiden race but between then and the day of the race has a win, it cannot then take part in its 'maiden'.

Graduation Race

A graduation race is designed to develop the capabilities of horses with limited experience. The Harvester Graduation Stakes, which Saumarez won at Sandown Park in April 1990, for example, was open only to horses which had not run more than three times. Other graduation races have similar conditions, such as being confined to horses who have won no more than one race.

Selling Race

A race in which the winner is sold at auction (with a reserve laid down) directly after the race, and in which other runners may be 'claimed' (bought) for an amount previously advertised. The owner of the winner may buy back the horse (in which case it is said to be 'bought in'), but a percentage of the proceeds of the sale goes to the racecourse. Selling races are usually the lowest form of British racing.

Auction Race

A race for horses which were bought as yearlings at public auction. Weight allowances are given to horses bought for lower sums.

Claiming Race

In a claiming race any runner can be claimed after the race for an advertised sum or more, and if the owner of any runner wishes it to carry less than the maximum weight the price at which it may be claimed is accordingly reduced. Thus the conditions for a claiming race may stipulate that the top weight to be carried is 9 stone 9 pounds and the maximum claiming price is £12,000, with a one-pound weight allowance for each £1,000 taken off the claiming price. If you put a claiming price of £6,000 on your horse when entering it, it will carry 9 stone 3 pounds. Claims for any individual horse are made in sealed bids – normally over the advertised amount – and are settled by the Clerk of the Scales, who awards the claim to the highest bidder. An owner can make a 'friendly claim' and claim his own horse back.

While most of the above sorts of race take place in National Hunt racing, and the very best jumping races are organized into a Pattern similar to that which applies on the Flat (see opposite page), there are others which are exclusive to jump racing:

Novices' Race

A novice hurdle or novice steeplechase is a race for horses which have not won a hurdle race or a steeplechase respectively before the current season. (Novice events are by no means confined to young horses:

Panegyrist only lost his novice tag when winning a steeplechase at Ayr in March 1989 at the ripe old age of fourteen.)

Hunter-Chase

A steeplechase for horses which have been regularly hunted during the current season, according to a Hunter's Certificate which must be endorsed by the Master of Foxhounds. Hunter-chases are popular targets for some top-class chasers in the twilight of their careers, but the regulations have been tightened to prevent these high-class horses cleaning up all the big prizes at the expense of more 'genuine' hunters.

National Hunt Flat Race

A National Hunt race which spares the runners the inconvenience of clearing obstacles. These races – popularly known as 'bumpers' – are an increasingly valuable testing ground for young jumping horses. They are confined to four-, five- and six-year-olds who have not run under the Rules of Racing except in NH Flat Races, ridden by amateur or conditional jockeys. No horse may run in more than three.

The racing progamme allows for variations on the basic categories of race. There are races in which all the riders are apprentices or conditional jockeys, or ladies, or amateurs; in which the runners can only be fillies, or colts, or mares, or (as in the case of a steeplechase at Warwick) horses aged ten years or over. At Kempton Park in June 1990 there was a ladies' race in which every rider had to be the wife, daughter or secretary of a trainer. The great variety of types of race is another of the enduring attractions of British racing.

The Pattern

Pattern races, or Group races, are the elite contests of flat racing: a series of tests for the best horses at all ages and at different distances, together they give the season its carefully constructed form, ensuring top-class and competitive racing on a Europe-wide scale.

The idea was born in the mid-1960s in response to worries about the lack of balance between British and French racing, and the Duke of Norfolk's Pattern of Racing Committee recommended in 1965 a system to embrace England, Ireland and France. (Germany and Italy joined later.) The aim of the Pattern was not to invent races but to grade existing races in such a way, according to the report of the Committee, as 'to ensure that a series of races over the right distances and at the right time of the year are available to test the best horses of all ages and . . . to ensure that the horses remain in training long enough and race often enough to be tested properly for constitution and soundness.' In addition to this noble aim in pursuit of the excellence of the Thoroughbred breed, the existence of the Pattern guarantees enthusiasts a constant stream of high-class racing throughout the season and makes it difficult for the best horses from several countries to avoid meeting each other regularly. The recommended system was finally implemented in 1971, with the Pattern races divided into three groups:

THE JUMPING PATTERN

A fresh Pattern has been introduced to the National Hunt season for the 1990–91 term to give more of a structure to the jumping season and bring a stronger emphasis to the mid-term period around Christmas. The Pattern divides into Grades 1, 2 and 3, and consists of 101 top races. Grades 1 and 2 consist of the big events in twelve different categories (according to the nature of the race and its distance), and each category has two Grade 1 races: thus juvenile hurdlers have Grade 1 events in the Finale Hurdle at Chepstow in late December and the Daily Express Triumph Hurdle at Cheltenham in March; the twin peaks for two-mile hurdlers are the Top Rank Christmas Hurdle at Kempton and the Bank of Ireland Champion Hurdle at Cheltenham; long-distance hurdlers have their Grade 1 events in the Long Walk Hurdle at Ascot in December and the Stayers' Hurdle at the Cheltenham Festival. Likewise, each category of steeplechasers has two big dates: the two-milers have the Castleford at Wetherby in December and the Queen Mother Champion Chase at Cheltenham in March; the three-mile novices the Butlin's Feltham Chase at Kempton on Boxing Day and the Sun Alliance at Cheltenham; and the three-mile chasers the traditional twin targets of the King George VI Rank Chase at Kempton on Boxing Day and the Tote Cheltenham Gold Cup in March.

In all there are twenty-four races in Grade 1, sixty-three supporting events in Grade 2, and fourteen big handicaps in Grade 3. This last grouping includes all the big handicap hurdles and chases.

Group 1

Classics and other races of major international importance.

Group 2

Races of international importance but at a level just below championship standard.

Group 3

Primarily domestic races regarded as preparatory contests for the higher groups (such as Classic trials).

Group 1 races are always run without penalties on a weight for age and sex basis, whereas penalties can apply in Groups 2 and 3 races and are based on previous performance in Pattern races.

Below Group races are **Listed races**, a set of races designed to identify racehorses of superior merit but below Group standard.

The Pattern is fluid, allowing the status of a particular race to be altered if appropriate: thus the Fillies' Mile at the Ascot September Meeting was raised from Group 2 to Group 1 in 1990 to reflect its regularly attracting the very best staying two-year-old fillies in training, and Doncaster's Flying Childers Stakes was downgraded from Group 1 to Group 2 in 1979 following its consistent failure to bring together the best sprinting two-year-olds. The idea is to space out the best races over similar distances for horses of particular age groups. So a four-year-old ten-furlong specialist might have the season mapped out around three Group 1 peaks: the Coral-Eclipse Stakes at Sandown Park in July, the Juddmonte International Stakes at York in August and the Dubai Champion Stakes at Newmarket in October.

There are something like 100 Pattern races each season in Great Britain, with about twenty at Group 1 level, thirty at Group 2, and fifty at Group 3. Of the twenty-four races designated Group 1 in the 1990 season (see panel), sixteen were covered by Channel Four.

The Classics

The five Classics – the One Thousand Guineas, the Two Thousand Guineas, the Derby, the Oaks and the St Leger – are the landmarks of the Flat season. They offer to three-year-old colts and fillies the challenge of having the speed to beat the best of the generation over a mile at Newmarket in the spring, the agility to do so again over one and a half miles of very different terrain at Epsom in the summer, and the stamina and resilience to win over a mile and three quarters at Doncaster in the autumn.

But they were not planned as a series. The five races were founded individually in the late eighteenth and early nineteenth centuries in response to the growing inclination to race horses at younger ages and over shorter distances than hitherto. Their grouping together into the Classic programme evolved later; and in the modern era, when specialization in racing is on the increase, for any colt to take the Triple

Crown by winning the three legs of the Classic programme for which he is eligible (the One Thousand Guineas and the Oaks are for fillies only) is a remarkable feat. For many people the Classics are still the ultimate test of the Thoroughbred.

The One Thousand Guineas

Run over 1 mile at Newmarket, for three-year-old fillies only, carrying 9 stone.

First Classic of the season, the One Thousand Guineas is the youngest of the five races; the first running in 1814, when a field of only five runners went to post, was won by Charlotte. In its early years the race was run over the Ditch Mile, a course much flatter and therefore less demanding than the Rowley Mile, to which the race was transferred in the early 1870s.

It is customary for One Thousand Guineas winners to be aimed for the second fillies' Classic, the Oaks, and several have won both races. But only the grey filly Tagalie in 1912 has ever won the One Thousand and the Derby: she took the Newmarket race at 20–1 and won at Epsom at 100–8. Two days after the Derby she was well beaten in the Oaks at 2–1 on. Recent winners have included many outstanding fillies, including Pebbles, who in 1984 won the first running sponsored by General Accident.

The Two Thousand Guineas

Run over 1 mile at Newmarket, for three-year-old colts and fillies: colts carry 9 stone, fillies 8 stone 9 pounds.

In 1809 Wizard beat seven rivals in the first Two Thousand Guineas, and the race has been run on the Rowley Mile ever since (except during the Second World War, when both Guineas races were transferred to the July Course, the Rowley course being requisitioned by the RAF). Like the One Thousand, it was first sponsored by General Accident in 1984.

The Two Thousand Guineas is the high point of the early part of the Flat season, and has produced some memorable races. In 1971 it provided one of the most hotly contested events of the post-war era, the top three in the betting going off at

6–4   Mill Reef
2–1   My Swallow
11–2   Brigadier Gerard

in a field of six. Brigadier Gerard swept past his rivals in the closing stages to win by an easy three lengths from Mill Reef on the only occasion that these two famous horses ever met. In 1985 Shadeed gave Lester Piggott his twenty-ninth and final Classic victory when pipping Bairn by a head, the following year the race saw Dancing Brave exhibit his exceptional ability in trouncing Green Desert, and in 1989 Nashwan powered up the hill to announce his arrival in the top bracket.

The Two Thousand Guineas has the distinction of holding the record for the number of entries in one race: 1,001 horses were entered for the 1974 running. Just twelve of them went to post.

The Derby

Run over 1½ miles at Epsom for three-year-old colts and fillies: colts carry 9 stone, fillies 8 stone 9 pounds.

The fastest recorded Derby was run by Mahmoud in 1936 in a time of 2 minutes 33.8 seconds. That was timed by hand. The fastest electrically timed Derby was by Kahyasi in 1988 at 2 minutes 33.84 seconds.

No event in the world compares with Derby Day; a great sporting occasion, it is also very much more than that, as hundreds of thousands of people crowd on to Epsom Downs, just a few miles outside London, to indulge in Britain's greatest annual celebration. What they are celebrating is not only the running of the most famous horse race in the world, a race which has given its name to imitations around the globe and which invariably captures the public imagination, but also the Derby as a social institution: it is a day when traditional class differences are forgotten, or at least disregarded, as the entire spectrum of society from the Royal Family down joins together for an unofficial public holiday.

This tradition goes back a long way. In the middle of the nineteenth century, the halcyon days of the Derby as pure festivity, the *Illustrated London News* noted:

> On Derby Day the patrician puts his pride into the pocket of his gossamer paletot [loose coat] and is perfectly ready to be hail fellow well met with the humblest of the working classes. None save the most ill-conditioned curmudgeons lose their temper at the witticisms levelled at them on the Hill or in coming and going. If things are thrown at you, just throw them back. But there are limits – oranges and lobster claws are just all right but not bags of flour or bad eggs.

For many decades in Victorian times parliament suspended business on Derby Day so that MPs could join the tumultuous throng on the Downs, and today there is still no event which generates such a widespread sense of popular excitement.

Such an occasion would have been far from the thoughts of the twelfth Earl of Derby and Sir Charles Bunbury when they hatched the plan which led to the first running of the race on 4 May 1780, and whether or not the story is true that they tossed a coin to see which man's name would be given to the race, it seems that the Earl was the principal proponent of the idea. For it was he who had organized the first running of the Oaks the previous year, an experiment considered such a success that it was decided to repeat the formula of a race at Epsom for three-year-olds, this time for both colts and fillies and to be run over a mile. (The distance was not increased to a mile and a half until 1784.) That first Derby – fittingly – was won by Sir Charles Bunbury's Diomed, and Bunbury was to win it twice more, with Eleanor and Smolensko.

The Derby was run at Newmarket during both World Wars, and was first sponsored by Ever Ready in 1984, when El Gran Senor, apparently coasting to victory halfway up the straight, had to give best to Secreto by a short head after a desperate struggle. Many runnings of the race have featured thrillingly close finishes, and the whole history of the Derby is full of spectacle, heroism and drama . . .

1844

The first horse past the post had been entered as the three-year-old Running Rein. He was, in fact, a four-year-old named Maccabeus, who had come under extreme suspicion the previous year when winning a two-year-old race at Newmarket as a three-year-old, the intrigue being masterminded by his owner Goodman Levy. A group of prominent Turf figures headed by Lord George Bentinck tried to prevent 'Running Rein' taking part in the Derby, but the Stewards decided that he should be permitted to run. He won from Orlando, whose owner duly sued Mr Wood, in whose name Running Rein had competed. The judge in the case, remarking that 'if gentlemen condescended to race with blackguards, they must condescend to expect to be cheated,' found against Wood, and the race went to Orlando. It is almost incidental to record the other happenings in this Derby. Another runner, Leander, was struck into by Running Rein and broke his leg. When he had been put down the vet examined his jaw and found him to be a four-year-old, though his indignant German owners claimed that he was actually six! The favourite, Ugly Buck, was the victim of deliberate foul riding, and the second favourite was both 'got at' the night before and pulled by his jockey to prevent his winning just in case the doping had not worked.

1865

The victory of the French-trained Gladiateur was a national humiliation which led to the horse's being nicknamed 'The Avenger of Waterloo'. He went on to win the Triple Crown, and was unplaced in the Cambridgeshire carrying 9 stone 12 pounds.

1913

Perhaps the most sensational Derby in the history of the race. The militant suffragette Emily Davison threw herself in front of King George V's horse Anmer as the runners came round Tattenham Corner, and died four days later from her injuries. Anmer was towards the rear of the field at the time, and meanwhile up front a furious race was developing. At the post the favourite Craganour beat the 100–1 outsider Aboyeur by a head after a good deal of bumping and deliberate barging, but the Stewards objected to the winner and the race was awarded to Aboyeur.

1921

The legendary Steve Donoghue rode six Derby winners: Humorist was his third, and the first in his sequence of three consecutive victories from 1921 to 1923. But Humorist is best remembered for his remarkable courage. Throughout his career he was subject to physical lapses which defied explanation, his health changing almost from day to day. Third in the Two Thousand Guineas, he started at 6–1 at Epsom and battled on bravely to win by a neck from the hot favourite Craig an Eran; but so distressed was he after the race that he could not be moved from Epsom until the following day. A few weeks later the head lad at trainer Charles Morton's stable at Wantage saw blood coming from under the door of his box. Humorist was dead, and was subsequently found to have been

Nashwan (Willie Carson) winning the 1989 Ever Ready Derby from Terimon (left) and Cacoethes (hooped sleeves).

The oldest jockey to win the Derby was John Forth, who was over sixty when riding Frederick to victory in 1829. The youngest – at least in this century – was Lester Piggott, eighteen when winning on Never Say Die in 1954. Walter Swinburn was an older eighteen when taking the 1981 race on Shergar. John Parsons is believed to have been sixteen when winning on Caractacus in 1862, but this has not been verified.

suffering from a tubercular lung condition. Winning the Derby in his physical state was the act of an exceptionally game horse.

1933

Hyperion was the smallest Derby winner for nearly a century, but he was wonderfully endowed in action and character and became the most popular horse of his time. Favourite for the Derby at 6–1, he won by four lengths from King Salmon. Despite a dismal season as a four-year-old Hyperion became an outstanding success as a stallion, being champion sire on six occasions. At stud he is said to have been fascinated by aeroplanes, watching them intently from his box as they moved across the sky. He died in 1960, having sired the winners of 752 races.

1953

Loyalties were divided for the Coronation Derby, with plenty of support for Aureole, owned by the newly-crowned Queen, and also for Pinza, ridden by Gordon Richards, just knighted and the greatest jockey of his age but still unsuccessful in the Derby despite twenty-seven attempts. At the line it was Pinza by four lengths from Aureole – possibly the most popular Derby result of all.

1962

Larkspur's year, but the victory of the Vincent O'Brien-trained colt was overshadowed by the fall of seven of the runners on the descent to Tattenham Corner. Victims of the pile-up were Hethersett (the favourite, who went on to win the St Leger), Romulus (later a top-class miler), King Canute II (who broke a leg and had to be destroyed), Crossen, Pindaric, Persian Fantasy and Changing Times. Larkspur never won again.

1980

Willie Carson had pumped Troy to a stunning seven-length victory in 1979, but the following year had to squeeze Henbit home by three quarters of a length from Master Willie. It transpired that Henbit had split a bone in a foreleg in the closing stages, so this ranks alongside Humorist's 1921 victory as one of the most heroic equine performances the Derby has ever seen.

1981

Shergar's ten-length victory over Glint of Gold was the longest officially recorded winning margin in the history of the race. Syndicated for stud duties at a valuation of £10 million after his three-year-old career, Shergar produced just one crop before his abduction from the Ballmany Stud in February 1983.

No horse has ever won all five Classics. In 1868 Formosa won the Two Thousand Guineas (dead-heating), One Thousand Guineas, Oaks and St Leger, while in 1902 Sceptre won the same four races and finished fourth in the Derby.

1986

Shahrastani's half-length defeat of Dancing Brave provoked a mighty controversy: had Greville Starkey on the runner-up lain too far out of his ground, demanding an impossible sprint from his horse in the straight? When they met again in Ascot's King George VI and Queen Elizabeth Diamond Stakes the following month Dancing Brave beat Shahrastani conclusively.

Aliysa, ridden by Walter Swinburn, beats Snow Bride and Roseate Tern (blinkers) in the 1989 Gold Seal Oaks. Sensation was to follow when her post-race dope test proved positive, but a year later the matter remained unresolved, causing the grotesque situation of the 1990 Oaks being run with the result of the 1989 still not finalized.

The Oaks

Run over 1½ miles at Epsom, for three-year-old fillies carrying 9 stone.

The Oaks is the second oldest of the Classics, having been first run in May 1779, three years after the first St Leger. The twelfth Earl of Derby, whose name was soon to be immortalized by the greater Epsom Classic launched the following year, instituted the Oaks and named it after his house near Epsom. His own Bridget won the inaugural running.

Four fillies have won the Derby as well as the Oaks: Eleanor (1801), Blink Bonny (1857), Signorinetta (1908), and Fifinella (1916), though even to attempt the double would be practically unthinkable today, as the Oaks is run only three days after the Derby. Pawneese and Time Charter were recent Oaks winners who went on to win Britain's most important middle-distance race open to older horses, the King George VI and Queen Elizabeth Diamond Stakes, but even their achievements do not match the extraordinary record of Cherimoya, who in the 1911 Oaks won a Classic in the only race of her life. She was ridden by Fred Winter, father of the great National Hunt jockey and trainer.

The Oaks was run at Newmarket during both World Wars, and was first sponsored in 1984, since when it has been run as the Gold Seal Oaks.

> Although fillies have their own Epsom Classic, it is not unknown for a filly to run in the Derby nowadays. Nobiliary in 1975 was the last filly to be placed in the Derby when runner-up to Grundy.

The St Leger

Run over 1 mile, 6 furlongs, 127 yards at Doncaster, for three-year-old colts and fillies: colts carry 9 stone, fillies 8 stone 9 pounds.

The St Leger, the oldest Classic, was first run on Cantley Common, Doncaster, in 1776, transferring to its present course on the Town Moor two years later. Named after a prominent local sportsman,

> The top Classic trainer is John Scott (1794–1871), who between 1827 and 1863 trained the winners of forty-one Classics, including sixteen St Legers.

At the opposite end of the racing spectrum from the Classics are point-to-points: many people's experience of racing begins with or is confined to a visit to their local meeting. Point-to-pointing (or hunt racing) is administered by the Jockey Club in association with the Masters of Foxhounds, and hunts stage their point-to-points (between February and May) to provide an important source of fund-raising. Horses running in point-to-points must be 'regularly and fairly hunted' to qualify, and their jockeys must be amateurs. But whereas originally point-to-pointers were hunters who went racing, the point-to-point field nowadays very often sees former steeplechasers competing (Bolands Cross is just one familiar name from the last year or two to go point-to-pointing after his retirement from racing under Rules). More significantly, it is often a nursery for future steeplechasers. Norton's Coin's path to 1990 Cheltenham glory began in Welsh point-to-points in 1986: he was pulled up on his first appearance, refused on his second and was beaten a distance on his third before notching up a sequence of four victories.

Point-to-point courses vary hugely – a few events are run on licensed racecourses, most take place on farmland circuits – and the meetings retain a strong local flavour, with many races restricted to horses owned by members of neighbouring hunts or, as in the photograph, by members of the host hunt: after a circuit of the Members' Race at the Vale of Aylesbury meeting at Kimble on Easter Saturday, 1990, there is little between the eventual winner Valued Opinion (Miss R. Smith, left), Jacob (Mr A. Johnson) and Mussel Bed (Mrs J. Wilkinson).

Lieutenant-Colonel Anthony St Leger, it was run over two miles until 1813, when its distance was reduced to one mile, six furlongs, 193 yards. Those 193 yards were reduced to 132 in 1826 and to the present 127 in 1969. Pushed around the country by the wars, the St Leger was run at Newmarket from 1915 to 1918, at Thirsk in 1940, Manchester in 1941, Newmarket in 1942–4 and York in 1945.

The only Classic run in the north, the St Leger has always attracted huge local support and is one of the highlights of the later part of the Flat season. Its prestige became rather dented for a while in the 1970s and there was even talk of opening it to older horses (as happened with the Irish St Leger), but the temptation was resisted, and although its proximity to the running of the Prix de l'Arc de Triomphe means that it is no longer automatically on the autumn agenda of the top three-year-olds, it has of late regained much of its lost reputation by attracting many top-class horses, not all of whom have been successful. Shergar's defeat in 1981 (he was fourth to Cut Above at 9–4 on) was a major sensation, and Alleged, who was to win the Arc twice, went down by a length and a half to the Queen's Dunfermline in 1977 after a protracted duel up the straight. Other notable occasions in recent years were the victories of Oh So Sharp and Sun Princess, both of whom had won the Oaks, of Reference Point, a brilliant Derby winner, and of Commanche Run, whose neck victory over Baynoun in 1984 in the first running sponsored by Holsten Pils gave Lester Piggott his record-breaking twenty-eighth Classic. But a local triumph in the St Leger is what really raises the roof at Doncaster, and when Apology won the race in 1874 (her third Classic win) ridden by Yorkshire jockey John Osborne, the cheering is said to have been heard at York Minster.

The same could hardly have been claimed in 1989. On the first day of the four-day St Leger meeting three horses fell in the Portland Handicap, and though the course was declared fit the third day saw another faller at about the same point in the straight: subsidence was discovered which made the course unfit for racing, and the remainder of the meeting was cancelled, the Classic itself being transferred to Ayr the following week when Michelozzo won by eight lengths.

THE INTERNATIONAL SCENE

There could be no better illustration of the international character of modern racing than the life of Triptych, the remarkable mare who died in May 1989 after a freak accident at Claiborne Farm in Kentucky. Bred in Kentucky from American-bred parents who had both been trained in France, she was bought as a yearling by Alan Clore, who put her in training in France with David Smaga. At the beginning of her three-year-old career she moved to the stables of David O'Brien in Ireland, and that year ran in Ireland, England and Canada. She spent some time in California before returning to Europe for her four-year-old campaign, this time to be trained in France by Patrick Biancone. That season (1986) she ran in France, England, Ireland, the USA and Japan; in 1987 she ran in France, England, Ireland and Japan, and in 1988 (by which time she had been sold to the American Peter Brant) in France, England, Canada, Ireland and the USA. She was ridden by jockeys from France, Ireland, the USA and the United Kingdom, and Tony Cruz, her regular partner in 1987, was born in Hong Kong. She had returned to Kentucky to be mated with Mr Prospector when the fatal accident happened.

Breeding Thoroughbreds has long been carried out on an international basis, and with the ease of modern transport it is becoming increasingly common for horses' racing campaigns to be planned on a global, rather than a national, basis. (It is also increasingly easy to make quick forays abroad: Triptych's visits to England and Ireland in 1987 were made by day-return.) The major countries with which British racing is involved are as follows.

Ireland

Ireland produces some of the world's finest Thoroughbred stock, especially steeplechasers, and although many of the best young chasing horses are sold to race in Britain, the continuing success of Irish bloodstock wherever it races pays eloquent tribute to the excellence of Irish breeding. In Ireland racing is a way of life, and it is no surprise that the Irish influence is widely felt in other areas of the sport: many Flat jockeys now based in England are Irish (such as Pat Eddery) or of Irish extraction, and there is a long and honourable tradition of jumping jockeys from Ireland, the most notable recent example being of course Jonjo O'Neill. The country boasts twenty-seven racecourses (see page 44), the grandest of which is The Curragh, situated on a vast plain about thirty miles outside Dublin and home of all the Irish Classics. Other courses which are often seen on British television include Leopardstown, near Dublin, on which are run the Vincent O'Brien Irish Gold Cup, the Ladbroke Hurdle, the Wessel Hurdle, and several other good jumping races; and Fairyhouse, north-west of Dublin, which is famous for staging the Irish Grand National in the spring.

The major Irish races are:

Irish Grand National

Fairyhouse, 3½ miles

First run in 1870, the Irish Grand National bears little relation to its Liverpool counterpart but has been won in its time by some famous horses – notably Arkle, who carried 12 stone to victory in 1964 as a seven-year-old after his first Cheltenham Gold Cup triumph over Mill House. Flyingbolt won the race in 1966, and Brown Lad won it three times. The only horse since the war to have won both the Irish and the Liverpool races is Rhyme 'N' Reason, who won at Fairyhouse in 1985 when trained by David Murray Smith and Liverpool in 1988 from the stable of David Elsworth, who in 1990 sent out Desert Orchid to take the race – the horse's first steeplechase outside England.

Irish Two Thousand Guineas

The Curragh, 1 mile

Often a consolation prize for horses beaten in the English Two Thousand Guineas (Shaadi won it in 1989 after being beaten at Newmarket), this is usually a high-class race. Triptych was the first filly ever to win when taking the race in 1985, and Don't Forget Me in 1987 the first horse to do the Newmarket–Curragh double since Right Tack in 1969. Don't Forget Me's trainer Richard Hannon repeated the double with Tirol in 1990.

Irish One Thousand Guineas

The Curragh, 1 mile

This race, too, often sees runners coming on from Newmarket. Recent winners have included very high-class fillies such as Cairn Rouge (1980), Katies (1984), Al Bahathri (1985), Sonic Lady (1986), Forest Flower (1987) and In The Groove (1990), though no filly has yet won the One Thousand and the Irish One Thousand.

Kahyasi (no. 7) beats Insan in the 1988 Budweiser Irish Derby.

Irish Derby

The Curragh, 1½ miles

One of the major international events of the Flat season, the Irish Derby is always an important contest. In 1962 the race received a massive injection of cash through its connection with the Irish Sweeps – that year the Irish Derby was worth £50,027, the Epsom Derby £34,786 – and today it is a natural target for the Epsom winner: since 1970 Nijinsky, Grundy, The Minstrel, Shirley Heights, Troy, Shergar, Shahrastani and Kahyasi have added the Irish Derby to victory in the English race. Salsabil in 1990 was the first filly to win since Gallinaria in 1900.

Irish Oaks

The Curragh, 1½ miles

First run in 1895, the Irish Oaks is now a major international contest. A staggering burst of acceleration in this race in 1973 introduced most of the racing world to Dahlia, who went on to become one of the best female racehorses of the modern era. Many winners of the Epsom Oaks have gone on to take the Irish, including Fair Salinia, who won it in 1978 on the controversial disqualification of Sorbus, and Diminuendo, who dead-heated with Melodist in 1988.

Irish St Leger

The Curragh, 1¾ miles

The Jefferson Smurfit Irish St Leger run on 8 October 1983 made Turf history as the first running of an English or Irish Classic race open to horses over the age of three – and it was won by the four-year-old filly Mountain Lodge. The decision to open the race to older horses reflected concern at the diminishing status of the race, run as it is so close to the Prix de l'Arc de Triomphe.

France

There are no bookmakers in France, and the betting monopoly of the Pari-Mutuel totalisator system allows a large proportion of the money wagered to be ploughed back into the sport, keeping the level of prize money high. So French races are very much on the agenda for British-trained horses, and not only the very best ones: many trainers like to take their early-season types to race at the seaside track of Cagnes-sur-Mer in February in order to get them into trim before the home season starts around Easter. France is of course a much larger country than Britain and this has led to a more centralized pattern of racing. There are two major training centres not far from Paris, at Chantilly and Maisons-Laffitte; race meetings are held regularly at Longchamp (in the Bois de Boulogne in Paris) and Saint-Cloud, not far from the centre of the city, and just outside the capital at Evry, Maisons-Laffitte and Chantilly. In August almost the whole racing community decamps to Deauville, on the Normandy coast. French racehorses have made many telling raids on the big British Flat races, and the French-trained Nupsala had the impertinence to win one of the top English steeplechases in 1987 when storming home in the King

George VI Rank Chase at Kempton. The major French races in which British horses seek revenge are:

> The balance of payments: British-trained horses won the equivalent of £3,960,364 in races abroad in 1989, while foreign-trained horses running in Great Britain won £365,875.

Poule d'Essai des Poulains

Longchamp, 1 mile

The French equivalent of the Two Thousand Guineas, this race has been won by many brilliant horses, such as Blushing Groom in 1977. In 1981 Recitation, trained by Guy Harwood, provided a rare British win.

Poule d'Essai des Pouliches

Longchamp, 1 mile

This is the French equivalent of the One Thousand Guineas, and the list of winners is glittering: it includes Allez France, Ivanjica, Dancing Maid, Three Troikas, Miesque and Ravinella.

Prix du Jockey-Club

Chantilly, 1 mile 4 furlongs

The French Derby, the Prix du Jockey-Club usually determines the identity of the best three-year-old in France. Since the war it has been won by such notable performers as Scratch II, Sicambre, Herbager, Right Royal, Val De Loir, Reliance, Sassafras, Youth, Acamas, Bikala, Assert and Caerleon (both trained in Ireland, Assert by David O'Brien and Caerleon by his father Vincent) and Bering. The first victory in the race by a British-trained runner came in 1989 when Sheikh Mohammed's Old Vic powered to a seven-length victory under Steve Cauthen, the second in 1990 when Pat Eddery drove Sanglamore to a hard-fought verdict over Epervier Bleu (see page 102).

Prix de Diane

Chantilly, 1 mile 2½ furlongs

This is popularly known as the French Oaks, though it is shorter than its Epsom equivalent: its distance proved an attraction for Henry Cecil's Indian Skimmer, who slammed Miesque in the race in 1987. Cecil won again with Rafha in 1990. Other notable recent winners have been Pawneese, who won this after taking the Epsom Oaks in 1986, and Highclere, who won for the Queen in 1974 after winning the One Thousand Guineas at Newmarket.

Grand Prix de Saint-Cloud

Saint-Cloud, 1 mile 4½ furlongs

This is one of the major middle-distance targets in mid-season. Sea Bird II won it in 1965, Rheingold took it twice, and Teenoso won on his way to victory in the King George VI and Queen Elizabeth Diamond Stakes in 1984.

Prix Royal-Oak

Longchamp, 1 mile 7½ furlongs

Although nominally the French equivalent of the St Leger, the Prix Royal-Oak has been open to four-year-olds and upwards since 1979, and has since then been won by good stayers such as Gold River and Ardross.

Prix de l'Abbaye

Longchamp, 5 furlongs

Just as the Prix de l'Arc de Triomphe is the culmination of the European season for middle-distance horses, so the Prix de l'Abbaye, run the same afternoon, is the sprinters' end-of-season target. There have been plenty of British successes in the race in recent years, with horses such as Gentilhombre, Double Form, Moorestyle, Marwell, Sharpo, Habibti, Double Schwartz, Handsome Sailor and Silver Fling giving the huge British contingent at Longchamp on Arc day something extra to invest on the big one. Not that this contingent can see much of the race in detail: it is run over a straight course so remote from the stands that it makes the sprint course at Sandown Park seem positively intimate.

Prix de l'Arc de Triomphe

Longchamp, 1½ miles

The Prix de l'Arc de Triomphe is the most important race run in Europe during the Flat season, for it brings together the cream of several generations. It invariably attracts an international field of the highest quality and provides a wonderful spectacle as the runners charge into the straight. Ribot took it twice, as did Alleged, and since Sea Bird II's stunning victory in 1965 (see page 20) such horses as Vaguely Noble, Mill Reef, Rheingold, Allez France, All Along and Rainbow Quest have confirmed their greatness in the race. Dancing Brave's triumph in 1986 is described on page 187 and illustrated on pages 104–5. Whatever wins the Arc is a great horse, but the race comes at the end of the season and racing memories can be short: how could Star Appeal, who had won the Eclipse Stakes in 1975, have started at 119–1 to win the Arc just three months later?

United States of America

Thoroughbred racing is the biggest spectator sport in the USA, though the atmosphere at many courses is closer to that of greyhound racing in Britain than to any British race meeting. The tracks are comparatively uniform in shape, and there is much less emphasis on the horse itself than there is in Britain: 'paddock inspection' is normally a fairly cursory activity, not the lingering study of the horses before the race which the

---

HONG KONG

There are two racetracks in Hong Kong – Happy Valley, where racing has taken place since 1846 and where night racing under floodlights has been an immensely popular feature since its introduction in 1973, and Sha Tin, built on reclaimed land and opened in 1978. Attendance at these tracks averages over 40,000 people per day, and the level of betting is huge, both on course and in the 129 off-course betting centres around the territory, with over £1,750 million staked annually – over £1 million per race. Many British Flat jockeys ride in Hong Kong during the winter.

THE BREEDERS' CUP

The inauguration of the Breeders' Cup programme in the USA in 1984 has changed the face of flat racing, for the staging of the richest day's sport anywhere in the world on Breeders' Cup Day in October or November – the timing and venue in America change from year to year – now offers a hugely valuable end-of-season target to the best horses from Europe and elsewhere.

The Breeders' Cup was devised by John Gaines, one of Kentucky's most famous breeders, as a way of combating the decline of racing in America by presenting the Turf equivalent of the Superbowl or the World Series – an event to which the whole of the sport would aspire, and to which the rest of the sporting world would pay attention. The funds needed to finance this extravaganza of racing were raised from breeders, who each make an annual payment of a sum equivalent to the stud fee of each of their stallions and make the foals of these stallions eligible through payment of an additional fee. (The scheme has a reciprocal arrangement with the European Breeders' Fund.) The Breeders' Cup fund puts money into several hundred American races, but primarily into the seven races on Breeders' Cup Day (see opposite).

Although it comes at the end of a long and hard European season, and although problems will remain while horses are allowed to compete in Breeders' Cup events in some states under the influence of drugs banned in Europe, the victories of stars such as Miesque and Pebbles will ensure that European horses continue to grace the richest international showcase that world racing provides.

British racegoer enjoys. Most tracks are left-handed ovals, most races are run on dirt, and the whole sport is geared towards betting: although there are no on-track bookmakers, some states allow off-track betting at the odds determined on the course by the totalisator system in operation. (Some states do not allow betting but still stage horse races.) But it would be unfair to characterize the American racing fan simply as a gambler, for certain horses do reach celebrity status, and these stars – Kelso, for instance, who was Horse of the Year five times between 1960 and 1964, or John Henry – are wildly fêted. John Henry, foaled in 1975, won thirty-nine of the eighty-three races he contested, including twenty-five Stakes races (the equivalent to European Group races), and the Arlington Million in 1981 and 1984. His career total of earnings was $6,597,947.

The backbone of the American season is the US Triple Crown, consisting of:

Kentucky Derby

Churchill Downs, Louisville, Kentucky, 1¼ miles

Preakness Stakes

Pimlico, Baltimore, Maryland, 1 mile 1½ furlongs

Belmont Stakes

Belmont Park, Long Island, New York, 1½ miles.

Since the war the Triple Crown has been won by Assault (1946), Citation (1948), Secretariat (1973), Seattle Slew (1977), and Affirmed (1978, ridden in all three by Steve Cauthen). Northern Dancer won the Kentucky Derby and the Preakness in 1964, as did Spectacular Bid in 1979 and Sunday Silence in 1989. Alydar was second to Affirmed in all three 1978 races.

The Triple Crown races are for three-year-olds, are run on dirt and take place early in the season (the Kentucky Derby on the first Saturday in May), so it is rare for a British horse to run in any of them. But Go And Go, trained in Ireland by Dermot Weld and ridden by Michael Kinane, became the first European-trained winner of a Triple Crown race when lifting the 1990 Belmont by eight and a quarter lengths; and Bold Arrangement, trained at Newmarket by Clive Brittain, was second to Ferdinand in the Kentucky Derby in 1986.

A race deliberately designed to attract an international field is the twelve-furlong **Washington International**, run on turf late in the year at Laurel Park, Washington DC. Horses participate by invitation only, and there have been many European winners since Wilwyn, ridden by Joe Mercer's brother the late Manny Mercer, won the inaugural running for England in 1952. Lester Piggott took it on Sir Ivor in 1968 (when his brilliant riding of a colt with suspect stamina brought much criticism on his head from the American racing press, unused to skills like his), on Karabas in 1969, and on the French-trained Argument in 1980. Other notable European winners have been Dahlia (1973), Nobiliary (1975), Youth (1976), April Run (1982), and All Along, steered to victory in 1983 by Walter Swinburn.

The **Arlington Million** was first run in 1981, at Arlington Park,

Pat Eddery drives Pebbles home a neck in front of Strawberry Road in the Breeders' Cup Turf at Aqueduct in November 1985.

Chicago. For three-year-olds and upwards and run on turf over a mile and a quarter, the race had guaranteed prize money of $1 million and since then has always attracted appropriately high-class fields of horses invited from all over the globe. The 1981 Million went to John Henry, who, two years later, was pipped to the post by Tolomeo, trained by Luca Cumani at Newmarket and ridden by Pat Eddery to register the first British win, starting at 38–1: the first victory by a British-based horse in a major American race since Karabas had taken the Washington International in 1969. The following year John Henry won his second Million at the age of nine, but 1985 provided the greatest British moment in the race when the hugely popular gelding Teleprompter, trained at Richmond in Yorkshire by Bill Watts, kept going relentlessly under Tony Ives to beat Greinton. Less than a month before the Arlington Park stands had been gutted by fire, but the race took place nonetheless, and in 1986 and 1987 the event was held with the crowd accommodated in temporary stands. The 1988 race was run in Toronto while new stands were being built in Chicago, returning to the reborn Arlington in 1989.

Two other countries belong to the European Pattern system – **Germany** and **Italy** – and horses from Britain, Ireland and France often raid the best races in these countries: for many trainers, the Classics in Italy provide much easier pickings than those at home.

Several Western horses travel to **Japan** for the Japan Cup, an invitation race over a mile and a half held in Tokyo in late November. It was first run in 1981; the 1986 Cup attracted horses from Britain, the USA, Canada, New Zealand and France as well as local runners, and in a desperate finish Jupiter Island, trained by the adventurous Clive Brittain and ridden by Pat Eddery, beat another British challenger Allez Milord by a head to carry off a first prize equivalent to £448,276. (Triptych, well down the field that year, ran in the race the following year and finished fourth, having won the Fuji Stakes two weeks earlier.)

The major race in **Australia** (where there are bookmakers on the course but not off it) is the Melbourne Cup, a two-mile handicap run at Flemington. At Talaq, who had finished fourth (at 250–1) behind Secreto in the Epsom Derby in 1984, won the Melbourne Cup in 1986, but its most famous winner remains the legendary Phar Lap, who triumphed under 9 stone 12 pounds in 1930.

BREEDERS' CUP RACES

Breeders' Cup Turf

1½ miles on grass

The victory of Pebbles, ridden by Pat Eddery, at Aqueduct in 1985 was at the time the highlight of English involvement in Breeders' Cup races and signalled the arrival of Breeders' Cup Day as the international championship of racing; and Indian Skimmer finished a commendable third in the 1988 running in Kentucky. But this race also provided Britain's gloomiest moment, when Dancing Brave failed to show his true ability and finished fourth behind Manila in California in 1986.

Breeders' Cup Mile

1 mile on grass

Last Tycoon won this for France in 1986, and Miesque ran out a brilliant winner in both 1987 and 1988. Zilzal flopped in 1989.

Breeders' Cup Juvenile

1 mile 110 yards on dirt for two-year-old colts and geldings

Breeders' Cup Juvenile Fillies

1 mile 110 yards on dirt for two-year-old fillies only

Breeder's Cup Classic

1¼ miles on dirt

This race, the richest of the day, produced memorable finishes in 1987 when Ferdinand just beat Alysheba and in 1989 when Sunday Silence held off Easy Goer.

Breeder's Cup Sprint

6 furlongs on dirt

Breeders' Cup Distaff

1 mile 1 furlong on dirt for fillies and mares only

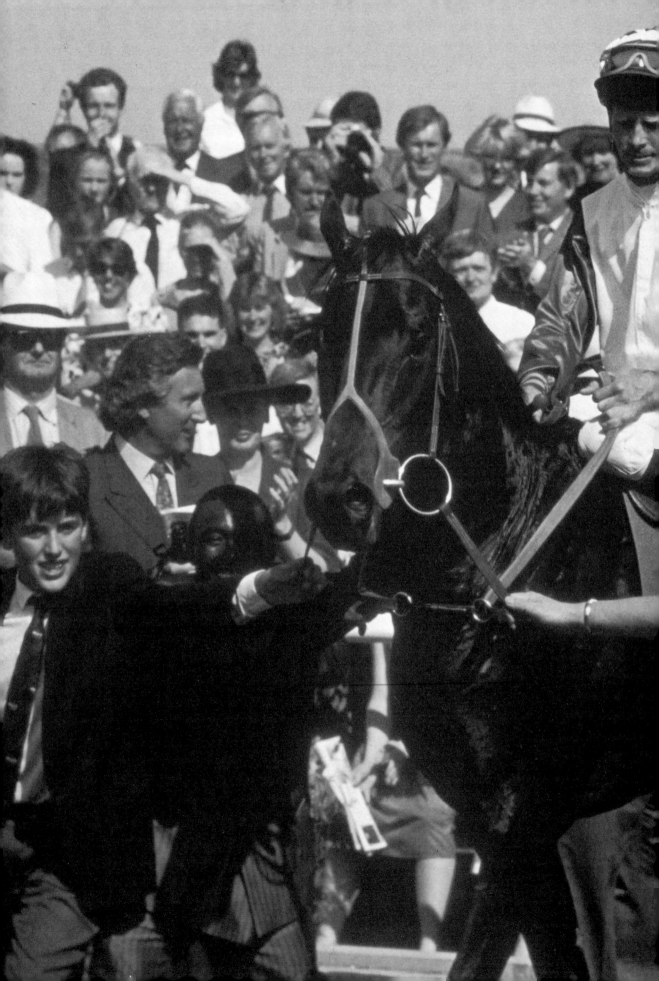

OWNERS, TRAINERS, JOCKEYS

Derek Thompson gave his first racecourse commentary – on a Cleveland point-to-point – at the age of fifteen, and was twenty-two when forming part of the BBC Radio commentary team on the 1973 Grand National, which is still his most memorable race (see page 182). He rode as an amateur on the Flat and over jumps, scoring his most notable victory in a private sweepstakes run for charity at Plumpton in 1980, when the Prince of Wales was among his beaten rivals. He has been presenting racing on television since 1982.

Previous pages:
Tirol (Michael Kinane) is led in after winning the 1990 General Accident Two Thousand Guineas: owner's wife Kate Horgan greets trainer Richard Hannon.

'*She'll drop anything for a jockey.*' *Not the most sensible line I've ever uttered on television, perhaps, but it unfortunately popped out when John McCririck was interviewing me one day at Kempton Park. I was referring to a masseuse who helped injured jockeys get back into the saddle quicker than most doctors would be able to, and I was trying to get across the fact that she would squeeze any jockey into her very busy schedule in an effort to get them fit again. It came out the wrong way, but such moments are all in a day's work on Channel Four Racing.*

Normally I ask the questions. Interviewing the owners, trainers, jockeys and others who make the news must surely be one of the best jobs in racing, as it brings me into contact with a wide range of fascinating personalities, from the excited young couple at Chester races who'd got married that morning, to His Highness the Aga Khan in the winner's enclosure at Epsom. Racing certainly brings together all strata of society and pitches them in together – rich and poor, good and bad, happy and sad.

Lester Piggott was undoubtedly the greatest of all the characters I've encountered during my career in racing. When I rushed up to him for a breathless interview as he was returning to the winner's enclosure after winning his ninth Derby on Teenoso a photographer frightened the horse just as I was asking the eternal question, 'What was it like?' 'F*** off!', came the reply, and the many millions who had just watched the Derby live around the world couldn't believe their ears: it was the one time I was glad that Lester had a speech impediment.

Trying to get the views of a beaten trainer or jockey isn't as easy as talking to the connections of the winner, and in the billion-dollar world of racing a word said out of place might take millions off the value of a future stallion – but on the whole we all get on well together. The same goes for the backroom boys and girls who are the real workers on Channel Four Racing: the presenters may be at the sharp end but they do have the most enjoyable part of the operation.

My encounter with the actor Larry Hagman is typical of my role. I bumped into J. R. Ewing and his glamorous wife Sue Ellen in the winner's enclosure at Longchamp shortly after Dancing Brave had won the Prix de l'Arc de Triomphe. 'Does the oil-rich J. R. Ewing own any racehorses?', I enquired. 'No, son,' he replied in his Texan drawl, 'I don't like anything that eats while I sleep.' You can't say fairer than that.

86

Owners, trainers and jockeys are the most visible of the thousands of people who participate in racing. They are supported in their pursuit of glory on the Turf by an army of others – stable lads, head lads, travelling head lads, box drivers, valets, farriers, vets and saddlers, not forgetting those who run and staff the studs, without whom there would be no horses to go to the races – but this trio have the leading roles: the trainer primes the horse for action, the jockey pilots it through the crucial few minutes of the race, and the owner pays the bills.

OWNERS

There is a story of an owner who, on being told by his trainer that his horse was still green, replied, 'He was brown the last time I saw him.'

Most racehorse owners, though, belie the outdated image of the rich but ignorant nuisance who owns horses simply for social reasons, and the nature of ownership over the last decade has changed immensely. On the one hand, ownership of the very best horses on the Flat is confined to a very small number of immensely rich people who build up huge strings of superbly bred horses by their own breeding operations and by shelling out unconscionable amounts of money at the yearling sales, so that big race after big race after big race is being fought out by jockeys sporting the colours of one of the Maktoum brothers, or Khalid Abdullah, or the Aga Khan or Robert Sangster. On the other hand, new regulations concerning syndicates and racing clubs mean that thousands of 'ordinary' people can now enjoy a genuine involvement with ownership for a fairly small outlay. Officially registered syndicates may not consist of more than twelve persons, but racing clubs (whose members make a one-off payment for a share) are increasingly popular with those of limited means but aspirations to rub shoulders with Hamdan Al-Maktoum in the winner's enclosure.

Owner Khalid Abdullah, trainer Roger Charlton (in his first season as master of Beckhampton) and jockey Pat Eddery scored a remarkable double in 1990 when Sanglamore won the Prix du Jockey-Club Lancia – the French Derby – at Chantilly on the first Sunday in June and Quest For Fame won the Ever Ready Derby at Epsom three days later. (This Derby double matched the feat of Marcel Boussac, Charles Semblat and Rae Johnstone with Scratch and Galcador in 1950.)

'I don't like anything that eats while I sleep': J. R. Ewing gives his views on racehorse ownership to Derek Thompson at Longchamp in October 1986. But racing is important for other soap characters. In *The Archers* both Jack Woolley and Brian Aldridge have owned racehorses, and on Derby Day 1983 Walter Gabriel had a playful accumulator: Clantime won the first at Epsom at 9–2, then his selection at Felpersham (the course near Ambridge) came in at a nice price, and Lester Piggott did the honours on Teenoso in the big one, netting Walter thousands.

RACING COLOURS

Racing colours must be registered annually with Weatherbys – the fee for 1990 was £15.00 (plus VAT) – and once registered cannot be taken by any other person. You do not actually have to own a racehorse to have racing colours: you could register in the expectation of future ownership in order to prevent anyone else from taking that combination of colours.

In bygone years subtle shades of colour could be registered. Lord Howard de Walden's colours are 'apricot', and the Duke of Devonshire's have been 'straw' since colours were first used on jockeys in 1762 'for the greater convenience of distinguishing the horses in running, as also for the prevention of disputes arising from not knowing the colours worn by each rider'. Nowadays the Jockey Club specifies eighteen basic colours in which new registrations must be made (white, grey, pink, red, maroon, light green, emerald green, dark green, light blue, royal blue, dark blue, mauve, purple, yellow, orange, beige, brown and black), and as all possible registrations in single colours have been claimed a new owner will now have to accept a combination of at least two. The Jockey Club has also standardized the design of the colours, so that only a combination of the designs reproduced on page 96 will be allowed. (Gone are the days when an owner could register colours with embellishments such as the large 'B' which graced the front and back of the colours of Mr John McShain, owner of Ballymoss and Gladness. The B stood for Barclay Stud, under which name he raced in the USA.)

A selection of famous racing colours is illustrated on page 97.

An extra dimension has been added to ownership – and an extra grotesquerie to the naming of horses – by allowing commercial companies to own racehorses, sometimes (though not always) for advertising purposes. That fine sprinter Moorestyle was probably the best company advertisement of recent years in terms of racing quality, and was undoubtedly a great asset in the balance sheet of his owners, Moores International Furnishings Limited. In the year that Moorestyle retired three horses of much lesser ability were neighbours in Denys Smith's yard: Geary's For Steel, Geary's for Strip, and Geary's Steel Stock are mainly memorable as examples of the overt use of horses' names for advertising – clearly Geary's was the place to go for steel.

There are over 18,000 owners registered with the Jockey Club. When registration (which in 1990 cost £29.00 plus VAT for an individual) is accepted the owner may deposit £200 into an account with Weatherbys. To this will be added winnings, and from it will be deducted entry fees and fees to the jockey. (Training fees are paid directly to the trainer.) When deductions exceed additions the owner must top up the account.

But what are the chances of making a profit by owning a horse? Apart from those owner–breeders such as Robert Sangster who operate on a vast scale with a view to making money (though Sangster can still claim that his years as an owner have been 'nothing but fun'), few owners are in it for monetary gain, and many are well aware that the odds are stacked against their prospering from this pursuit. The basic training fee per horse will be upwards of £130 per week, to which must usually be added charges for the attentions of the vet and the farrier, entry fees, transport costs, insurance premiums, jockeys' fees, and various registration fees. So in very round numbers it will cost £10,000 a year to keep a horse in training – much more if the horse is with one of the top Flat trainers.

Even with the minimum race value (that is, the total to be won by all placed horses) raised in 1990 to £3,000 for a flat race, £2,700 for a steeplechase and £2,000 for a hurdle, a horse at the lower level is clearly unlikely to pay its way, and around two thirds of all horses in training fail to win a race at all. Some 1,300 registered owners did win a race in the 1989 Flat season (excluding all-weather): Sheikh Mohammed's 130 victories with 90 winning horses netted him £1,296,933 (and he won £800,337 in place money); Sheikh Rashid Al Khalifa's solitary winner brought him £1,576.

The history of the Turf is peopled by famous owners from a variety of backgrounds – royalty, aristocracy, show business, commerce, even politics . . .

Sir Winston Churchill was seventy-five before he first registered as an owner, but he had long been a keen racing enthusiast. He became a member of the Jockey Club and owned several renowned horses, notably the grey Colonist II, who won thirteen races (including the Jockey Club Cup and – appropriately – the Winston Churchill Stakes), and came second in the Ascot Gold Cup. High Hat was one of the best middle-distance horses of his generation, beating Petite Etoile at Kempton Park and finishing second to St Paddy in the Jockey Club Stakes; he was fourth in the Prix de l'Arc de Triomphe in 1961. Vienna won six races and was placed in the St Leger, Coronation Cup,

Hardwicke Stakes, Champion Stakes and Prix Ganay, and became the sire of the great Vaguely Noble. Sir Winston's racing colours – pink, chocolate sleeves and cap – live on in the scarf of Churchill College, Cambridge.

A far cry from Sir Winston in temperament, if not in physique, was **Dorothy Paget**. One of the great eccentrics of the century, she raced on a vast scale between the wars, financing her operation with the fortune she had inherited at the age of twenty-one. Once an accomplished horsewoman herself, riding side-saddle in point-to-points, her curious life-style included obsessive eating, and she soon weighed in at over twenty stone. She disliked human company – especially men, whose proximity reportedly inclined her to vomit – and surrounded herself with a bevy of female minders. She kept odd hours, dining at 7 a.m., sleeping through the day and getting up for breakfast at 8:30 p.m., then spending the night consuming vast meals and phoning her trainers. She expected them to be adaptable to such eccentricities, but (not surprisingly) her tyrannical ways led to friction: horses would be shuffled around between trainers at her whim. But her nomadic string included some star performers, notably Golden Miller, who won the Cheltenham Gold Cup five times from 1932 to 1936 and remains the only horse to have won the Gold Cup and the Grand National in the same year. (When she planted a kiss on Golden Miller's nose after one of his victories, a racegoer speculated that this was probably the first occasion on which she had kissed a member of the opposite sex: 'And he's a gelding,' pointed out another.) She owned Insurance, twice winner of the Champion Hurdle, and two other Champion Hurdle winners: Solford, ridden to victory by one Sean Magee in 1940, and Distel in 1946. She also owned Straight Deal, who took the wartime Derby at Newmarket in 1943, and Mont Tremblant, winner of the Cheltenham Gold Cup as a novice in 1952. Another of her horses, Tuppence, does not figure in the records of great races but was the subject of one of the oddest gambles of modern times. He was backed from odds as long as 200–1 in the week before the 1933 Derby, and started at 10–1 – a 'steamer' to end all steamers – to finish nineteenth of twenty-four runners behind Hyperion. (Tuppence later dead-heated for a race at Hamilton Park, netting his owner £56.) Certainly much of the money bringing his Derby odds tumbling so dramatically could have been Dorothy Paget's, for she was an inveterate punter: her largest stake was reputed to have been £160,000, on an 8–1 on chance. To say that it duly obliged (which it did) seems to underplay the magnitude of the wager. But her curious daily routine made orthodox punting rather awkward, and such was the trust with which she was regarded by one of her bookmakers that he allowed her to phone him in the evening and bet on races which had already taken place. Dorothy Paget – truly a big owner – died in 1960.

It is a tribute to the allure of British and Irish racing that it has attracted the involvement of many owners from overseas – not only the Aga Khan and the Maktoums, but also famous American figures such as Raymond Guest, owner of Derby winners Larkspur and Sir Ivor and of the great chaser L'Escargot; Paul Mellon, whose Mill Reef is one of the Turf's immortals, and whose black and gold colours are still a familiar sight in

> Lord Derby's famous colours are registered as 'black, white cap', yet the silks include one white button. When Tommy Weston was getting changed to ride Lord Derby's Sansovino in the 1924 Derby he nervously got part of the white stock which he wore round his neck caught around the black button of his jacket – so that it looked as if he had one white button. The horse won, and to this day that white button has remained (unofficially) part of Lord Derby's colours.

Dorothy Paget.

The Aga Khan in the unsaddling enclosure at Epsom after Kahyasi's victory in the 1988 Ever Ready Derby.

┌─ **SHOW BUSINESS** ──────

Racing is a great entertainment, and has long had close links with show business, with many actors and actresses, singers and other entertainers drawn to the British racing scene – among them Lily Langtry, whose horses were raced under the name of 'Mr Jersey'; Gregory Peck, who owned some good steeplechasers, including Owens Sedge and Different Class, third in the 1968 Grand National; and James Bolam, whose best horse has been Credo's Daughter, a game chasing mare of the 1970s. Singer Billy Fury owned Anselmo, fourth in the 1964 Derby, while Gainsay won the Ritz Club National Hunt Chase at the 1987 Cheltenham Festival for Errol Brown of the group Hot Chocolate. And it's not only in ownership that the showbiz connections can be found. George Formby was an apprentice jockey before embarking on his legendary singing career: he rode in Lord Derby's colours at the age of ten.

British races; and silver tycoon Nelson Bunker Hunt, owner of Dahlia, Empery and Youth. Grundy was owned by the Italian aristocrat Carlo Vittadini, Pebbles in her early racing career by the Greek shipping magnate Marcos Lemos, who also owned Petingo, sire of Troy; Bolkonski and Wollow, who won the Two Thousand Guineas in successive years, were owned by the Italian Carlo d'Alessio; and Secreto, who pipped El Gran Senor in the 1984 Derby, by Luigi Miglietti from Venezuela.

The Aga Khan

The Aga Khan, Imam (spiritual leader) of the Shia Muslims, was born in 1936, grandson of the Aga Khan who was a major figure in European racing in the middle part of the century, winning the Triple Crown in 1935 with Bahram and the Derby on four other occasions, with Blenheim, Mahmoud, My Love and Tulyar. The present Aga Khan built up his racing interests during the 1970s and enjoyed spectacular success throughout the following decade. He won the Derby, Irish Derby and King George VI and Queen Elizabeth Diamond Stakes in 1981 with the ill-fated Shergar, and the Derby twice more with Shahrastani in 1986 and Kahyasi (who carried his second colours, the green and chocolate hoops made famous by his grandfather) in 1988: his first colours (green, red epaulets) were carried in that race by Doyoun, who had added to the Classic haul by taking the 1988 Two Thousand Guineas.

Khalid Abdullah

Khalid Abdullah is a Saudi prince who has become one of the biggest owner–breeders in modern racing. His Known Fact became the first Arab-owned English Classic winner when taking the 1980 Two Thousand Guineas on the disqualification of Nureyev (see page 183), and his colours of green, pink sash and cap, white sleeves have since then been carried by many well-known horses, among them the brilliant milers Rousillon and Warning, and Rainbow Quest, who won the 1985 Coronation Cup and Prix de l'Arc de Triomphe. His Dancing Brave was one of the outstanding horses of the post-war period, winning in 1986 the Two Thousand Guineas, the Coral–Eclipse, the King George VI and Queen Elizabeth Diamond Stakes, and a

Robert Sangster and his wife greet jockey Michael Hills at Newmarket in April 1989 after Nomadic Way had won the Carter Street Garage Citroen BX Handicap.

memorable Prix de l'Arc de Triomphe (described on page 187). Dancing Brave was controversially beaten in the 1986 Derby, and Abdullah was also placed in the Epsom Classic with Damister (third in 1985) and Bellotto (third in 1987). But he finally won the race with Quest For Fame in 1990, three days after his Sanglamore had won the French equivalent, the Prix du Jockey-Club. Khalid Abdullah has more than 150 horses in training in Britain, and his Juddmonte Stud operation has bases in Berkshire, County Meath and Kentucky.

Robert Sangster

Emerald green, royal blue sleeves, white cap, emerald green spots – how many famous horses have carried those colours! The Minstrel, El Gran Senor, Golden Fleece, Alleged, Detroit, Assert, Sadlers Wells, Caerleon, Solford, Pas De Seul, Hawaiian Sound, Lomond – all have played their part in building up Robert Sangster's massive international owning and breeding interests. His first success as an owner was a far cry from the exploits of those star names: Chalk Stream, trained by Eric Cousins, won a small race at Haydock for the 24-year-old Sangster in 1960. After that humble beginning he acquired more horses, and in the early 1970s decided to become involved in the breeding side. In partnership with John Magnier he founded the Coolmore Stud in Ireland, and in 1975 formed a syndicate of big owners (including Stavros Niarchos and Danny Schwartz) to breed and race horses to be trained at Ballydoyle by Vincent O'Brien. The first crop – not all of which raced in Sangster's colours – included The Minstrel, Be My Guest, Artaius, Godswalk and Alleged. Sangster's own Swettenham Stud, in Cheshire, has bred many fine horses (such as Dibidale, El Gran Senor and Sadler's Wells), but his breeding interests range all over the world. It was the international spirit of Sangster's operation, particularly his widespread importation of the best American blood, which helped to change the character of racing.

H. J. Joel with Ballyhane at Sandown Park in December 1987. One of the most successful owner–breeders of the modern era, Jim Joel won many big races (including the 1967 Two Thousand Guineas and Derby) with Royal Palace, and among other notable performers who carried his famous colours of black, scarlet cap on the Flat were Picture Play (One Thousand Guineas, 1944), Light Cavalry (St Leger, 1980), Fairy Footsteps (One Thousand Guineas, 1981), Connaught, Major Portion and Welsh Pageant. In 1987, at the age of 92, he won the Grand National with Maori Venture.

Even Sangster, though, has his limits, and his buying power at the world's top yearling sales now tends to be eclipsed by that of the major Arab owners. (After his Nomadic Way had won the marathon Cesarewitch in 1988 Sangster declared, tongue only partly in cheek: 'I don't usually go in for slow horses – but these days these are the only races the Arabs will let us win'.) In 1984 he purchased the famous training establishment at Manton in Wiltshire, with first Michael Dickinson (who departed in 1986) and then Barry Hills as his trainer.

Royalty

Racing has for long been known as the Sport of Kings, and today the active involvement of the Royal Family in breeding, owning and riding racehorses is one of the great boons of the sport. Her Majesty the Queen has some thirty horses in training, the Queen Mother's passion for National Hunt racing is as strong as ever, and the riding exploits of the Princess Royal bear witness to a new generation of Royal participation in the sport.

Charles II, the first English king to show a real enthusiasm for organized racing, holds the distinction of being the only reigning monarch to ride the winner of an official horse race. His patronage of Newmarket established the town as the centre of British racing, and Charles won The Plate there in 1671 and 1674: 'I do assure you the king won by good horsemanship,' wrote Sir Robert Carr of his second victory. William of Orange owned and bred racehorses, winning a match at Newmarket with the engagingly named Stiff Dick.

It was Queen Anne who next exerted great royal influence on the Turf, establishing Ascot racecourse in 1711: the Queen Anne Stakes remains the traditional opening race at Royal Ascot. George II's third son, the Duke of Cumberland, bred Herod and Eclipse, and George IV instituted the Royal Procession at Ascot. Queen Victoria bred the winners of eleven Classics, though she never set foot on a racecourse after the death of Prince Albert. Her son the Prince of Wales founded the Sandringham Stud and bred Persimmon, who won the Derby for him in 1896, and Diamond Jubilee, who repeated the feat in 1900. As King Edward VII he won his third Derby with Minoru in 1909. George V was less keen than his father, though he won the One Thousand Guineas in 1928 with Scuttle, but George VI, who had little interest in racing until his accession, won five Classics: in 1942 the brilliant Sun Chariot took the One Thousand Guineas, Oaks and St Leger; in the same year he won the Two Thousand Guineas with Big Game and in 1946 the One Thousand again with Hypericum.

In Queen Elizabeth II the British racing scene has a patron who is not only highly knowledgeable about the sport (especially about breeding) but also a keen racegoer. Success as an owner came early in her reign, her Aureole running second to Pinza in the Derby in 1953 shortly after the Coronation. Aureole matured into a top-class four-year-old, winning the King George VI and Queen Elizabeth Stakes in 1954 (having again found Pinza too good for him in the 1953 running), and had a fine career at stud, siring the 1960 Derby winner St Paddy and two winners of the St Leger in Aurelius and Provoke. The Queen's first Classic winners were Carrozza, who snatched the Oaks by a short head under Lester Piggott in 1957, and Pall Mall, winner of the Two Thousand Guineas in 1958. Highclere, the grand-dam of Nashwan, won the One Thousand Guineas in 1974 and then took the Prix de Diane at Chantilly. In 1977, the Queen's Jubilee year, Dunfermline fittingly provided two more English Classic victories in the Oaks and – after an unforgettable duel with Alleged – the St Leger.

If a triumph in the Queen's colours excites any Flat meeting, the Queen Mother holds a very special place in the affections of the National Hunt community. For she, more than any other individual,

> Unknown Quantity's win in the royal colours in the Arlington Handicap (Grade 1) at Arlington Park, Chicago on 12 August 1989 recorded the Queen's first ever victory in the USA, and her first Group 1 or Grade 1 success since 1982. Her Marienski won the Bernard Baruch Handicap (Grade 2) at Saratoga on 12 August 1990.

was responsible for raising the status of the jumping game from that of a poor relation to the Flat to the position it enjoys today. A succession of famous horses have carried the 'blue, buff stripes, blue sleeves, black cap, gold tassel' to victory in top races: Manicou, The Rip, Makaldar, Laffy, Double Star, Gay Record, Antiar, Oedipe, Escalus, Inch Arran, Colonius, Isle Of Man, Game Spirit, Sunyboy, Tammuz, and The Argonaut among them. Two others in particular recall notably memorable, and very different, occasions. Special Cargo, who won the Grand Military Gold Cup at Sandown Park three times, will always be remembered for his last-gasp victory in the Whitbread Gold Cup on the same course in 1984, a race which many people (including Graham Goode: see page 185) regard as the finest steeplechase of all time.

The Queen Mother at Sandown Park on Whitbread Gold Cup Day, April 1989.

And what of Devon Loch? His fate in the 1956 Grand National will be for ever the epitome of defeat snatched out of the jaws of victory. For having seen off his rivals in the world's greatest steeplechase with a superb display of jumping, Devon Loch (ridden by Dick Francis) was bounding up the Liverpool run-in to certain triumph in front of his owner and the young Queen and Princess Margaret when, fifty yards from the winning post, he seemed to leap at an imaginary obstacle and slid down to the turf, leaving ESB to stride past and take the race. No one can say for sure why he did it: Dick Francis thinks that the crescendo of noise greeting a winner who would have been the most popular victor in the history of the race scared the horse: 'I have never heard in my life such a noise. It rolled and lapped around us, buffeting and glorious, the enthusiastic expression of love for the Royal Family and delight in seeing the Royal horse win.' Whatever the reason for Devon Loch's sensational slither, the Queen Mother stifled her disappointment, writing a few days later to the horse's trainer Peter Cazalet, 'We will not be done in by this, and will just keep on trying.'

By the day of her ninetieth birthday in August 1990 she had owned the winners of 380 jumping races and four on the Flat, and it was appropriate that Special Cargo and The Argonaut (who had added the 1990 Grand Military Gold Cup to his companion's treble in the race) should join the parade in London in June to celebrate her life.

The Prince of Wales owns racehorses and rode a few times over fences in the 1980–81 season, taking a well-publicized tumble from Good Prospect at the Cheltenham National Hunt Festival. Under pressure to give up such a dangerous pursuit, he was quoted as saying: 'I wish people could only understand the real thrill, the challenge of steeplechasing. It's part of the great British way of life, and none of the sports I've done bears any comparison.' The Prince bred Devil's Elbow, who seemed to have given him his first victory as an owner in a novices' hurdle at Worcester in December 1988; then the post-race dope test proved positive and the horse was disqualified. Trainer Nick Gaselee was cleared of intentionally administering the offending substances, but the Prince had to forgo the £680 first prize.

The Princess Royal being given the leg-up by trainer David Nicholson for her first ride in a steeplechase, on Cnoc Na Cuille at Kempton Park in February 1987.

The Princess Royal has become an accomplished amateur jockey under the tutelage of trainer David Nicholson, and rides regularly under both codes. In 1987 she won the top ladies' race of the season, on Diamond Day at Ascot, for Michael Stoute on Ten No Trumps; and the following year took (appropriately) the Queen Mother's Cup at York on Insular, her first victory shown live on Channel Four.

The Maktoums

'When we were small boys we were riding horses,' Hamdan Al-Maktoum explained in a newspaper interview in July 1990 when asked why he and his brothers so loved horse racing: 'It's part of our culture. Our involvement here started as a hobby, and now it's a very strong hobby.' A very strong hobby indeed. Even though the Maktoum brothers have been part of the scene for a decade the facts and figures still boggle the mind. Together they own some 1,500 horses. Sheikh Mohammed has about 600 in training, Sheikh Hamdan 290. Sheikh Mohammed and Sheikh Hamdan were first and second in the table of leading owners for the 1989 Flat season, with Sheikh Maktoum Al-Maktoum fifth and their cousin Mana Al-Maktoum (owner of Zilzal) sixth. Horses owned by these four men won 265 races worth £3,401,448 in win prize money in Britain alone, with place money bringing the takings up to £4,610,769. But it's an expensive hobby as well. Each of the four brothers owns a breeding operation, and each spends heftily at the sales. At the yearling sales in Kentucky in July 1988 the family shelled out a reputed $30 million, in 1989 possibly twice that figure; at the same sale in 1990 the figure of over $32 million spent by the Maktoums in two days for fifty-nine horses does not take account of purchases handled by agents. But whatever they cost, the achievements of the horses who have run in the Maktoum colours are legion. When Sheikh Mohammed's Belmez beat his Old Vic in the 1990 King George VI and Queen Elizabeth Diamond Stakes at Ascot, the victory represented the sixth Maktoum triumph from eleven Group 1 races run so far that season in Britain, and was simply the latest point in a lengthy sequence of big-race success brought off by such as Nashwan, Oh So Sharp, Salsabil, Pebbles, Bairn, Awaasif, Indian Skimmer, Musical Bliss, Soviet Star, Touching Wood, Wassl, Polish Precedent, Elmaamul, Mtoto, Shadeed, Shareef Dancer, Ma Biche, Reprimand, In The Wings, Creator, Unfuwain, Al Bahathri, Dayjur, Diminuendo . . .

The Maktoum brothers are the sons of Sheikh Rashid bin Saeed Al-Maktoum, ruler of Dubai, the tiny oil-rich state which forms part of the United Arab Emirates. Maktoum Al-Maktoum (colours: royal blue, white chevron, light blue cap) is the oldest of the four, and was the first to own a Classic winner: his Touching Wood, second to Golden Fleece in the 1982 Derby, went on to win the St Leger. Sheikh Maktoum followed up with Ma Biche in the 1983 One Thousand Guineas and Shadeed in the 1985 Two Thousand; his Shareef Dancer won the Irish Sweeps Derby in 1983, and he has also owned fine sprinters in Green Desert and Cadeaux Genereux. His bloodstock interests include the Gainsborough Stud near Newbury.

With the achievements of Nashwan in 1989 and Salsabil, Dayjur, Mujtahid and Elmaamul in 1990 the second oldest brother Sheikh Hamdan has challenged the younger Sheikh Mohammed for the position of the leading light of the brothers. Before Nashwan his best horses had been Unfuwain and the filly Al Bahathri, beaten a short head by Oh So Sharp in the 1985 One Thousand Guineas and a game winner of the Irish One Thousand. His colours of royal blue, white epaulets, striped cap, have become a familiar sight in big races all over

When Alydaress won the Irish Oaks in July 1989 Sheikh Mohammed achieved the unusual feat of owning four winners of this Classic in three years, having won it with Unite in 1987 and owning the dead-heaters Diminuendo and Melodist in 1988.

the world: he won the Melbourne Cup with At Talaq in 1986. Sheikh Hamdan's breeding operation is run as the Shadwell Estate Company, the flagship of which is the Nunnery Stud near Thetford in Norfolk: here Nashwan, Unfuwain and Green Desert took up stud duties.

Sheikh Hamdan Al-Maktoum leads in Salsabil (Willie Carson) after her victory in the Gold Seal Oaks at Epsom in June 1990.

Sheikh Mohammed races and breeds on the grandest scale, with 200 or so broodmares in addition to his 600 horses in training around the world. He started developing his racing interests in earnest in the late 1970s, but had to wait until 1985 for his first Classic winner when Oh So Sharp, whom he had bred, took the One Thousand Guineas: she then won the Oaks and the St Leger. Sheikh Mohammed bought Pebbles after she had won the One Thousand Guineas in 1984, and she went on to win the Eclipse Stakes (the first filly to do so), the Champion Stakes (sponsored since 1982 by the Maktoum family) and the Breeders' Cup Turf in 1985 – the year that Sheikh Mohammed first became leading owner. Other famous fillies to have raced in his colours (maroon, white sleeves, maroon cap, white star) include the winners of the 1987 and 1988 Oaks in Unite and Diminuendo, the 1989 One Thousand Guineas winner Musical Bliss and the brilliant Indian Skimmer. He has even made an impact on the National Hunt scene, his Kribensis winning the 1990 Champion Hurdle. Like his brothers, Sheikh Mohammed maintains his own international breeding interests – notably at the Dalham Hall Stud, Newmarket, where Dancing Brave and Reference Point are among the resident stallions – but he still buys prodigiously at the yearling sales: his most famous purchase was that of Snaafi Dancer for $10.2 million dollars in 1982 (see page 21).

Sheikh Ahmed (yellow, black epaulets) is the youngest of the four brothers. His best-known horses have been Wassl, winner of the Irish Two Thousand Guineas in 1983, and Mtoto, who took the Eclipse Stakes in 1987 (from Reference Point) and 1988 (from Shady Heights) before winning the King George at Ascot. Sheikh Ahmed owns the Aston Upthorpe Stud in Oxfordshire, where Mtoto stands.

With so many hundreds of horses in training and a control of so many of the best bloodlines, the Maktoums dominate British (and indeed world) flat racing. Opinions are divided about the effects of this, some resenting the concentration of so much power in so few hands and the situation where even small races at minor courses go to the family (leaving minute pickings for the smaller operator), but most applauding the way in which the Maktoums' investment in the sport in Britain has raised it once again to a position of pre-eminence on the world stage. Less headline-grabbing than the big races won and the mammoth amounts paid at the sales are the sums of money the family has put into the infrastructure of the sport: the all-weather Al Bahathri Gallop at Newmarket, for instance, was a gift to the racing community of the town from the Maktoums.

Racing may be the Maktoums' hobby, but they all hold government positions in Dubai (Sheikh Mohammed is Minister of Defence of the UAE, Sheikh Hamdan is Finance Minister) and sometimes sport must take second place. In early August 1990 the Sheikhs and their entourages were not to be seen on British racecourses. They had more important business back home.

JACKET

SLEEVES

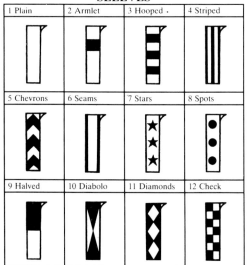

CAP

The official designs for racing colours, as specified by Weatherbys

Her Majesty Queen Elizabeth II

Her Majesty Queen Elizabeth
the Queen Mother

The Aga Khan

Robert Sangster

Hamdan Al-Maktoum

Sheikh Mohammed

Maktoum Al-Maktoum

Khalid Abdullah

H. J. Joel

Owners' colours: nine sets of familiar silks

Opposite page: Brigadier Gerard (Joe Mercer) wins the Queen Elizabeth II Stakes at Ascot in September 1972 from Sparkler, the penultimate victory in a career in which he was beaten only once in eighteen races.

Two famous racehorses make their way to the start: *left*, the gelding Teleprompter (Tony Ives) at Ascot, and *below*, Pebbles (Pat Eddery) before her victory in the Breeders' Cup Turf at Aqueduct, New York, in 1985.

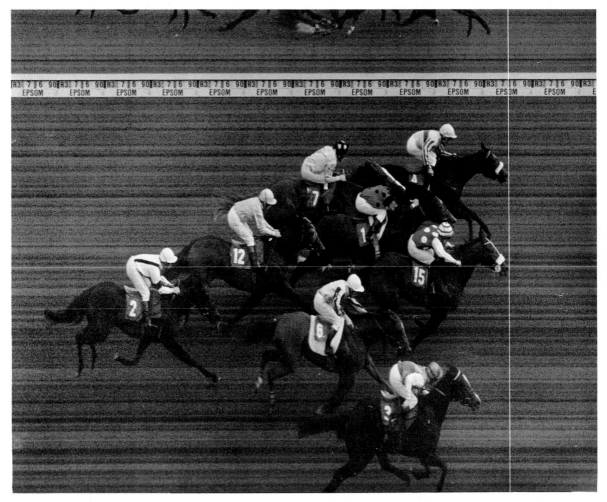

A colour photo-finish print. The finish of the Stanley Wootton Handicap at Epsom on 7 June 1990, with Lyndseylee (no. 4) and Maison Des Fruits inseparable in front of Lake Mistassiu (no. 3), Night At Sea (no. 1), Reel Foyle (no. 6), Rancho Mirage (no. 7), Deceit (no. 12) and Rivers Rhapsody (no. 2). The distances were: dead heat, head, head, neck, short head, half a length, three quarters of a length.

The international dimension of racing. *Above:* Triptych (American-bred, and at the time English-owned, French-trained, and ridden by Tony Cruz, born in Hong Kong) beats Celestial Storm (American-bred, American-owned, trained in England by the Italian Luca Cumani and ridden by Ulsterman Ray Cochrane) in the 1986 Dubai Champion Stakes, run that year on the July Course at Newmarket. *Below:* Tony Bin (English-bred, owned and trained by Italians, ridden by another Ulsterman, John Reid, and destined for stud in Japan) holds off Mtoto (English-bred, Arab-owned, English-trained, ridden by the South African jockey Michael Roberts) in the 1988 Ciga Prix de l'Arc de Triomphe at Longchamp.

British-trained winners in two overseas Derbys in 1990. *Above:* Sanglamore (Pat Eddery, pink cap) just gets the better of Epervier Bleu (Dominic Boeuf) in the Prix du Jockey-Club Lancia at Chantilly on 3 June. *Below:* Salsabil (Willie Carson) strides home from Deploy (Walter Swinburn) in the Budweiser Irish Derby at The Curragh on 1 July.

Left: Prince Khalid Abdullah at last wins Flat racing's most prestigious prize, and leads in Quest For Fame (Pat Eddery) after winning the Ever Ready Derby at Epsom on 6 June 1990. *Below:* Queen Elizabeth the Queen Mother receives the Horse and Hound Grand Military Gold Cup from her daughter at Sandown Park on 9 March 1990 after The Argonaut's victory.

Dancing Brave (Pat Eddery) surges to the front in the 1986 Trusthouse Forte Prix de l'Arc de Triomphe at Longchamp. Second was Bering (number 14), third Triptych (left), fourth Shahrastani (green colours, mostly obscured behind Bering), fifth Shardari (brown cap) and sixth Darara (sheepskin noseband).

Crisp (Richard Pitman) sweeps over
Becher's Brook on the second circuit
of the 1973 Grand National.

Opposite page: above, at the last fence in the 1984
Whitbread Gold Cup Special Cargo (Kevin Mooney, left)
comes into focus as Plundering (pink colours) sets off for
the line closely pursued by Diamond Edge (partly
obscured). *Below:* Tirol (Michael Kinane) surges home in
the 1990 General Accident Two Thousand Guineas at
Newmarket.

Opposite page: two famous Cheltenham Gold Cups. *Above:* Dawn Run (right) seems held at the last fence in 1986 by Forgive 'N Forget (left) and Wayward Lad, while at the same stage of the 1989 race (*below*) the grey Desert Orchid comes to tackle Yahoo.

Two sides of being a jockey. *Right:* Lester Piggott rides a finish at Newbury, and Richard Dunwoody (*below*) experiences the frequent fate of the jump jockey when taking a spill from Celtic Barle in the Sun Alliance Novices' Hurdle at Cheltenham in March 1989.

Graham Goode's card for the 1990 Ever Ready Derby at Epsom. Graham makes a note at the head of the sheet of the win and place prize money (£576,417) and the numbers of wins that the runners have scored out of their total number of outings (thirty out of sixty-nine). He calls the race mainly by identifying the jockeys' colours, but takes account of special physical characteristics – Linamix is a dark grey (spot the colour sample to the left of his colours), Kaheel has a white blaze ('wh face'), Zoman has a white sock and a white face. He also notes the equipment – Mr Brooks has a red visor, Sober Mind blinkers, Treble Eight a sheepskin noseband. The card points out that this Derby is Walter Swinburn's tenth ride in the race, that he has won previously on Shergar and Shahrastani, and that he has ridden twenty-nine winners already in the 1990 season. Michael Kinane (River God) was second in the Derby on Carlingford Castle, while five jockeys (listed in the lower right-hand corner) are having their first ride in the race. Along the foot of the sheet he draws the colours of the jockeys in their draw position: Quest For Fame is drawn 10, with Duke Of Paducah at 1 on the inside of the track – to the right looking towards the stalls. Over to you, GG!

Opposite: The finish of the Three Chimneys Dewhurst Stakes at Newmarket in October 1988: Scenic (Michael Hills, near side) dead-heats with Prince Of Dance (Willie Carson).

110

Lester Piggott and Teenoso are led in after their triumph in the 1983 Derby. Derek Thompson (left) looks more exhausted than the horse – or is he pondering what he has just heard from Lester's lips (see page 86)?

TRAINERS

'They're more complicated,' said Henry Cecil of fillies during his interview with Brough Scott on Channel Four Racing in April 1989. 'I think women are more complicated than men. But they're fascinating. Most of the fillies I've had have had a little temperament, but you've got to accept that and let them enjoy themselves and have their little quirks and things, and in the end they turn out very well. I think you've just got to take them very gently, rather like women – if you're too hard on women they probably turn round and slap you in the face.'

The trainer of One In A Million, Fairy Footsteps, Oh So Sharp, Diminuendo and Indian Skimmer is entitled to have views about training fillies, but horse psychologist is just one of the many roles at which a good trainer must excel. He (or she) must be a diplomat and a public relations expert in dealing with owners and with the press. He must be able to administer what can amount to a substantial business. He must have sufficient knowledge of bloodlines and the bloodstock business to be able to buy and deal successfully. Above all, he must have the ability to get horses fit and ready, physically and mentally, to run in races. And, in the words of the Jockey Club rule, 'Every trainer shall conduct his business of training racehorses with reasonable care and skill and with due regard to the interests of his owners and to the safety of his employees and agents and of the horses in his charge.'

There are around 900 trainers in Great Britain licensed by the Jockey Club. Of this number, some 400 are 'permit holders', licensed to train for steeplechases, hurdle races and National Hunt Flat races only horses which are the property of the trainer or his immediate family. Horses are trained all over the country and in a variety of settings: Red Rum's stable was behind a second-hand car showroom on a busy street in Southport, and he galloped on the local beach. ('If a

Salsabil (with work rider Tony Nelson) goes clear on the all-weather gallop at John Dunlop's Arundel stables, March 1990.

horse has ability,' said his trainer Ginger McCain, 'you can train it up the side of a mountain or down a mineshaft.') A complete contrast is the magnificent training estate of Manton in Wiltshire. And there are towns and villages which revolve around racehorse training. The major one after Newmarket is Lambourn in Berkshire, the home of some forty trainers; the Yorkshire towns of Malton and Middleham are others.

The number of horses which a trainer has in his care varies enormously. Henry Cecil had 211 horses listed as being in his charge in *Horses in Training* for 1990, in two separate yards in Newmarket; Michael Stoute had 191; Barry Hills 159; Luca Cumani 187; Guy Harwood 164; and John Dunlop 126. The top jumping trainers tend to maintain smaller establishments than their equivalents on the Flat: Martin Pipe had 107 horses. Many trainers had only a couple.

Whatever the size of the operation, the key to the art of training any racehorse is to combine a regular routine with a carefully worked out programme of exercise and feeding in order to bring the horse to its peak at just the right moment – to have it 'trained to the minute'. A horse cannot be kept at its best for long stretches of time, nor can it be expected to be at maximum fitness for every single race it runs, so the trainer will run it in lesser races in order to bring it to top fitness for the really important occasions. (When its racing season has finished it will be 'roughed off', and probably turned out in a field to relax after the rigours of training.)

The cycle of the Flat trainer's year begins in the autumn, when the stable receives the new intake of yearlings from studs and from the sales. Most of these will have learnt the basics of what is required of them (see 'Breaking in' panel) by the turn of the year, though the trend nowadays is to bring the best horses along more slowly, so that a horse being thought of as a candidate for the Derby (run two seasons after it arrives in the stable as a yearling) might not race until the autumn of its two-year-old season, and thus will not need to be hurried. Humbler yearlings will be taught their trade more quickly with the aim of winning races early the following year before the cream of the crop starts racing.

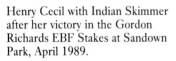

Henry Cecil with Indian Skimmer after her victory in the Gordon Richards EBF Stakes at Sandown Park, April 1989.

BREAKING IN

The timing of when a horse is 'broken in' – taught how to be ridden – depends on when it will go into training. A horse destined to run on the Flat will be broken towards the end of its second year, whereas a horse which will be kept as a 'store' for racing over jumps without racing on the Flat will not be broken until much later: Arkle was not broken until he was nearly four.

The horse will have worn a halter and been led from its days as a very young foal and will be used to human company, but nevertheless breaking in is a tricky and crucial operation, usually entrusted to a highly experienced stable lad.

The whole process normally takes two to three weeks (though the revolutionary method of the American Monty Roberts, illustrated on Channel Four Racing in the spring of 1989, reduces this period to a couple of days), and cannot be rushed. The horse must get used to the feel of a bit in its mouth, and is introduced to this peculiar sensation by means of a mouthing bit, to the mouthpiece of which are attached jangling 'keys' with which the youngster can fiddle with its tongue. To this bit are attached long reins: the lad walks behind the horse and gets it used to feeling the signals coming through the reins to its mouth, and then teaches it to lunge – to walk and trot in circles on the end of a single long rein. Then comes the roller, a padded girth fitted in the position where there will later be a saddle: the reins are fitted through rings on the roller to replicate the feel of the rider's hands on the reins. Next the roller is replaced by a saddle, so that the horse can become accustomed to a larger item on its back. At each stage the horse will continue to be lunged and be taken walking with the unfamiliar equipment to get it used to these strange sensations. Eventually comes the big moment when it will be 'backed' – when for the first time it will feel a human being on its back. A lad will lean across the horse, then lay across its back for a few moments, then for longer – all the while making the horse amenable to the new sensations – and before long he will sit quietly and loosely astride it. Then the horse will be lunged with the lad sitting astride and, when it is clear that it accepts as normal the presence of the rider, the lungeing rein will be removed and the horse will be properly ridden – quietly at first by walking and trotting, but soon cantering and getting used to the company of other horses by engaging in a gentle canter up the gallops, usually with an older horse to show the way.

A horse which will run on the Flat must also be introduced to starting stalls. The yearling is loaded into the stalls and at first will walk out, then trot out, when the front doors are opened. When it is used to that it will be ridden out of the stalls more forcefully and be allowed to canter for a few hundred yards.

The more advanced education comes when the horse is taught how to keep itself balanced while negotiating bends and how to stretch out at the gallop. It is not until these crucial stages that the trainer will learn the potential racing ability of the new racehorse.

The Trainer's Team

The personnel which a trainer normally has under his command are:

Assistant Trainer

Often an amateur jockey and usually working in the stable in order to learn the skills of the job before setting up as a trainer himself, he is the trainer's understudy. Assistant trainers often move around from one yard to another (sometimes going abroad in order to gain a breadth of experience), and most well-known trainers have spent time as an assistant: Guy Harwood was assistant to Bryan Marshall, Roger Charlton to Jeremy Tree, and Henry Cecil to his step-father Cecil Boyd-Rochfort.

Head Lad

The head lad (a very big yard might have several) is a crucial person in the yard, ensuring the smooth running of the place in all aspects relating directly to the horses and to the stable lads and stable lasses who look after them. The job demands an exceptionally high level of knowledge of horses and the training business, and it is not surprising that many of today's top trainers once served as head lads – Barry Hills with John Oxley, for instance, and Clive Brittain with Noel Murless.

Travelling Head Lad

To the travelling head lad falls the vital responsibility of seeing that the stable's runners get to the races and supervising the horses' stay at the course. He will often represent the trainer if the latter cannot attend himself.

Stable Lad

The lad (or lass) knows the individual horse better than anyone, as he or she spends time grooming it and generally looking after it in its box. The lad will not necessarily ride it in its work: often a more experienced lad or a work rider will do this. A stable lad will normally look after several horses, and fame (though not riches) can come to those who have the famous in their charge – witness Alison Dean with her 'Herbie', better known as Reference Point, and Desert Orchid's dedicated attendant Janice Coyle. Notoriously underpaid yet usually devoted to the horses in their charge, stable lads are the unsung heroes and heroines of racing.

Stable Jockey

Should it have one, the stable's retained jockey is a vital member of the team and will work closely with the trainer in planning the campaign of each horse, riding work, advising on the purchase of fresh horses, and so on.

Several footballers have had a close involvement with racing. Francis Lee, who won 27 international caps for England, made a new career as a trainer. Mike Channon was an owner and breeder – he bred Jamesmead, who won the Tote Gold Trophy at Newbury in 1988 – before taking out a trainer's licence for 1990. Many other soccer stars – including Peter Shilton and Kevin Keegan – have owned racehorses.

Apprentice

The stable apprentice will 'do his two' (in practice, probably four or five) while pursuing his aim of learning the art of race-riding.

Stable Secretary

The secretary is partly an accountant (looking after the yard's books, arranging the payment of wages, sending accounts to owners), partly a record keeper, and partly a personnel officer.

In addition, a big yard might have its own feedman (responsible for the feeding routine of each horse) and tackman (who would maintain the equipment). And it would certainly have its own farrier (see panel).

A Day in – and out of – the Stable

Everyday stable routine is a vital part of the training business, and has changed little in 200 years. Horses for the most part enjoy routine and can become keyed up – for good or ill – if it is disturbed: in the later part of his spectacular career Arkle would become overexcited when his mane was plaited before a race, and in order to cut down on this unnecessary expenditure of nervous energy his mane was left unplaited for what turned out to be his final two races. The daily timetable varies depending on the time of year (horses cannot work in the dark), but the routine in a fairly large stable would be approximately as follows:

6:30 a.m.
The head lad opens the yard and gives each horse its first feed of the day. He checks the horses for any problems which have have occurred or developed during the night, and the stable lads arrive to muck out the boxes and give the horses a light grooming before saddling up the 'first lot' – the first string of horses which will go out for exercise.

7:30 a.m.
When the first lot are mounted the trainer will probably ask the lads to walk them around the stable yard so that he can see if they are walking sound (the head lad having already reported any special problems to him), and as soon as they are ready they move off. Racehorses undergo many different forms of exercise, walking for miles around the roads, especially when building up towards the new season, and trotting and cantering as they are brought towards true fitness. They will seriously gallop ('work') only twice a week when they are in full training, either on grass or on purpose-built gallops of peat, woodchip or other surfaces specially designed to be resistant to the vagaries of the weather. (They will also benefit from the occasional swim – excellent exercise without putting stress on the legs.)

Often a trainer will get permission to gallop a horse on a racecourse after racing: although horses like routine they also appreciate a change, and many horses will work better or more informatively at a racecourse than they would on the familiar home gallops.

THE FARRIER

George Windless may not be a name familiar in the annals of the Turf, but his importance in Charlottown's 1966 Derby victory cannot be underrated. For Charlottown, a well-backed third favourite for the Epsom Classic, trod on his own off forefoot when being mounted in the paddock by Scobie Breasley, and wrenched off the shoe. He had 'spread a plate'. As trainer Gordon Smyth's farrier, George Windless had the delicate task of replacing the offending shoe on a horse that suffered from thin-soled feet, so that Charlottown could take his place in the field. Windless did his job adeptly, as – a few minutes later – did horse and jockey.

A farrier's role is usually less dramatic, and less public, but no less important for that. For without being comfortably shod a racehorse cannot race. The racing 'plate' which a horse wears in the race is normally made of aluminium – light but sturdy – as opposed to the iron-based shoes which it will wear about the stable and for exercise. Trainers differ in how long before a race they will have the horse fitted with its racing plates: some will have them put on several days before the race, others leave it until the actual day. Whenever it is done, the farrier's skills are vital, for the shoe is attached by thin nails driven into the wall of the hoof, and a nail hammered in a centimetre off target can ruin months or even years of preparation.

To minimize this risk – particularly for horses with sensitive or thin hooves – some trainers are fitting 'stick-on' shoes which are attached by means of strips glued down to the wall of the hoof.

Work is timed to fit in with a horse's next race, its main pre-race gallop normally taking place four or five days before the competition, with a 'pipe-opener' two days before the race to clear its wind. The trainer will position himself in a spot from where he can see as much of the gallop as possible and will assess each horse as it comes by, usually expecting his working horses to start off at half speed and gradually increase the pace towards the end of the gallop. A trainer can discover how good a horse is before he races it by galloping it with another horse whose ability he is well aware of, at carefully calculated weights, and word of a trial that shows up something special can often get round very rapidly: Nashwan became favourite for the Two Thousand Guineas in 1989 on the strength of reports of one spectacular gallop at West Ilsley.

Jumping horses will be 'schooled' over hurdles or fences in addition to their usual work, but most trainers do not school a horse once its season has begun (other than if its racing performance suggests that it needs a refresher course).

9:00 a.m.
The return from exercise is a crucial moment, for the lads will have to report to the trainer any occurrence of the dreaded cough. With the first lot returned, the lads leave each horse with a net of fresh hay and go off for their own breakfast. This is the most important human meal of the racing day, giving the trainer and the lads (and often the stable jockey) the opportunity for a relaxed discussion about the horses in their care.

10:00 a.m.
Second lot goes out. Often this includes horses who are not in serious work, either because they are backward or because they have recently run in a race: once a horse is fit it will maintain that fitness for a while (witness the victories of Feroda on consecutive days at the Liverpool Grand National meeting in 1989, or Chaplins Club's extraordinary feat of winning seven races in nine runs over just nineteen days in 1988), but if it has no imminent engagements after running it will be let down before being built up to its next peak.

11:30 a.m.
Second lot returns. This leaves only a few horses with special needs to go out: some horses may be exercised individually because of temperament or a particular condition.

Meanwhile the contingent which is to go racing is getting prepared. The travelling head lad is responsible for ensuring not only that the stable's runners are ready, but that they are accompanied to the course by all the necessary accoutrements – such as the owner's colours and the horse's passport (see page 171) – before supervising the loading of the runners into the horsebox and setting off for the races.

12:30 p.m.
The horses receive their lunchtime feed, under the watchful eye of the head lad, who will take a quick look at each horse as the feed goes round.

2:00 p.m.
Early afternoon is the quiet time in a racing stable, and the lads have a couple of hours off.

4:00 p.m.

Evening stables. As the third feed of the day is served, the trainer (or, if he is away at the races, the assistant trainer) and the head lad go round each horse and discuss its condition with its stable lad. Is there any heat in its legs? Is it eating up? Is it giving off any of the tell-tale signs which advertise an unhappy horse – crib-biting, weaving, box-walking?

The lads finish work at about 6 p.m., and tranquillity descends on the stable. Not that the trainer's day is done: there are future races to study and entries to arrange, for placing horses to compete in and to win races suitable to their true ability is a key part of the trainer's job. There are owners to phone, queries from the racing press to deal with, and a hundred other tasks.

A trainer never stops, but there is something magical about a racing stable, with its air of efficient calm contrasting with the hectic excitement of the racecourse. 'The nicest thing about training is going out with the horses in the morning and going round them in the evening,' says Henry Cecil, one of many great trainers . . .

Henry Cecil

Henry Richard Amherst Cecil was born on 11 January 1943, ten minutes before his identical twin brother David. A fortnight before his birth his father had been killed in action in North Africa. In 1944 his widowed mother married Captain Cecil Boyd-Rochfort, a legendary figure who the previous year had been appointed trainer to King George VI: he continued as Royal trainer after the accession of Queen Elizabeth II, preparing many of the Queen's horses for big-race victories. Henry Cecil became his assistant trainer in 1964 and took charge of the famous stables at Freemason Lodge in 1968 on Boyd-Rochfort's retirement. His first winner came when Celestial Cloud prevailed by a short head in the Newby Maiden Stakes for amateur riders at Ripon on 17 May 1969; in the same season he won the Eclipse Stakes with Wolver Hollow and the Observer Gold Cup with Approval.

Since those early days Henry Cecil has established himself at the very peak of his profession. He won his first English Classic with Bolkonski in the 1975 Two Thousand Guineas and took the race again with Wollow in 1976, the first year he was champion trainer. On the retirement of Sir Noel Murless (whose daughter Julie he had married ten years earlier: they divorced in 1990) he moved his horses into Murless's stables at Warren Place in Newmarket. Leading trainer again in 1978 and 1979, he set a twentieth-century record for winners trained (128) in 1979, the year he took the One Thousand Guineas with One In A Million and pulled off the Cup treble at Ascot, Goodwood and Doncaster with Le Moss (who repeated the achievement the next year). He won the 1980 St Leger with Light Cavalry for Jim Joel and the 1981 One Thousand Guineas for the same owner with Fairy Footsteps, but had to wait until 1985 for his first victory in the Derby, Steve Cauthen powering home aboard Slip Anchor. The same year Cecil sent out Oh So Sharp to win three Classics and became the first trainer in British Turf history to saddle the winners of races worth over £1 million – £1,148,189 in all. In 1987 Reference Point gave him his second Derby and third St Leger: that year he set a

A horse which consumes its food enthusiastically and shows the benefit is known as a 'good doer', and any horse's intake of food is carefully adjusted according to its individual needs and tastes and to its racing and training programme. The traditional basic diet is corn – oats (too much of which can get a horse over-excited) and bran (what is left when the flour is milled from wheat) – and hay. Many trainers now feed their charges on 'racehorse cubes', manufactured compounds which ensure a balanced diet of high-quality feed. The drawback of cubes is that they can be contaminated by substances prohibited by the Jockey Club, and the trainer feeding cubes has less control over exactly what he is giving his horses. Other common foodstuffs are dried sugar beet, maize, boiled barley, linseed, molasses, and carrots and apples. A bran mash is a sort of porridge in which the bran is supplemented by oats, treacle or other ingredients to make it more appetizing, and perhaps some Epsom salts as a laxative.

Other additives are more bracing. Arkle's basic feed when in training was a mixture of mash and dry oats mixed up with six eggs and supplemented by two bottles of Guinness, and Mandarin enjoyed a Mackeson: on his retirement he had two bottles a day delivered to him from the local pub in Lambourn, courtesy of Colonel Bill Whitbread, whose company sponsors the famous handicap chase in which he was thrice runner-up. But unsupervised eating can cause problems: the good hurdler No Bombs once filched his lad's Mars Bar, ingesting a prohibited substance which the 'work, rest and play' delicacy contains. He ran, won, failed the dope test, and lost the race.

fresh record of winners trained – 180. Diminuendo won him another Oaks in 1988, and Michelozzo a fourth St Leger in 1989, in which year his Old Vic won the Irish Derby and the Prix du Jockey-Club. In 1990 Rafha won the Prix de Diane (the French Oaks), with another Cecil horse Moon Cactus second, and the King George brought a memorable moment in his extraordinary career when his pair Belmez and Old Vic fought out a rousing duel up the Ascot straight to finish first and second. Other horses to come under Cecil's magic spell include Ardross, Kris, Buckskin and Indian Skimmer.

But the figures and statistics, the list of big races won and great horses trained, only partly explain why Henry Cecil is such a cult figure in modern racing. His phenomenal success at his job is complemented by a very obvious attachment to the horses who make that success possible, and that endears him to the racegoing public.

Michael Stoute

Guy Harwood (*left*) and Michael Stoute at Sandown Park, April 1989.

Born in Barbados in 1945, Michael Stoute moved to Britain at the age of nineteen to join the Yorkshire stable of Pat Rohan, following this with spells at Newmarket with Doug Smith and Tom Jones before setting up there on his own account in 1972. Classic success came with Fair Salinia in the 1978 Oaks (she also won the Irish and the Yorkshire Oaks), and in 1981 he was leading trainer for the first time, principally through the memorable exploits of Shergar, whom he sent out to win five races that year, including the Derby, the Irish Derby and the King George. He also won the Irish Derby in 1983 with Shareef Dancer (who had been beaten in a handicap at Sandown on Whitbread Gold Cup Day in April), and took his third English Classic with Shadeed in the 1985 Two Thousand Guineas. Shahrastani brought him his second Epsom Derby and third Irish Derby in 1986; he won the Oaks again with Unite in 1987, the Two Thousand Guineas with Doyoun in 1988 and his first One Thousand Guineas with Musical Bliss in 1989. (He thus became the first trainer this century to win an English Classic in five successive seasons.)

Guy Harwood

Guy Harwood, born in 1939, took out a licence to train at Pulborough in Sussex in 1966, but it was not until 1981 that he landed a Classic, when To-Agori-Mou won the Two Thousand Guineas. The exploits of Dancing Brave in 1986 confirmed his position among the top trainers, bringing home another Two Thousand Guineas as well as the the Eclipse, the King George and the Prix de l'Arc de Triomphe. Among other notable horses trained by Harwood are Kalaglow (Eclipse and King George in 1982), the milers Rousillon and Warning and the dual Ascot Gold Cup winner Sadeem.

Dick Hern

Hethersett, Provoke, Brigadier Gerard, Highclere, Bustino, Dunfermline, Troy, Henbit, Bireme, Cut Above, Sun Princess, Nashwan – Major Dick Hern has trained Classic winners for three decades. (And

> When Heaven-Liegh-Grey won at Brighton on 8 August 1990, Jack Berry became only the second northern-based trainer this century to saddle 100 winners during a Flat season. The other was Dobson Peacock in 1932.

Minster Son was sent out from Hern's West Ilsley stables to win the 1988 St Leger when the yard was temporarily under the control of his assistant Neil Graham while the Major recuperated after heart surgery. This came in the wake of a serious hunting accident in 1984.) To Hern's roll of honour must be added Ela-Mana-Mou and Petoski, both winners of the King George VI and Queen Elizabeth Diamond Stakes, and old favourites such as Bedtime. But the one with whom his name will for ever be associated is Brigadier Gerard: beaten only once in eighteen races, this wonder horse supplemented his Two Thousand Guineas success in 1971 with victory in a stream of big races, including the Sussex Stakes, the Queen Elizabeth II Stakes, and the Champion Stakes; and as a four-year-old he won the Eclipse and the King George, and the Queen Elizabeth II Stakes and Champion Stakes again. For many people 'The Brigadier' was the best British-based horse since the war, and provided unforgettable evidence of Hern's skills.

Major Dick Hern receives his award after Nashwan's victory in the General Accident Two Thousand Guineas at Newmarket, May 1989.

John Dunlop

The exploits of Salsabil in 1990 brought John Leeper Dunlop (born 1939) back into the very front rank of British trainers. Not that he had ever really left it, though he was thirteenth in the list of trainers in 1989, the £446,747 earned by his horses in win and place money less than a quarter of the total of the leading trainer Michael Stoute. Salsabil's victory in the One Thousand Guineas (soon followed by the Oaks) was Dunlop's fifth Classic, following Shirley Heights (1978 Derby: he also won the Irish Sweeps Derby), Quick As Lightning (1980 One Thousand), Circus Plume (1984 Oaks) and Moon Madness (1986 St Leger). Other famous horses to have come under his care at his stables in the park of Arundel Castle in Sussex include the wonderfully fast filly Habibti, that fine miler Posse, Balmerino (second in the Arc) and the Ascot Gold Cup winner Ragstone.

John Dunlop, 1990.

David Elsworth

In The Groove's storming victory in the Goffs Irish One Thousand Guineas on 26 May 1990 proved yet another landmark in the training career of David Elsworth: his first Classic. This notable prize was added to a huge haul of top National Hunt events and confirmed Elsworth as the best dual-purpose trainer since Vincent O'Brien concentrated on the Flat. Many of his greatest jumping moments were of course brought about by Desert Orchid, but he has also won the Grand National with Rhyme 'N' Reason (1988), the Triumph Hurdle with Heighlin, the Queen Mother Champion Chase twice with Barnbrook Again and countless other big races with old favourites such as Combs Ditch, Lesley Ann and Floyd. And don't forget that his Mighty Flutter was third in the 1984 Derby! Having ridden as a professional jump jockey between 1957 and 1972, David Elsworth first took out a training licence for the 1978–79 season (after a spell out of racing, part of which he spent as a stallholder at country markets in Wiltshire and Dorset). He now trains at Whitsbury Manor Stables, near Fordingbridge in Hampshire.

Fulke Walwyn

In the first full jumping season after the war, 1946–47, Fulke Walwyn took the trainers' title by sending out the winners of sixty races. He was champion trainer for the following two seasons and again in 1957–58 and 1963–64. His training of the Queen Mother's string after the retirement of Peter Cazalet led to many famous successes, and among the horses who have benefited from the Walwyn touch are Mandarin, Mont Tremblant, Taxidermist, Mill House, The Dikler, Charlie Potheen, Dramatist, Diamond Edge and Special Cargo; he trained Team Spirit to win the 1964 Grand National, having taken the race as a jockey on Reynoldstown in 1936. By the end of the 1988–89 season he had trained, in addition to his one victory in the National, the winner of the Cheltenham Gold Cup four times, the Champion Hurdle twice, the King George VI Chase five times, the Hennessy Gold Cup six times, and the Whitbread seven times. He retired in June 1990.

Martin Pipe

In the 1988–89 jumping season Martin Pipe trained the winners of 208 races worth £589,460, embodying an extraordinary strike rate of wins to runs of 37 per cent. Any suggestion that this achievement was in any way freakish was demolished by Pipe's 1989–90 term: the strike rate slipped to 35 per cent, but he trained 224 winners of races worth £668,659. It was the twelfth consecutive season that he had improved on his previous score, the fifth time he had trained the highest number of winners and the second time he had been champion in terms of prize money: his win and place earnings came to £792,544. Much of this recent record-breaking is linked to his association with Peter Scudamore. But another factor is the up-to-date and sophisticated nature of his yard, at Nicholashayne in Somerset, where he was established by his father David, a well-known bookmaker in the region. Pipe's attention to detail is fabled, as is his ability to turn out horses at the peak of their fitness.

Martin Pipe supervising exercise.

JOCKEYS

Pity the poor jockey. What other sportsman so regularly exposes himself to the merciless attentions of thousands of spectators – millions when the race is on television – who know for a fact that they could do his job as well as he, and who have invested money in the expectation of his displaying his skills with a proper regard for that investment? He should have kicked on earlier . . . he shouldn't have gone for that gap . . . he came much too soon . . . he got boxed in. Disgruntled punters are free with their advice to a jockey who has deprived them of profit, yet half an hour earlier, when everything was going to plan, that same jockey was the hero of the race. Hero or villain, the jockey plays the most public human role in racing.

There are about 150 professional jockeys licensed by the Jockey Club to ride on the Flat, plus another 300 or so apprentices. Over jumps some 700 hold licences, of whom about half are 'conditional' jockeys (see page 136). In addition there are around 600 amateur riders. Many, though by no means all, professional jockeys are paid a 'retainer' with a particular stable, which allows that trainer first call on his services. Sometimes a jockey's retainer is with an owner, as with Pat Eddery's arrangement to ride horses owned by Khalid Abdullah (no matter who trains them), or Willie Carson's to ride those belonging to Sheikh Hamdan Al-Maktoum. A top jockey might have more than one retainer, but if so they will be in a strict order of priority. Trainer Mark Tompkins had second claim on Ray Cochrane in 1990, should he not be required by Guy Harwood; Pat Eddery's second retainer was from owner Maktoum Al-Maktoum. The amount of each retainer must be registered at Weatherbys' *Racing Calendar* office: Lester Piggott's demand for the 1982 season for a sum of £45,000 from trainer Henry Cecil's owners over and above his registered retainer of £10,000 set in motion the events which led to his imprisonment for tax fraud.

The retainer is quite separate from riding fees, and an agreement must not be based on a jockey riding for a lower fee than that laid down in the Jockey Club Rules. These stipulate that from the summer of 1990 a jockey riding on the Flat will earn £49.00 per ride, over jumps £66.80 per ride, plus VAT if applicable. (In addition, the owner must pay a percentage of the fee into the Professional Riders' Insurance Scheme.) If an amateur rider is put up, the fee is normally paid by the owner to the Jockey Club (so that an owner cannot save money by avoiding the use of professional jockeys). A jockey may also expect a 'present' from a winning owner, and top jockeys may negotiate an arrangement whereby they receive a share in the stallion value of the winners they ride in Group races. But very few jockeys are rich, and against all their earnings are set considerable expenses – primarily travel: in Britain alone a professional jockey may have to cover between 50,000 and 60,000 miles per year, by car, aeroplane and helicopter.

Moments like this are an occupational hazard of a jump jockey's life: Paul Leach in difficulty at Sandown Park.

American jockey Chris Antley won nine races in one day at Aqueduct, New York, and The Meadowlands, New Jersey, on 31 October 1987.

Yet a few jockeys can become among the top earners in sport, and it is not hard to see why. For their skills can make the difference between a horse winning and losing a race, and if that race is the Derby or the Prix de l'Arc de Triomphe or one of a few other top events, winning will increase the value of the horse to mind-boggling sums. But what is the essence of their skills? It is a commonplace of racing that the good jockey is the one who makes fewer mistakes than the ordinary one, rather than the one who will win many races which an ordinary jockey would not. A few, of course, have that exceptional knack: 'The difference between a very good jockey and the absolute top,' trainer John Dunlop told Simon Barnes in *Horsesweat and Tears*, 'is that the very best will *sometimes* win you races you shouldn't have won. Pat Eddery can do this, Steve Cauthen can do it. And Lester Piggott, of course, was the man who could do this to a quite exceptional extent. Willie Carson at his best can do it too.'

Jockeys do not win races: horses win races. But most races are won by the jockey's complementing the horse's ability in making it as straightforward as possible for the horse to win – by responding to the particular manner of that horse's style of racing. Thus a good jockey does not set the pace on a horse with doubtful stamina, but will keep it covered up until the right time to produce it for its run to the winning post. Some horses have instant acceleration, some take longer to work up to top speed (and some, of course, have no acceleration at all). Some horses 'stop' when they find themselves in the lead, so have to get their heads in front at the last possible moment, while some like to lead all the way. The trainer will point out such foibles to the jockey before the horse is mounted, and will instruct the jockey on the best way of riding the race. Sometimes a trainer's pre-race instructions may not fill the jockey with confidence: when Charlie Fenwick was being given the leg-up for his victorious ride on Ben Nevis in the 1980 Grand National, trainer Tim Forster's instructions were: 'Keep remounting.'

A good jockey will also be a shrewd judge of pace (that is, he will know whether the runners are moving too slowly or too fast, given the distance of the race and the condition of the going), and will be able to adapt to the way a race is run, so that if no jockey wishes to make the pace he may decide to put his horse in front in order to ensure a true gallop, even though that was not the original intention. A jockey riding up the inside rail may find that he is surrounded by other runners at the moment he needs to make his run: does he pull back so as to be able to get round to the outside of the field, or sit tight in the hope that one of the runners in front may tire and roll away from the rails, thus creating a gap? Such decisions must be made in a split second during a race which is being run at about 35 m.p.h., and call for iron nerve and acute judgement: get it wrong and there's no shortage of vociferous advice from racegoers as you dismount.

Nor can most jockeys drown their sorrows in a few pints of bitter and a Cornish pasty, for the constant battle against weight which many jockeys have to wage forms an austere backcloth to everyday existence, at least during the season. The carefully structured and controlled range of weights which horses carry in Flat races harks back to an age when people generally (and, indeed, horses) were significantly smaller than they are today, and have not been adjusted upwards to take

Victor Morley Lawson, owner of several good horses including Popsi's Joy, was sixty-seven when he rode his first winner, Ocean King at Warwick in October 1973.

124

account of the body-building effects of National Health orange juice. Thus today's jockeys need to be uncommonly light in order to ply their trade. Top weight in a Flat race is likely to be somewhere between 9 and 10 stone, with the bottom weight in a handicap around 7½ stone – so, given the preponderance of horses towards the bottom of the handicap, the lighter a jockey can ride at, the more rides he will be able to get. This means that most jockeys have to subject themselves to fierce discipline in order to keep their weight low: the traditional diet by which a jockey keeps appetite at bay consists of champagne and cigars, though in reality most exist on a very small breakfast of tea and toast, no lunch, and a light supper. (The weight range in National Hunt races is around 2 stone higher than for the Flat, reflecting the jumping game's origins in the hunting field, where underfed riders are not a common sight.)

The aim, of course, is to keep to a starvation diet and at the same time keep the body fit and strong, for to control over 1,000 pounds of horseflesh through a race demands a level of fitness which participants in many other sports would envy, and a jockey's body needs to be at maximum fitness to minimize the effects of the injuries which may blight a riding life.

A National Hunt jockey can expect to fall roughly once every eleven or twelve rides, though only 4 per cent of falls result in a significant injury (the most common one being a broken collar bone), and it is a source of constant amazement how easily jump jockeys seem to shrug off the effects of falls. When Kevin Mooney's name appeared on the number board to ride in the last race at Cheltenham one Saturday in January 1988 many racegoers believed it to be there in error, for about an hour earlier Mooney had taken a terrible fall off Ten Plus, the horse landing on top of him and leaving him motionless and apparently seriously injured. But Mooney was back in the saddle for the last race, testimony to the almost unbelievable toughness of the professional jockey. Occasionally injury has a permanent effect, and the history of the profession is peppered with instances of jockeys whose riding careers were brought to an unscheduled end through mishap. Some jockeys have paid the ultimate price which their highly dangerous profession can demand, including Manny Mercer (brother of Joe), killed at Ascot in September 1959 when thrown on the way to the start, Brian Taylor, who died as a result of a fall at the end of a race in Hong Kong in December 1984, and jump jockeys Doug Barrott, who died after a fall at Newcastle in 1973, and Viv Kennedy, who suffered fatal head injuries in a hurdle race at Huntingdon in August 1988.

Every jockey must obtain a Medical Record Book from the Jockey Club, in which his injuries are recorded: this should be shown to the Medical Officer at the race meeting before the jockey weighs out. A jockey who has a bad fall can be barred from riding until such time as the Medical Officer specifies, and such restrictions are noted in his Medical Record Book.

Fred Archer, the most famous jockey to ride in Britain before Gordon Richards, succumbed not to injury but to the battle against weight. Archer was unusually tall for a jockey, and although he weighed only 6 stone when taking his first Classic, the Two Thousand Guineas on Atlantic in 1874 – the first year he was champion jockey, at the age of

Nineteen-year-old Lanfranco Dettori's victory on Line Of Thunder at Chepstow on 27 August 1990 made him the first teenager to ride a century of winners in Britain since Lester Piggott (an older nineteen) in 1955.

Fred Archer, as caricatured by *Vanity Fair*'s 'Spy' in 1881.

seventeen – he gradually found keeping himself to a reasonable riding weight a terrible struggle. He used an extremely strong purgative, known as 'Archer's Mixture' ('I tried it myself when I was riding races,' wrote the trainer George Lambton, 'and from my own experience I should say it was made of dynamite'), and the effort of wasting took its toll on him mentally and physically. But his riding record was phenomenal: 2,748 winners from 8,084 rides, including twenty-one Classics. (Among his five wins in the Derby was the 1880 victory of Bend Or, whom Archer rode with one arm strapped to a steel brace under his silks, having been savaged by a horse at Newmarket less than a month before.) In October 1886 he wasted fiercely in order to ride St Mirrin in the Cambridgeshire at Newmarket, but he put up one pound overweight and the horse was beaten by a head. Archer's wasting had brought on a fever. He rode for a few more days, going down to Lewes for what turned out to be his last ride, then returned to Newmarket for medical attention. On 8 November 1886 he shot himself in a fit of delirium.

A lesser jockey of the period shortly after Archer, but one ultimately of more lasting influence, was the American **'Tod' Sloan**. For he it was who revolutionized British race-riding by popularizing what is now the universal jockey's seat based on very short stirrup leathers, the jockey crouched up over his mount's neck rather than – as Archer would have ridden – in a much more upright posture (though contemporary photographs of Sloan riding show that his length of stirrup leather was still very much longer than is common in today's Flat jockeys). 'He rides like a monkey on a stick,' wrote the famous contemporary society magazine *Vanity Fair*, 'but he wins races.' Sloan had not invented the style (which was deemed to be effective as it cut down wind resistance on a jockey during a race), but he made it a common sight on English racecourses, and he enjoyed a good deal of success. He was a brilliant judge of pace and a fine tactician, and mastered the art of riding a race from the front: to 'do a Tod Sloan' became rhyming slang for going out on your own – hence 'on your Tod'.

But Sloan's temperament did not match his riding ability. In his famous book *Men and Horses I Have Known* George Lambton tells how he had engaged Sloan to ride a two-year-old filly at Kempton Park, only to learn that Sloan had declared himself too tired after riding another Lambton horse in the previous race:

> I went to Sloan and told him he must ride. With his funny American twang he replied, 'That was the meanest horse I've ever ridden. I'm tired to death, and I can't ride any more.' But I insisted and weighed him out. When he came into the paddock he lay on his back in the grass, repeating, 'It's no use: I can't ride.'
>   Bobette, who was a beautiful little filly, was walking about close by. Sloan, still lying on his back, asked, 'Is that my horse?' When I said, 'Yes,' he was on his feet in a moment, and all his depression and lassitude disappeared. He won the race easily. Sloan was like that: when he was full of life and confidence he could do anything, but when he was down he could do nothing, and would get beaten on the best thing in the world.

Between 1897 and 1900 Sloan rode 254 winners (including one Classic winner) from 801 mounts in England, and in 1899 had earned the huge retainer of £5,000 from Lord William Beresford. But he fell foul of the Jockey Club on account of his betting, and his licence to ride was not renewed. He was deported from England in 1915 for running an illegal gaming house in London, and died in the charity ward of a Los Angeles hospital in 1933. At the height of his career in England *Vanity Fair* had said of him: 'He is a great little jockey who is popular; but he is hardly so polite as a good American should be.'

The *Vanity Fair* portrayal of Tod Sloan, 1899.

More popular and much more polite was **Steve Donoghue**, who dominated the jockeys' championship during and following the First World War, taking the title annually from 1914 until 1923, when he tied with the then apprentice Charlie Elliott; and the cry of 'Come on, Steve!' was a familiar shout for long after. Donoghue rode the winners of fourteen Classics, including the Derby six times, on Pommern, Gay Crusader, Humorist, Captain Cuttle, Papyrus and Manna. His name will for ever be associated with two other immortals of the Turf – The Tetrarch, who ran only as a two-year-old but whose achievements in that one year (1913) give him a claim to be the fastest horse ever seen in England, and Brown Jack, on whom Donoghue won the Queen Alexandra Stakes at Royal Ascot for six consecutive years from 1929 to 1934. Their final victory gave rise to some of the most emotional scenes ever seen on a British racecourse. 'Never will I forget the roar of that crowd as long as I live,' wrote Donoghue. 'All my six Derbys faded before the reception that was awaiting Jack and myself as we set out to return to weigh-in. I don't think I was ever so happy in my life.'

But we must not forget the exploits of the great jockeys in the other code, for National Hunt racing has created riding legends of its own – none more acclaimed than **Peter Scudamore** (see page 128). Scudamore's achievements are remarkable, but he is the latest in a long line of jump jockeys whose names adorn the annals of the winter game. Before the Second World War jumping was very much the inferior code, but three jockeys stood out: **Fred Rees** and **Billy Stott**, who each won the jockeys' championship five times, and **Gerry Wilson**, who won it six times just before the war and rode Golden Miller when that great horse won the Cheltenham Gold Cup and the Grand National in 1934, winning the Gold Cup again on him in 1935. (Golden Miller was ridden by four different jockeys for his five Gold Cup victories.) The immediate post-war period dominated by **Tim Molony**, champion jockey from the 1948–49 season until 1951–52 and again in 1954–55; and the fifties belonged to **Fred Winter**, champion four times: 1952–53 and 1955–56 to 1957–58. He rode to victory in the Grand National on Sundew (1957) and Kilmore (1962) and was to win it twice more as a trainer in the 1960s; his greatest feat as a jockey was to steer Mandarin to victory in the Grand Steeplechase de Paris in 1962, a race described on page 182. **Stan Mellor** became the first jump jockey to ride more than 1,000 winners, and **Jonjo O'Neill**'s record of 149 winners in a season in 1977–78 stood until Peter Scudamore's 1988–89 term, the early eighties having seen keen rivalry between Scudamore and **John Francome** (see page 132).

Great jockeys all, but none so dear as the one who will bring home your next winner.

The Jockey Club Rules prohibit jockeys from:

– betting, or instructing any person to bet on their behalf, or receiving any proceeds from any bet on horse racing;

– owning or part-owning a horse participating in any race (with the exception of hunter-chases);

– receiving presents in connection with any race other than from the owner of the horse ridden.

Peter Scudamore weighing out at Devon and Exeter.

1989–90

Peter Scudamore did not in the 1989–90 season match his achievements of the 1988–89 term described on this page, not least because his season was cut short when he stopped riding in early May, as a result of continuing problems caused by a wrist injury incurred in a fall from Huntworth at Cheltenham on 18 April. None the less he was champion jockey (for the sixth time) with 170 wins from 523 rides (a strike rate of one in three), and was 68 winners ahead of his nearest rival Richard Dunwoody. Of those 170 wins (considerably more than any other jump jockey has ever scored), 122 were on horses trained by Martin Pipe.

SCUDAMORE'S SEASON 1988–89

'It's easier riding winners than losers,' said Peter Scudamore at Towcester races on the evening of 27 April 1989. He spoke with some authority, having just marked up his 200th winner of the record-breaking 1988–89 term. By the time the season ended, on 3 June, he was champion jockey for the fifth time (including the title shared with John Francome in 1981–82), with the extraordinary total of 221 winners: his strike rate was at the previously undreamt-of level of one win out of every three rides, and 168 of those winners started favourite. He was the first jump jockey in history to break the 200 barrier (and only three Flat jockeys have achieved the feat), and had smashed Jonjo O'Neill's record of 149, set in 1977–78.

Peter Scudamore was born on 13 June 1958, the son of Michael Scudamore, who won the Grand National the following year on Oxo. He rode his first winner, Rolyat, at Devon and Exeter in 1979, and it was less than three years later that he tied with John Francome for the championship, during his time as stable jockey to David Nicholson. He subsequently became first jockey to Fred Winter, winning the Champion Hurdle for him on Celtic Shot in 1988.

But it was his close association with trainer Martin Pipe in the 1988–89 season which broke records for them both. In the first race of the season, the Dimplex Tango Handicap Chase at Newton Abbot on 30 July, Scudamore rode Rahiib for Pipe. Starting at 11–10 on, it won by a head. His other rides that afternoon all lost, but by the end of August he had ridden twenty-three winners, all but two of them trained by Pipe; by the end of October it was fifty-three (the fastest half-century in jumping records), forty-five of them for Pipe. And so it went on. He reached the century at Ludlow on 20 December (the hundredth winner was Sayfar's Lad, another Pipe runner), by which time the team was achieving not only quantity but quality, having won the Hennessy Cognac Gold Cup with Strands of Gold and the Edward Hanmer Memorial Chase at Haydock with Beau Ranger. Scudamore had also won the Mackeson Gold Cup on Pegwell Bay. Another big race followed for Pipe and Scudamore when Bonanza Boy sauntered home the easy winner of the Coral Welsh National, and the 150 came up with Anti Matter's victory at Warwick on 7 February. The Cheltenham Festival in March was a minor embarrassment, for Scudamore managed only one winner, and both Pipe's winners at the meeting were ridden by other jockeys. But Pipe had trained 142 of Scudamore's first 200, and by the end of the season the partnership had brought home 158 winners – over forty per cent of their runners were successful.

Many factors made Peter Scudamore's phenomenal season possible: the mild winter meant few cancelled meetings, he mercifully kept free from injury, and the Pipe stable was spared widespread illness. But the major reason was Scudamore's superb jockeyship – his tactical sense, judgement, and fearless determination when putting his horse at a fence. In 1988–89 Peter Scudamore was simply the best, by a very long way.

Lester Piggott

Lester Piggott was twelve when he rode his first winner, The Chase at Haydock Park on 18 August 1948. When he rode his last, Full Choke at Nottingham on 29 October 1985, he was a few days short of his fiftieth birthday. For nearly four decades he dominated British race-riding, taking the jockeys' championship eleven times, winning a record twenty-nine English Classics and hundreds of other big races at home and abroad. He won 4,349 races from 19,809 rides on the Flat in Britain, a record which makes him the second most successful jockey (behind Gordon Richards) in British Turf history. In addition, he won twenty races over hurdles and over 800 races overseas. On his retirement from the saddle he set up as a trainer, but sent out runners for only two seasons before being sent to prison for tax fraud in October 1987.

The bare facts of Piggott's extraordinary life in racing do little to convey the magic he wove during his riding career. Bred for racing (his father Keith was a trainer and jockey, his grandfather had ridden the winners of two Grand Nationals, his mother was a member of the famous jockey-producing Rickaby family), he was the complete jockey: a superb judge of pace, fearless, almost unbeatable in a close finish, hard on a horse when he thought it necessary yet unsurpassed at being able to coax the best out of a reluctant or non-staying partner, completely cool yet fiercely competitive. This last aspect of his character led him into trouble on many occasions, not least when at the age of eighteen in 1954 he fell foul of the Royal Ascot Stewards for his riding of Never Say Die (on whom he had won his first Derby that year) in the King Edward VII Stakes. Piggott had supposedly ridden dangerously in going for a gap just after the turn into the home straight, and the incident is still, a third of a century later, the subject of debate and disagreement. He was suspended from riding until further notice, the Stewards of the Jockey Club (to whom the case was referred) advising him that they had 'taken notice of his dangerous and erratic riding both this season and in previous seasons, and that in spite of continuous warnings, he continued to show complete disregard for the Rules of Racing and for the safety of other jockeys.'

Piggott himself calmly put such reversals behind him, and in 1955 replaced Sir Gordon Richards (who had retired in 1954) as jockey to Noel Murless: the top riding job in British racing. The partnership won several Classics and saw Piggott take his first jockeys' title in 1960, but it was not a formal arrangement, and when in 1966 Piggott decided to ride Vincent O'Brien's Valoris in the Oaks rather than the Murless runner, Varinia, Murless announced that their partnership was over. Valoris duly won the Classic, and Piggott and Murless patched up their differences, enabling the jockey to ride several other big winners for the stable. In 1967 he won the jockeys' championship as a freelance, and in 1968 deepened his already close association with the Vincent O'Brien stable, putting in one of his most brilliant performances in producing Sir Ivor with a dazzling burst of finishing speed to win the Derby. In 1970 he landed the Triple Crown with Nijinsky, though he was criticized for coming too late on the colt in the Prix de l'Arc de Triomphe when beaten a head by Sassafras. Controversy surrounded Piggott again before the 1972 Derby, in which he replaced Bill

---

LESTER PIGGOTT'S CLASSIC WINNERS

Two Thousand Guineas

Crepello 1957
Sir Ivor 1968
Nijinsky 1970
Shadeed 1985

One Thousand Guineas

Humble Duty 1970
Fairy Footsteps 1981

Derby

Never Say Die 1954
Crepello 1957
St Paddy 1960
Sir Ivor 1968
Nijinsky 1970
Roberto 1972
Empery 1976
The Minstrel 1977
Teenoso 1983

Oaks

Carrozza 1957
Petite Etoile 1959
Valoris 1966
Juliette Marny 1975
Blue Wind 1981
Circus Plume 1984

St Leger

St Paddy 1960
Aurelius 1961
Ribocco 1967
Ribero 1968
Nijinsky 1970
Athens Wood 1971
Boucher 1972
Commanche Run 1984

Williamson as rider of Roberto. Whether this was a case of Piggott 'jocking off' the other rider or whether he was an innocent by-stander as the owner exercised his right to have whichever rider he could get for his horse, Piggott produced one of his fiercest finishes to get Roberto home by a short head from Rheingold – and the same determination was in evidence when he drove The Minstrel home a neck ahead of Hot Grove in the 1977 Derby.

Towards the end of the 1980 season O'Brien and Piggott parted company, and in 1981 Piggott became stable jockey to Henry Cecil at Warren Place, the Newmarket yard where he had had such a long association with Noel Murless. The new arrangement got off to a flying start when Piggott rode Fairy Footsteps to take the One Thousand Guineas – just days after he had been dragged under the front door of the Epsom stalls by Winsor Boy, a terrifying accident which left the jockey with a severely injured ear. He was champion jockey for the last time in 1982, and for his final season in 1985 Piggott returned to freelance status. (Cecil snapped up four Classics that year with his new stable jockey, Steve Cauthen.)

Many other famous horses apart from his own Classic winners in Britain have benefited from the Piggott touch: Alleged, Dahlia, Shergar (on whom he won the 1981 Irish Derby in a canter), Ardross, Park Top, Sagaro, Moorestyle, Rheingold, Aunt Edith, Meadow Court, Zucchero, Zarathustra – the roll of honour goes on and on. But Piggott was as determined and as effective in a small race on a mediocre horse as in any Derby, and it was this quality which made him a man to have on your side. Hence the devotion he attracted from punters: they knew that he wanted the horse to win just as much as its backers did.

Lester Piggott has always been an enigmatic character, and stories of his carefulness with money were part of the fabric of racing gossip for decades. But few people were prepared for the revelation that he was being investigated for possible tax fraud, and the shock when he was convicted and sentenced to three years in prison in October 1987 reverberated throughout the racing world. His OBE, awarded in the 1975 New Year Honours, was stripped from him. He was released on parole on 24 October 1988, a year and a day after conviction.

However sensational the postscript to Lester Piggott's riding career, it is the memory of him in the saddle which will live on. Unusually tall for a Flat jockey (hence his nickname 'The Long Fellow'), his distinctive riding posture, bottom stuck high in the air ('I've got to put it somewhere,' he said), made him an unmistakable and unforgettable sight on the racecourses of the world.

Gordon Richards

Gordon Richards was the most successful jockey in the history of British racing. His career total of 4,870 winners from 21,843 rides has never been in danger of being exceeded (the second highest total is the 4,349 of Lester Piggott, who had a slightly inferior strike rate); he was champion jockey twenty-six times and rode the winners of fourteen Classics.

Born in Shropshire on 5 May 1904, one of twelve children of a miner, he had his first ride in public in 1920 and his first winner, Gay

> Lester Piggott fought a constant battle with his weight: for most of his career he rode at around 8 stone 5 pounds, nearly 2 stone below his natural weight.

Lord, in an apprentice race at Leicester, in 1921. (On returning to unsaddle he was asked why he had taken the horse so wide round the bends, and he replied that he had been told that Gay Lord needed a longer trip.) He was champion jockey for the first time in 1925, and for the 1932 season accepted a retainer from the immensely powerful Fred Darling stable at Beckhampton: he subsequently rode for the stable until Darling's retirement in 1947.

In 1933 Richards's seasonal total of winners was a record-breaking 259. On 3 October that year he won on his last ride at Nottingham, then all six races at Chepstow the next day, and the first five at Chepstow the day after. In the sixth race he was aboard a 3–1 on shot called Eagle Ray: 'I did not think that I could possibly be beaten,' he wrote, but Eagle Ray finished third, beaten a head and a neck. Gordon Richards had ridden the winners of twelve successive races, a world record.

Another memorable Richards year was 1947, when his total of 269 winners set a fresh record which will probably stand for ever. The same year, though, saw one of his most sensational defeats, on Tudor Minstrel in the Derby. Tudor Minstrel had won the Two Thousand Guineas by eight lengths and seemed a certainty for the Epsom race, starting at 7–4 on. In his autobiography *My Story* Gordon Richards recalled the race:

Gordon Richards

> I have never, in the whole of my life, had such an uncomfortable ride at Epsom. Every time I held him up, he fought me. Every time I let him down to go, he shot off to the right. Either way, he was making certain that he lost the race. The whole race was a nightmare, but he still finished fourth.
>
> Then the letters began to arrive. Hundreds of them, and telegrams as well. Some incredibly impertinent people even telephoned. I was told that I had pulled the horse's head off. The kindest suggested that I was incapable of riding a donkey.
>
> As a matter of fact, I find donkeys very difficult to ride.

Lack of stamina combined with his refusal to settle caused Tudor Minstrel's downfall, but Richards finally got his desperately sought-after victory in the Derby with Pinza in 1953, just after he had been knighted in recognition of his services to racing. This partnership went on to win the King George VI and Queen Elizabeth Stakes, but in 1954 Richards was forced to retire after the Queen's filly Abergeldie reared and fell on him in the paddock at Sandown Park, causing severe injuries. His career as a trainer produced several very good horses, including Pipe of Peace, winner of the Middle Park Stakes in 1956 and third to Crepello in both the Two Thousand Guineas and the Derby the following year; Court Harwell, second to Ballymoss in the 1957 St Leger; and Reform, who beat Taj Dewan and Royal Palace in the Champion Stakes in 1967. His final year of training was 1969, after which he acted as racing manager for Sir Michael Sobell and for Lady Beaverbrook, on whose behalf he and Major Dick Hern paid 21,000 guineas for the yearling who was to be named Bustino. Gordon Richards died on 10 November 1986.

He had an unorthodox riding style, more upright than today's jockeys and often with a loose rein. Yet his mounts did not get unbalanced and

GORDON RICHARDS'S
CLASSIC WINNERS

Two Thousand Guineas

Pasch 1938
Big Game 1942
Tudor Minstrel 1947

One Thousand Guineas

Sun Chariot 1942
Queenpot 1948
Belle of All 1951

Derby

Pinza 1953

Oaks

Rose of England 1930
Sun Chariot 1942

St Leger

Singapore 1930
Chulmleigh 1937
Turkhan 1940
Sun Chariot 1942
Tehran 1944

horses ran extremely straight for him. He used his whip as an encouragement, not a punishment, yet was rarely pipped in a close finish. A model of integrity and modesty, he was loved by the racing community and punters alike.

John Francome

John Francome winning the Piper Champagne Cheltenham Gold Cup in 1978 on Midnight Court.

John McCririck's appellation 'Greatest Jockey' sits well on John Francome. The supreme stylist among jump jockeys of the modern era, he rode the winners of 1,138 races during a career which ended in 1985. His strike rate of winners to runners was superior to those of both Gordon Richards and Lester Piggott.

The son of a Swindon builder, Francome laid the foundations of his exceptional horsemanship as a young show jumper; but despite winning international honours in the sport, he left it to join Fred Winter's stable in Lambourn in 1969. He won his first race on his first public ride under National Hunt Rules when steering Multigrey to victory at Worcester on 2 December 1970 (in his second ride he fell and broke a wrist), and became first jockey to Winter on Richard Pitman's retirement. The jockeys' championship fell to him first in the 1975–76 season, and he took the title seven times in all.

Although he never rode a Grand National winner – Rough and Tumble's second to Ben Nevis in 1980 was the closest he got – he partnered many great horses. His coolness on Sea Pigeon in the 1981 Champion Hurdle, when he delayed his challenge until halfway up the run-in before sweeping to victory past Pollardstown, was quite remarkable, and he won the Cheltenham Gold Cup on Midnight Court in 1978. Another horse with which he will always be associated is Burrough Hill Lad, on whom he won the Welsh National in 1983 and the Hennessy Cognac Gold Cup and the King George VI Chase in 1984. He also landed the King George on Wayward Lad in 1982, and won several races on Lanzarote. His final victory was on Gambler's Cup at Huntingdon on 8 April 1985.

In his autobiography *Born Lucky* John Francome avows that 'riding was my job and horses just the tools I worked with,' but that disarming comment belies his exceptional horsemanship. No National Hunt jockey in history has been better at presenting a horse at a fence – his show-jumping ability and training showing through in his knack of measuring the stride to ensure a fluent jump; he was an exemplary judge of pace and an astute tactician. He was also notable for his sportsmanship: in 1982 Peter Scudamore was well ahead in the jockeys' championship when he sustained a bad injury, putting him out of action for the rest of the season. Francome caught up with his absent rival but himself stopped competing for the season when their scores were level, allowing Scudamore to share the title. For one with such a record, 'Greatest Jockey' seems about right.

Willie Carson

William Hunter Carson was born in Stirling on 16 November 1942. His first riding success was a six-length victory on Pinker's Pond in an apprentice handicap (worth £181 10s) at Catterick on 19 July 1962, and he has hardly looked back since. He was champion jockey for the first time in 1972 (following eight successive championships by Lester Piggott) and since then has only once failed to ride a century of winners or more in a season. That once was in 1984, when he was sidelined by injury, but even in 1981, when he took a horrific fall from Silken Knot in the Yorkshire Oaks in August and was out for the rest of the season, his total was already 114. Quality has gone hand-in-hand with quantity. He won his first Derby on Troy in 1979, his second on Henbit a year later, and his third in 1989 on Nashwan, on whom he also won the Two Thousand Guineas (also won on High Top in 1972, Known Fact in 1980 and Don't Forget Me in 1987), the Eclipse (which he would land again on Elmaamul in 1990) and the King George VI and Queen Elizabeth Diamond Stakes (to follow up victories on Troy in 1979, Ela-Mana-Mou in 1980, and Petoski in 1985). He won the Oaks on Dunfermline for the Queen in 1977, on Bireme in 1980, on Sun Princess in 1983 and on Salsabil in 1990; the One Thousand Guineas on Salsabil; and the St Leger on Dunfermline, Sun Princess and in 1988 on Lady Beaverbrook's Minster Son, whom he bred. Carson was forty-seven years old at the start of the 1990 season, but age could not wither him nor custom stale his inimitable way of pumping home the winners, and the weekend which brought June into July also brought perhaps his finest hours. On the Friday he rode five winners at Newmarket and Goodwood, and then on the Saturday at Newcastle became only the third jockey this century to notch up six victories at one fixture, entering the record books alongside Gordon Richards's 1933 feat at Chepstow (see page 131) and Alec Russell's in 1957 at Bogside. On 30 June 1990 Willie Carson won on Arousal, Soweto, Al Maheb (in the Northumberland Plate), Ternimus, Tadwin and Hot Desert. But the weekend was not over yet, for on the Sunday he was at The Curragh for two more wins, a two-length victory on Time Gentlemen setting him up to partner Salsabil to her famous routing of the colts in the Budweiser Irish Derby. On the Monday evening he rode four more winners to bring his total for the four days of the long weekend to seventeen. Understandably, he took the Tuesday off, but less than two months later he was rearranging the record books again: his victory on Joud at Newmarket on 24 August 1990 brought his career total of wins in Great Britain to 3,112, taking Carson past Doug Smith's total to make him the third most successful jockey in British racing history, behind Gordon Richards (4,870) and Lester Piggott (4,349).

Willie Carson – jockey and breeder – with Minster Son after winning the Holsten Pils St Leger in 1988.

Pat Eddery

Pat Eddery had his first winner at the age of seventeen when riding Alvaro to victory at Epsom in April 1969. Apprenticed to 'Frenchie' Nicholson, the greatest tutor of young jockeys (who also gave a start to Paul Cook, Tony Murray and Walter Swinburn), Eddery first displayed his exceptional talents when riding five winners from seven mounts at Haydock Park one Saturday in August 1970, and was leading apprentice in 1971 with 71 winners. His apprenticeship over, he joined Peter Walwyn, becoming champion jockey for the first time in 1974, the year he also won his first Classic, the Oaks on Polygamy: 'You'd have

Pat Eddery at Sandown Park, 1988.

had to shoot her to stop her,' was his post-race comment. He retained the title for the following three seasons. The high point of his time with Walwyn was undoubtedly the 1975 summer campaign of Grundy, who won the Derby and Irish Derby before beating Bustino in the King George VI and Queen Elizabeth Diamond Stakes at Ascot, widely held to be the race of the century. Eddery's riding of Grundy that day was testament to his great qualities as a jockey – acute judgement of pace with the ability to read the rapidly changing circumstances of a race, strength and determination in a close finish and a wonderful rhythmical drive to help his horse see out the punishing final stages.

Eddery's next English Classic win was on Scintillate for Jeremy Tree in the 1979 Oaks, and in 1980 he won the Prix de l'Arc de Triomphe on Robert Sangster's Detroit. That year he started riding for Vincent O'Brien, and in 1981 he won the Irish Two Thousand Guineas and Sussex Stakes for the stable on King's Lake. The following year he won his second Derby on Golden Fleece (who never ran again), in 1983 the Two Thousand Guineas on Lomond, and 1984 was marked by his association with El Gran Senor, on whom he won the Two Thousand Guineas and the Irish Derby but whose failure by a short head to get back at Secreto in the Derby after a ding-dong struggle through the last furlong brought upon the jockey charges of over-confidence from the riders in the stand. But in 1985 he really asserted himself on the international stage by taking the Irish Derby on Law Society, the Coronation Cup and Prix de l'Arc de Triomphe on Rainbow Quest, and the Champion Stakes and Breeders' Cup Turf on Pebbles. He won the St Leger for John Dunlop on Moon Madness in 1986 and in the same year took over from Greville Starkey the ride on Dancing Brave, winning the King George and the Arc. His association with this great horse led to a lucrative retainer with Dancing Brave's owner Khalid Abdullah, for whom he has ridden such fine horses as Warning and the English and French Derby winners of 1990, Quest For Fame and Sanglamore.

The retirement of Lester Piggott at the end of the 1985 season left a gaping hole at the top level of British jockeyship. For many people, Pat Eddery has filled it.

Steve Cauthen

Salisbury races on Saturday 7 April 1979 was one of those occasions which no one who was there will forget. Heavy rain had turned the course into a quagmire for the unusually large crowd which the running of the Guineas Trials had brought to this delightful Wiltshire track. When some of the Stewards drove up the course before the Two Thousand Guineas Trial to decide whether the race was possible in the appalling conditions, their vehicle got stuck in the mud. Racegoers could not tell what was going on, though their spirits were raised when a scruffy little pony somehow managed to get on to the course and canter, in solitary splendour, past the stands. The public address system had broken down, so that the big race (won by Lake City, trained by Ryan Price) was run without racecourse commentary. It was all gloriously chaotic.

But what sort of introduction to British racing was this for Steve Cauthen, the young American jockey who had migrated to ride for Barry Hills and whose debut that day had packed the Salisbury stands and solidified the traffic jams? Cauthen had arrived on the British racing scene in a blaze of publicity. In America he had been a phenomenon, riding his first winner in 1976 shortly after his sixteenth birthday. In 1977 'The Kid' had become The Six Million Dollar Man, riding 487 winners for prize money in excess of that figure. In 1978 he won the American Triple Crown on Affirmed. But following a period when his phenomenal winning spell was mirrored by an equally phenomenal run of losing rides, he accepted an offer from Robert Sangster to move to England. His first ride in the country on that memorable afternoon proved to be a winning one as he booted home Marquee Universal for Hills in the first race. A month later he won his first Classic, on Tap On Wood in the Two Thousand Guineas, and since then Steve Cauthen has become an integral part of British Flat racing.

To adapt to the vagaries of British racing after the uniformity of American tracks is a huge challenge for any jockey, but Cauthen rose to it, winning fifty-two races in that 1979 season with Hills. In 1984 he became the first American since Danny Maher early in the century to be champion jockey, and in 1985 he replaced Lester Piggott as stable jockey for the powerful Henry Cecil stable. That year he won four of the five Classics, taking the One Thousand Guineas, Oaks and St Leger on Oh So Sharp and riding a brilliant front-running race on Slip Anchor in the Derby – thereby becoming the first jockey in history to have won both the Epsom Derby and the Kentucky Derby. When he won the jockeys' title in 1985 with 195 winners it was the highest total since Gordon Richards's 231 in 1952: and he bettered that score with 197 after a memorable battle with Pat Eddery in 1987, when he won two more Classics on Reference Point. Diminuendo in the 1988 Oaks and Michelozzo in the 1989 St Leger provided more Classic success.

> The youngest jockey to ride in a recorded race was Frank Wootton, who rode in South Africa at nine years and ten months. He was champion jockey in England from 1909 to 1912.

Steve Cauthen on Chimes Of Freedom after winning the Coronation Stakes at Royal Ascot, 1990.

When the Flat season proper (that is, the turf season) began in March 1990, apprentice Alex Greaves had already ridden eighteen winners since the official commencement of the Flat season on 1 January. Those eighteen were part of her total of twenty-three wins in all-weather races, well ahead of any other jockey. Her first victory on turf came on Joe Bumpas at Catterick on 28 March, and though she would not stay in the vanguard of the jockeys' race once Eddery, Carson, Cauthen and company got into full swing, she had made her mark.

On 10 June 1935 Harry Beasley rode his filly Our Mollie in a flat race for amateur riders at Baldoyle at the age of 83.

APPRENTICE

An apprentice is a young Flat jockey who is tied by annually renewed contract to a licensed trainer, under whom he will learn the skills of race-riding. A boy or girl can become an apprentice at sixteen, but can no longer ride as an apprentice jockey once the age of twenty-four has been reached.

An apprentice may claim a weight allowance – that is, the horse he rides in a race will carry less weight than he would if ridden by a fully-fledged jockey, in order to compensate for his rider's lack of experience. (In certain big races the claiming of allowances is not permitted.) The allowances are:

7 pounds until he has won 10 races; thereafter
5 pounds until he has won 50 races; thereafter
3 pounds until he has won 75 races.

(Races confined to apprentices are excluded from these totals.)

Given the weight allowances, it can be very tempting for an owner and trainer to put up a good apprentice on a horse in a competitive handicap where to carry less weight would confer an important advantage. But many apprentices find it a struggle to get rides once they have lost their claim, as they then have to compete on equal terms with more experienced jockeys.

CONDITIONAL JOCKEYS

The conditional jockey is National Hunt racing's equivalent of the Flat apprentice. A conditional jockey must be under the age of twenty-five, and from the beginning of the 1989–90 season may claim allowances (which may not be claimed in the Grand National or in the more valuable weight-for-age races) as follows:

7 pounds until he has won 15 races; thereafter
5 pounds until he has won 25 races; thereafter
3 pounds until he has won 40 races.

AMATEUR JOCKEYS

There are two categories of licensed riders who take part in races without receiving a fee. Category A amateur riders may ride in any Flat or National Hunt event confined to amateur riders, while Category B riders may ride against licensed professional jockeys under National Hunt Rules (on the Flat there are no events in which male amateurs may ride against professionals). Many top jump jockeys have begun their riding careers as amateurs, but the Jockey Club takes a dim view of an amateur who appears to be having too may rides in 'open' races, thus depriving a professional jockey of the mount.

Lady jockeys: the winning team of British amateur riders at the Champagne Lanson Ladies International Challenge at York in May 1989. Left to right: Joanna Winter, Elaine Bronson, Amanda Harwood, Sharon Murgatroyd, Carolyn Eddery and Jennie Goulding.

LADY JOCKEYS

Women were first allowed to ride under Jockey Club Rules in 1972, and the first ladies' race was run at Kempton Park on 6 May, when the Goya Stakes was won by Meriel Tufnell on Scorched Earth at 50–1. Some 229 runners were ridden by ladies that year, and not all the criticism levelled at the early female style of race-riding came from Male Chauvinist Pigs: Louie Dingwall, one of the legendary female trainers and then in her eighties, threatened to apply for a jockey's licence because she could 'ride the backside off these girls'. Since 1975 women have been allowed to ride as professional jockeys, and with the Sex Discrimination Act becoming law that year they generally have to ride against men, though there are still some races confined to lady jockeys – notably the race run at Ascot as a curtain-raiser to the King George VI and Queen Elizabeth Diamond Stakes in July. Lady jockeys are now an established part of the racing scene.

Women riding over fences was a much less novel idea than lady riders on the Flat, for ladies' races have long been an important element in point-to-point racing. Women were first allowed to ride under National Hunt Rules in 1976, the first winning lady rider being Diana Thorne at Stratford on 7 February. Since then lady jump jockeys have made such a significant impact that it is no longer a cause for much comment if a runner in a big race is ridden by a woman. The first woman to ride in the Grand National was Charlotte Brew: her mount Barony Fort refused four fences out in the 1977 running. The first woman to win a race over the Grand National course at Liverpool was Caroline Beasley, who won the Foxhunters' Chase on Eliogarty in 1986. On the same horse in 1983 she had scored the first female riding triumph at the Cheltenham National Hunt Festival, where Gee Armytage rode two winners in 1987. In 1984 the Irish Grand National at Fairyhouse was won by Mrs Ann Ferris on Bentom Boy, and her sister Rosemary finished third.

...TSHOOF   4-8-10
                 B Hanbury
...23/13111353-1
[7.8f]
b c Sadler's Wells (USA) - Steel Habit by Habitat
   1989 (Apl) 7f soft (Leicester); (May) 7f 122y
good/firm (Chester); (Jun) 1¼m 110y good/firm
(York) lstd; (Jun) 1¼m good/firm (Kempton). £30,636
   1990 (Apl) 1¼m firm (Kempton).
(£3,980).

                           DRAW: 2
   April 6, Kempton, 1¼m , firm, £3,980: 1
BATSHOOF (4-9-6, Pat Eddery,8), tracked
leaders, led one furlong out, pushed out.
(11/10 fav op 8/11 tchd 5/4) 2 Marine Diver
(4-8-11,1), 3 Jehol (4-9-0,7),; 15 Ran. ½l, ¾l, 1l,
20l, 7l; 1½l, sht-hd, 2l, 6l, ½l. 1m 59.53s (b
1.97s). SR: 65/55/56/51/20/-.
   RACECHECK: Wins 0, pl 1, unpl 8.

   Sept 7 1989, York, 1m 1f , good to firm,
£10,965: 1 Opening Verse (3-8-9, inc 2lb ow,3)
2 Greenwich Papillon (3-8-10,4), 3 BATSHOOF
(3-8-10, B Raymond,5), waited with, improved two furlongs out, not extra. (11/8 fav
op 11/10 tchd 6/4); 5 Ran. 1½l, sht-hd, 1½l, 5l.
1m 51.20s (a 2.70s). SR: 50/46/45/34/22.

   Aug 22 1989, York. See ILE DE CHYPRE

   June 17 1989, York, 1¼m 110y (3-y-o) (Listed
Race), good to firm, £9,418: 1 BATSHOOF
(8-10, Pat Eddery,3), held up, headway on bit
three furlongs out, led inside final furlong,
cleverly. (4/1 op 9/4) 2 DOLPOUR (8-10, W R
Swinburn,5), tracked leaders, led three
furlongs out, headed inside final furlong,
kept on well, no chance with winner. (11/2 op
7/2) 3 Lypheor's Honour (8-10,2),; 6 Ran. ¾l,
5l, 10l, 4l, 6l. 2m 7.75s (b 0.25s). SR:
67/65/55/33/19/5.

DOLPOUR   4-8-10
4/21212-   **M R Stoute**
b c Sadler's Wells (USA) - Dumka (FR) by
Kashmir II [6.9f]
   1989 (May) 1¼m good/firm (Leicester) mdn;
(Aug) 1¼m 22y good (Windsor) lstd. £9,649.

                         DRAW: 8
   Oct 21 1989, Newmarket, 1¼m (3-8-10,1), 2
good, £255,745: 1 Legal Case (3-8-10,1), 2
DOLPOUR (3-8-10, W R Swinburn,5), well in
touch, ran on over two out, every chance
when edged right well inside final furlong,
rallied close home. (4/1 fav tchd 9/2) 3 ILE DE
CHYPRE (4-9-3, W Carson,8), led, quickened
well inside final furlong, wandered left and
edged well inside final furlong, came
under pressure final furlong,; 10 MONASTERY
... ,; ... tori,9), chased front rank
...tchd 11/2) ... (btn
20/1 ... 3l. 2m 2.95s

OBSERVATION POST   4-8-10
11/222-   **B W Hills**
b c Shirley Heights [11.8f] - Godzilla by Gyr (USA)
[13.3f] 1988 7f good (Newmarket); 1m 50y good/
soft (Nottingham). £11,090.

   July 2 1989, Curragh, 1½m (3-y-o) (Group 1),
good, £366,500: 1 Old Vic (9-0,3), 2 OBSER-
VATION POST (9-0, W Carson,7), well placed
early, good progress on rails in straight,
stayed on strongly, not match for
winner. (12/1) 3 Ile de Nisky (9-0,5),; 8 Ran.
2½l, 5l, 2½l, hd, 8l. 2m 29.90s (b 3.
83/75/70/60/55/54.

   May 17 1989, York, 1¼m 110y (3-
2), firm, £74,232: 1 Torjoun (9-0,
VATION POST (9-0, M Hills
steady headway three out,
approaching final furlong,
quicken. (11/10 fav op 5/4 t
(9-0,7),; 7 Ran. 2l, 2½l, ¾l.
1.02s). SR: 68/64/59/57/55

   May 5 1989, Newmark
to firm, £14,490: 1 Prin
OBSERVATION POST
up in last place, dis
until inside final f
near finish. (9/4
Ibrahim (8-10,5),;
1.15s). SR: 79/7

RELIEF PITCH...
40/5232132212...
b c Welsh Ter...
Northern Dan...
   1989 (Jun) ... good
1¼m good ...

   Apr
firm.
dar
R
E

          8-11
...ys Smith
... Green God

...ndn; (Aug) 7f

         DRAW: 4
See MISSIONARY

...y, 7f (2-y-o) , good,
...AY (8-11, B Rouse,5);
...ongs out, pulled out
... well to lead inside last.
   2 Marquetry (8-11,1), 3
... Ran. 1l, 1½l, 2l, 12l. 1m
...R: 49/46/41/35/-.

...York, 6f (2-y-o) mdn, good to
...KARINGA BAY (9-0, T Ives,8),
driven when pace quickened
... out, ran on strongly to lead
...uarantee (9-0,7),; 8 Ran. Nk, 8l, ¾l,
op 8/1 tchd 12/1) 2 Contract Law
...2l, hd. 1m 11.70s (a 1.20s). SR:
-/-.

          8-11
      Major W R Hern
... (USA) [8.3f] - Highclere by Queen's
...SKI (USA)
...eyev (USA) [9.9f]
...7f good/firm (Newmarket Jly crs)
          DRAW: 2
... (2-y-o) (Group 2),
... (8-10,6), 2
...on (8-10,1), ...
...8)

March 14, Che... [
Listed Race) [Open...], 2 Le...
New Halen (9-9-7,7*), P FOUR...
King Of The Lot (7-10-9), **hit sixth, behind...**
138, N Doughty), **pulled up before tenth.** (7/1 op 6/1 tchd 8/1);
Ran. 8l, 2l, 4l, 5l, 6l, nk. 4m 58.40s (b 1.60s).
RACECHECK: Wins 2, pl 4, unpl 6.

March 3, Newbury, 2½m Hcp chase
[Open,140], good, £8,656: 1 Gembridge Jupiter
(12-10-9), 2 FOUR TRIX (9-11-8, **138**, G
McCourt), **in touch, challenged three out,
kept on same pace.** (7/2 op 3/1 tchd 4/1); 5
Chief Ironside (10-11-10), ; 8 Ran. 6l, 10l, 20l, 5...
9.40s (a 13.40s).
RACECHECK: Wins 1, pl 1, unpl 6.

KILDIMO 10-11-7
/1401022/P542F3-F4F   **G B Balding**
b g 9 Le Bavard (FR) - Leuze by Vimy **1985-86**
(Worcester) 2½m h good/firm 2½m h good
(Cheltenham); **1986-87** 2½m h good/firm
ch soft (Cheltenham); 3m h good/soft; 3m
(Towcester); 3m ch good (Cheltenham); 3m
110y ch soft (Ayr) **1987-88** 3m ch soft
(Cheltenham); 3m 1f ch good (Wincanton).
£59,465.
LWR (89+90): -   TR: 158

March 15, Cheltenham, 3¼m chase, good to
firm, £67,003: 1 Norton's Coin (9-12-0), 3 Desert Orchid (11-12-0), 2 Toby
Tobias (8-12-0), J Frost), **chased leaders**
KILDIMO (10-12-0, J Frost), **chased leaders
till weakened 14th, fell next.** (50/1 op 33/1 tchd
66/1); 12 Ran. ¾l, 4l, 7l, 12l, 1l, 15l, 2½l. 6m
30.90s (b 9.10s). SR: 87/86/82/75/63/57.
RACECHECK: Wins 2, pl 2, unpl 3.

March 3, Hereford, 2m 3f chase, soft, £3,265:
1 Fu's Lady (8-10-12), 2 Ruststone (10-10-8,7*),
3 Duhallow Boy (10-10-3,7*), 4 KILDIMO
(10-10-10, J Frost), **held up, some headway
ninth, ridden and no impression from three
out.** (11/8 op Evens); 6 Ran. 15l, ¾l, 3l. 4m
55.00s (a 23.50s).
RACECHECK: Wins 0, pl 3, unpl 12.

Feb 22, Wincanton, 3m 1f chase (Listed
Race), good to soft, £8,415: 1 Cavvies Clown
(10-11-6), 2 Cool Ground (8-11-0), 3 Golden
Friend (12-11-6), F KILDIMO (10-11-6, J Frost),
**last after mistake third, mistake ninth, lost
touch 14th, rallied to second three out, well
held when fell last.** (9/4 op 7/4 tchd 5/2); 4
Ran. 25l, 30l. 6m 32.40s (a 18.40s).

Dec 17 1988, Ascot, 3m Hcp chase, £13,840: 1
Ballyhane (7-10-4), 2 Sun Rising (10-10-8,bl), 3
Castle Warden (11-10-3), 4 KILDIMO (8-12-0, every
Smith Eccles), **led second to fourth, every
chance till ridden and weakened two out**
(5/1 op 5/1 tchd 6/1), P Scudamore); 5 Ran. Nk, 5l, 7l. 6m 16.00...
F STRANDS OF GOL... **fell third.** (13/8 jt-fav...

4-8-10
P T Walwyn
Bases Loaded (USA) by
...m (Kempton) mdn; (Aug)
...auville) lstd. £25,622.
DRAW: 1
...market, 1m 1f (Group 3), good to
: 1 Terimon (4-8-10,1), 2 Citi-
...,4), 3 Pirate Army (4-8-10,10), 7
...TCHER (btn 5¼l) (4-8-10, Pat
**well placed, no extra final furlong,
two out, ridden four out,**
...10 Ran. Sht-hd, ½l, 1½l, 11½l,
49.15s (b 1.35s). SR: 73/75/70/68/67/64.
...ECHECK: Wins 0, pl 0, unpl 0.

Sept 15 1989, Goodwood, 1¼m (Group 3),
...od to soft, £18,114: 1 Legal Case (3-8-6,1), 2
reenwich Papillon (3-8-6,3), 3 Indian Queen
(4-9-2,v,5), 4 RELIEF PITCHER (3-8-6, G
Baxter,4), **led five furlongs, soon outpaced.
inside final two furlongs, headed**
(5/2 op 2/1 tchd 11/4); 5 Ran. 4l, 3l, ¾l, 25l. 2m
12.54s (a 7.04s). SR: 72/64/68/56/16.

Sept 2 1989, Kempton, 1m 3f 30y (Group 3),
...to firm, £26,730: 1 Assatis (4-9-5,1), 2
...PITCHER (3-8-4, G Baxter,2), **chased
...tering straight, ridden and ran
...just caught.** (5/1 op 5/1
...); 5 Ran. Hd, 3l, 8l.
52/36/40/24/14.

(Liste...
£16,032: ...
Golden Minstre...
(12-9-13,7*), 4 MR...
...tage), **left in lead till three
lead 16th till three
last.** (7/1 op 5/1 tchd 11.5...
5l, 11½l, 1½l. 6m 11.5...
...7/2.

...Hcp chase [Ope...
...(9-10-0), 2 B...
(9-10-0), 5 M...
(8-10-0), **prom...
Jan 12, A... 11...
good, £11,355: 3 Macroom (8-10-0), **bet...**
(9-11-11), **151**, A Tory,5*), **prom...**
(11-11-6, **151**, A Tory,5*), **well be...
jumped slowly 13th, well...
blundered two out.** (13/2 op 6/...
MEMBERSON (btn 49½l+) (12-1...
Upton,3*), **always behind.** (50...
Ran. 7l, 3l, 15l, 20l, 2½l, ...
6.20s). SR: 58/76/48/57/38/1...

SAM DA VINCI
B1512222322-40UP23
ch g Saucy Kit - Fortilage by **1985**
h firm (Doncaster) 1985...
(Nottingham) 1986-87 3...
well); 3m ch firm (Che...
soft (Fakenham); 3m...
3m ch good/firm (Che...
good (Market R...
(Cheltenham); 3m...
£23,577.
LWR (89+90):

April 16,
(Listed Rac...
1 Lacida...
(8-10-7,5...
Brennan...
two, w...
5/2);
RAC...

...ERSON ...A30064613U
Miss Stalbridge...
P D...

Jim McGrath, Channel Four
Racing's form expert and paddock
commentator, is a director of the
Timeform organization.

'The reason Con loses at the races, while he always wins at cards, is
that he can't shuffle the horses!' That statement (which I found in The
Jockey Who Laughed, *a collection of racing anecdotes edited by former
top Australian jockey Roy Higgins and journalist Tom Prior) was
attributed to an anonymous Greek taxi-driver, and as a supposedly
sound exponent of the art of thumbing through the form book I can
sympathize: if only we could 'shuffle' the horses when toiling over the
ifs, buts and whys of, say, the Ayr Gold Cup . . .*

*To those of you hoping to learn that we on Channel Four Racing
have devised a foolproof formula for finding winners I have to offer our
apologies: no such formula exists. But I hope that the next few
paragraphs will convince even the most sceptical among you that we can
offer just a few hints to assist in finding that elusive 'good thing'.*

*Most horses, like most humans, follow patterns of behaviour. For example,
two of the best ten-furlong horses around in 1990 were Relief Pitcher and the
Eclipse winner Elmaamul. Viewed from the rail of the paddock or on
Channel Four, they presented a stark contrast: Relief Pitcher often became
edgy and sweated up, whereas Elmaamul adopted an altogether calmer
demeanour, remaining cool and laid-back. Watch horses, and in particular
the better ones: knowing how they react before a race can be a definite help in
predicting how they might perform in it.*

*Never forget that any horse unable to act effectively on the prevailing
going is most unlikely to run to form. Horses' actions differ, and very
few are able to give the same level of performance on firm and on heavy:
the more they race the better we are informed about which going suits
them ideally. When assessing handicaps on the Flat (in particular those
for four-year-olds and upwards) a quick glance at the winning
performances of each animal can prove of more benefit than hours of
cross-referencing through past races.*

*Horses for courses is another useful guide. Some tracks do appear to
bring out a performance from a horse that other tracks cannot. Keep an
eye out for horses moving up in distance. Those noted 'staying on well'
or 'running on strongly' are often the types needing another furlong or
two: Off the Record and Absonal were just two examples in the first half of
the 1990 Flat season of horses who became more effective the further they
raced.*

*It was the late Phil Bull of Timeform who described racing as a 'great
triviality'. In essence that is true, but for hundreds of years millions of
people throughout the world have been fascinated by this most baffling
and inexact of sports. We on Channel Four are sometimes baffled by it
too, but we hope we keep you entertained and occasionally point you
towards a winner.*

Previous pages:
Whitbread Gold Cup day form in the
Sporting Life.

According to the prep-school philosopher Nigel Molesworth, 'every boy ort to equip himself for life by knoing a bit about horse racing,' and he advises his readers about how to put their money on: 'You do this with a bookie or the tote as even a fule kno. What every fule do not kno however is which horse to put the money on and bring back a dividend. To kno this you hav to study form . . . Everything is right. DANDRUFF hav won over the distance, it hav two ancestors from the national stud, a french owner, trained on meat, sits up in its stable, lest . . pig . . . . up, firm going THE LOT. BASH ON THE WINE GUMS.' Dandruff, the 51–1 on favourite in the 3:30 at Sponger's Park, is unplaced in a field of five, but Molesworth, undaunted, is soon lining up his next bet.

His method is to follow the advice of newspaper tipsters, but the interpretation of form is not nearly as difficult or mysterious as many people imagine. Form is simply information about a horse's past performances, and by amassing information about the going, the course, the style of running, the jockey, the trainer, the time of the race, the distance of the race, the distance between the horse and the other horses, and so on, the student of form can assess which horse in a race has the best chance based on those past performances. In practice, of course, it is not quite so simple. There is the occasional truly freak result, as when Foinavon won the 1967 Grand National only because he was so far behind the rest of the field before the sensational pile-up at the twenty-third fence that he was able to avoid the mayhem. More usually, there is the factor which might reasonably not be predicted – such as Desert Orchid's defiance of the form-book in staying three miles to win the 1986 King George VI Rank Chase at Kempton, thus causing a rethinking of his preferred trip, or Mtoto's victory in the 1988 King George VI and Queen Elizabeth Diamond Stakes at Ascot on ground much softer than he was previously thought to have been happy with. So form is constantly changing, and the more a horse runs, the more your overall picture of him will be coloured in: if Foinavon's victory did not make him seem a better horse, certainly Desert Orchid's victory in the King George necessitated a rethink.

The problem, though, is *how* to interpret the form accurately and profitably – how much significance to attach to each of the different elements which together comprise the overall picture. For instance, the most direct form link between Nashwan and Cacoethes, who were vying for favouritism for the 1989 Derby during the week before the race, was that they had once raced against each other, in a two-year-old race at Ascot. That Nashwan had beaten Cacoethes by over five lengths that day – eight months before the Derby – was part of the form picture, but a relatively unimportant part of it, direct as the connection between the two horses on that running may have been: it was Cacoethes' first ever race, and he would not have been expected to be at peak fitness or thoroughly versed in how to run; by the time of the Derby a variety of other factors had filled out the form picture, and the obvious element –

```
SALSABIL                              9-0
121-1                            J L Dunlop
b f Sadler's Wells (USA) - Flame Of Tara by
Artaius (USA) [10.3f]
  1989 (Sep) 6f 60y (Nottingham) mdn; (Oct) 1m
good/soft (Longchamp) Gp1
  1990 (Apl) 7f 60y good (Newbury) Gp3.
£88,796 (£22,782).

                                    DRAW: 5

   April 20, Newbury, 7f 60y (3-y-o) (Group 3),
good, £22,782: 1 SALSABIL (9-0, W Carson,3),
held up in touch, ridden to lead two furlongs
out, quickened clear, impressive. (11/4 op
2/1) 2 Haunting Beauty (9-0,8), 3 London Pride
(9-0,5), 6 LAKELAND BEAUTY (btn 12l) (9-0,
W Newnes,7), always about same place.
(33/1); 8 Ran. 6l, hd, 4l, hd, 1½l, sht-hd, 20l. 1m
31.63s (a 4.03s). SR: 73/55/54/42/41/36.
RACECHECK: Wins 0, pl 0, unpl 0.

   Oct 8 1989, Longchamp, 1m (Group 1), good
to soft, £63,063: 1 SALSABIL (2-8-9, W
Carson,4), always prominent, sixth straight,
led one furlong out, driven out. (13/2) 2
Houseproud (2-8-9,5), 3 Alchi (2-8-9,2), 0
PALACE STREET (2-8-9, W R Swinburn,11),
always rear. (30/1); 15 Ran. 2l, sht-hd, nk, ½l,
½l, 1½l, sht-hd, sht-hd, 3l, 2½l. 1m 40.30s.
   Sept 22 1989, Newbury. See FREE AT LAST
```

This is the *Sporting Life*'s version of Salsabil's form before the 1990 One Thousand Guineas. The heading gives the horse's name; the weight she will carry; her form figures, with the most recent run on the right and the dash indicating the end of last season; her trainer; her breeding, with (in square brackets) the average winning distance of the progeny of her sire aged three and over in the British Isles since 1985; her previous victories, with the nature of each race ('mdn' is a maiden race, and so on) and the prize money she has won (with this season's haul in parentheses). She is drawn 5. Then come the relevant details of her previous races: date, course, type of race, going, prize money, finishing position, weight, jockey, draw, the manner in which she ran, her starting price and betting moves. Then are listed the other placed horses and a full entry for sixth-placed Lakeland Beauty, who is also in the One Thousand and whose direct form with Salsabil is obviously material to her chance: she was beaten twelve lengths in the Newbury race, in which eight ran, the distances were six lengths, a head, four lengths (etc.), and the time of the race was 1 minute 31.63 seconds, 4.03 seconds above standard time. Then follows the *Life*'s 'speed ratings' of the first six horses and a summary of subsequent runnings of the horses in that race (though in this instance none of them has run since). Details of Salsabil's run on 22 September 1989 can be found in the entry on Free At Last, who beat her on that occasion.

READING FORM

3.40 10 DECLARED	General Accident 1000 Guineas Stakes (Group 1)		1m Row	TV CH4

£110,000 added **For** three yr old fillies only **Weights** 9st each **Entries** 87 pay £400 **Forfeit** 51 pay £850 **Confirmed** 13 pay £400
Penalty Value 1st £110,493 **2nd** £40,887 **3rd** £19,619 **4th** £8,018 **5th** £3,184 **6th** £1,250
POSTMARK

1	22111- FREE AT LAST[209] C	G Harwood	3 9-00	A Clark 4	124
	Gerald Leigh –brown, beige chevrons on body.				
2	21-3 HASBAH[16]	H Thomson Jones	3 9-00	R Hills 1	129
	Hamdan Al-Maktoum –royal blue, white epaulets, striped cap.				
3	1-1 HEART OF JOY (USA)[16] C	M R Stoute	3 9-00	W R Swinburn 10	129
	John C Mabee –maroon, yellow cross of lorraine and sleeves.				
4	2213-2 IN THE GROOVE[16]	D R C Elsworth	3 9-00	S Cauthen 2	129
	Brian Cooper –grey and maroon (halved), sleeves reversed, grey and maroon quartered cap.				
5	416-6 LAKELAND BEAUTY[13]	W G A Brooks	3 9-00	W Newnes 9	114
	Mrs J Harmsworth –grey, red epaulets, red cap.				
6	31- NEGLIGENT[195] C	B W Hills	3 9-00	Pat Eddery 3	130
	Mrs J M Corbett –royal blue, silver striped sleeves, blue and red hooped cap.				
7	3510-2 PALACE STREET (USA)[19]	G B Balding	3 9-00	J Williams 6	111
	Miss B Swire –lilac, rose quartered cap.				
8	11- RA'A (USA)[188]	H Thomson Jones	3 9-00	G Duffield 8	116
	Hamdan Al-Maktoum –royal blue, white epaulets, striped cap.				
9	1-4 SALLY ROUS[16]	G Wragg	3 9-00	G Carter 7	123
	Sir Philip Oppenheimer –black and white (halved), sleeves reversed, red cap.				
10	121-1 SALSABIL[13] D	J L Dunlop	3 9-00	W Carson 5	140◀
	Hamdan Al-Maktoum –royal blue, white epaulets, striped cap.				
LAST YEAR:	MUSICAL BLISS (USA)	M R Stoute	3 09 00	W R Swinburn	

BETTING FORECAST: 6-4 Salsabil, 3 Heart of joy, 6 Negligent, 13-2 Hasbah, 9 In the Groove, 16 Free At Last, Sally Rous, 100 Lakeland Beauty, Palace Street, Ra'a

The card for the 1990 General Accident One Thousand Guineas as published in the *Racing Post*. The race is due off at 3.40 p.m., with ten declared runners, a Group 1 race over one mile of the Rowley Mile course, televised on Channel Four. Then follow the race conditions and details of the entries: 87 horses were entered at £400 each; at the forfeit stage 51 were kept in the race at £850 each; and 13 were confirmed as runners at another £400 each (though only ten of those now run). After the calculations described on pages 63–4, the Penalty Value for the race works out at £110,493, with £40,887 to the second and so on down to £1,250 to the sixth.

Free At Last will carry number 1. The form figures before her name indicate that she has not run this season (there is no figure to the right of the dash which indicates the change of term), but last season she was second in her first two races and won her remaining three. (In National Hunt form these figures are augmented by letters such as 'F' for 'fell', 'B' for 'brought down', 'U' for 'unseated rider', 'P' for 'pulled up', 'R' for 'refused'.) It is 209 days since Free At Last's previous race, and the capital 'C' in the box indicates that she has won over the course of today's race (as has Heart of Joy). At the bottom of the list, 'D' after Salsabil's name shows that she has won over today's distance – the only runner to have such a qualification. ('BF' would mean beaten favourite in its previous race.) Free At Last is owned by Gerald Leigh (whose colours are given) and trained by Guy Harwood; a trainer from an overseas base would have the fact signalled by his name. She is a three-year-old, will carry 9 stone, will be ridden by A. Clark and is drawn 4. (The Postmark column is a rating arrived at by the *Post*'s own handicapper: Salsabil on 140 is the highest rated.) Note that Heart of Joy, Palace Street and Ra'a were foaled in the USA.

that they had run against each other at level weights – became almost irrelevant. It is the choice of what is relevant and what is not which makes the study of form so fascinating and (potentially) so rewarding.

Where do you find this vital information? The specialist racing daily newspapers – the *Sporting Life* and the *Racing Post* – will give you a comprehensive and detailed account of the form of each horse in each race. But it takes a lot of studying if you are to benefit from it fully, so it may be easier to rely on the interpretation which the expert journalists in these and other papers have undertaken on your behalf. Of course, you may disagree with all the experts if your own reading of a race or a particular line of form seems to you to be more convincing: rarely is a race run completely true to form, and if Nashwan's wonderful victory in the 1989 Ever Ready Derby was predicted by most experts, who could have thought that Terimon would run on to finish second at 500–1, the longest-priced horse ever placed in the Derby?

Form is fact, but it must be tempered by judgement: it can be taken at face value, or it can be amended by a personal interpretation, weighted depending upon the circumstances of the race. Whatever the personal input, though, there are certain key factual elements to be taken into account.

Distance of the Race

Most horses have a range of ideal race distances, and what this ideal is may not always be obvious even to those most closely involved with it. Sheikh Mohammed's Ajdal won the top two-year-old race of the season, the Dewhurst Stakes over seven furlongs, in 1986, then as a three-year-old won the Craven Stakes and disappointed when fourth in the Two Thousand Guineas and third (and subsequently disqualified when his jockey Walter Swinburn failed to weigh in) in the Irish Two Thousand – all races over one mile; his pedigree suggested he might stay further so he ran in the Derby (one and a half miles), finishing down the field behind Reference Point after being close up two furlongs from the post – a run which suggested lack of stamina. So he was switched from middle-distance races to sprinting, and proved an instant success, winning three of the major sprint races – the July Cup, the William Hill Sprint Championship and the Vernons Sprint Cup, over six, five and six furlongs respectively.

The first indication of the probable best distance for a horse is its breeding, as stamina, like speed, is hereditary. One of the few doubts over Nashwan before the 1989 Derby was whether he would stay the one and a half miles, as his sire, Blushing Groom, had not won over further than one mile and had palpably failed to stay when third to The Minstrel in the 1977 Derby. But Nashwan's dam Height of Fashion was by the St Leger winner Bustino, had herself won at one and a half miles, and her offspring Unfuwain and Alwasmi had both shown their best form at one and a half miles. Thus on balance it looked as if Nashwan *would* stay, and so indeed it proved: inheriting his sire's speed and his dam's stamina, he strode clear of his rivals to record a five-length victory.

In Nashwan's case, before the Derby there was no direct evidence from races longer than a mile on which to judge his stamina, and

Although some national
newspapers give a very brief
digest of the form for the major
races of the day, the main
sources of detailed form are the
two racing papers, the *Sporting
Life* (established 1859) and the
Racing Post (established 1986).
Both appear daily (except
Sundays) and give a very
comprehensive run-down of the
form of each runner that day, as
well as expert interpretation of
that form. In addition to the
immediate concern of finding the
day's winners, both offer a range
of other useful information to
anyone interested in racing:
results and reports of the
previous day's racing in Britain
and overseas, entries and weights
in future races, profiles of and
interviews with leading Turf
personalities, articles on all
aspects of the sport (both are
especially strong on breeding),
detailed statistics and a wide
range of racing news. The
Sporting Life also publishes the
weekly *Weekender*, which
concentrates on the weekend's
racing but also includes the
previous week's results and
articles by regular columnists.

In both the *Sporting Life* and
the *Racing Post* you will find
advertisements for services
offered by those who have done
all the homework for you (and
have often supplemented it with
inside information from racing
stables) and are prepared to
divulge their findings for a small
consideration, either by post or
by recorded telephone message.
Some of the shrewdest pundits in
racing (including trainers and
Channel Four Racing presenters)
offer telephone tipping and
information services.

racecourse performance is always the most reliable indicator of any
aspect of form. Of course, several factors affect how far a particular
performance testifies to a horse's stamina – the pace at which the race
was run, the state of the going, the nature of the track – and these must
be weighed up and interpreted. For instance, any horse which is
running on at the end of a truly run race over two miles at Newmarket in
heavy going may reasonably be assumed to be able to stay the distance,
whereas the winner of a slowly run race over the same distance on firm
going around the much tighter track at Chester could not, on that
evidence alone, be said to have the same stamina. The question of
stamina, in fact, is rarely clear-cut. Some experts think that the Derby
course of a mile and a half can suit a horse which truly stays no more
than a mile and a quarter, as much of it is downhill: Sir Ivor in 1968 is
one instance of a horse who won the Derby but showed that one and a
quarter miles was his ideal trip. More curiously, it is often the case that
the four and a half mile Grand National sees fine performances from
horses whose optimum trip elsewhere is around two and a half miles:
in recent years such old favourites as Classified and The Tsarevich
have regularly run well in the National although their best distance
was two and a half to three miles, and Gay Trip, winner in 1970, also
came into this category (as did Crisp, whose exploits at Liverpool are
described on pages 182–3).

Bear in mind that running over a trip longer than really suits it can
blunt a horse's speed when it is returned to a shorter distance: three of
the most sensational defeats of the past twenty years were when
Nijinsky lost the 1970 Prix de l'Arc de Triomphe, when Brigadier
Gerard failed in the 1972 Benson and Hedges Gold Cup and when
Grundy was beaten into fourth in the same race in 1975 a few weeks
after his epic race with Bustino in the King George VI and Queen
Elizabeth Diamond Stakes: in each case there was a variety of reasons
for defeat, but it is interesting to note that all three horses were running
over a shorter distance than in their previous races.

Going

Most horses show a preference for a particular state of the ground,
though some can act equally well on any going. Preference for a
particular kind of going can be passed on from generation to
generation, so in the absence of conclusive racecourse evidence useful
information can be gleaned from the horse's breeding. In addition,
some horses are obviously physically more suited to a certain sort of
going by virtue of their action or conformation: a horse with very
straight pasterns ('straight in front') will tend to lack suppleness and so
may well be uncomfortable on firm ground, which can easily cause
jarring. The size of the feet does not necessarily point to a going
preference; the action of the horse is more important, for a horse with a
high, round action (that is, one which brings the knees of its forelegs
high in each stride) is likely to go well on soft or muddy going, while the
animal with a more economical 'daisy-cutting' stride will probably go
well on fast ground but will be less effective on soft. And if it seems to
'float' over the ground on good going it may well get stuck in the soft.

Obviously the chances of a horse with an apparent preference for a certain sort of going will be subject to the weather: the hefty gamble for the 1989 Ever Ready Derby on Cacoethes, widely expected to prefer fast ground, dried up as the Epsom conditions did the opposite. But having the 'wrong' ground does not of course mean that the horse will not win: Desert Orchid won the 1989 Cheltenham Gold Cup in very heavy ground, which he was known to dislike; nevertheless in terms of strict form he ran below his best – because of the going. When assessing the chances for any race it is folly to discount the importance of the going, though any horse should be able to act effectively on good ground. On extremes of going – very hard or very heavy – always pay serious attention to the chances of horses who have won or run well on similar going in the past.

Class

Form is relative. A close-up sixth in a Classic is probably a much better performance than a victory in a lowly race, and it is important that the class of a race which makes up part of the form is taken into account. Detailed form in the specialist racing papers will give the prize money of the past race in question, and will state if it was a Group race (see page 69), so the class of the race can be easily assessed. Generally Group 1 form will be of a very high order, and those who forget the old adage that Classic form is the best form sometimes miss out on a decent winner: On The House won the Sussex Stakes at 14–1 in 1982, the year she took the One Thousand Guineas, and Roberto was 12–1 when supplementing his Derby victory in 1972 with his sensational triumph in the Benson and Hedges Gold Cup – though it hardly seemed a generous price beforehand, as one of his rivals was Brigadier Gerard. The quality of the form of any race becomes established as the runners proceed to run well subsequently ('frank' or 'advertise' the form) or to disappoint ('devalue' the form).

Time

The study and use of race times can be immensely complicated, and most casual punters have only a vague notion of how important an element of form the matter of time can be, generally leaving it to the time experts in the racing press to advise them as to what is significant.

Horses do not race against the clock, and compared with human athletes they have shown little improvement in times over the last fifty years. The fastest recorded victory in the Derby is still that of Mahmoud in 1936, timed by hand; the fastest electrically timed Derby was Kahyasi's 1988 win. But if record times are not in themselves important, the comparison of the times that different horses take to win different races over the same course can be very significant, and to this end the concept of the standard time has been introduced. The standard time on the Flat is a time for each distance at each course adjusted to a horse carrying 9 stone on good or firm ground, and is calculated by taking the average of the ten fastest runnings over that distance on that course. Courses vary hugely, and standard times will reflect this variety. At Epsom in early 1990 the standard time over five furlongs was 55 seconds; at Sandown Park, with its stiff uphill finish,

┌ **RACEFORM** ────────

The official form book is published by Raceform Ltd (who are also responsible for the compilation of such vital information as standard times). Among other Raceform products are the Private Handicap, which gives a rating for every runner in most races, and the Raceform Note Book, which offers highly informed and detailed assessments of the running and future potential of selected runners in all races. Between them Raceform and Timeform (see page 143) offer serious students of form all they might need.

SECTIONAL TIMING

Horses are not necessarily running their fastest at the end of the race, and the plotting of time taken to run certain portions of the race – 'sectional timing' – can be highly revealing, as it can show where in the race the pressure was really applied, whether the winner was tiring towards the end, and so on. In some countries sectional times are recorded officially, but in Britain it is mostly left to a small number of dedicated enthusiasts, who time by hand (usually against the evidence of video recordings) and publish their findings in the racing press. For instance, the impression that Nashwan was tiring towards the end of his Coral–Eclipse Stakes victory in 1989 was confirmed by Michael Tanner's sectional timing. After a very fast first six furlongs had been set by the pacemakers, Nashwan clocked the penultimate quarter (that is, from half a mile out to two furlongs out) more than one and a half seconds quicker than the leading horses: this was the effort which demanded his maximum speed and took him past the leader Opening Verse, leaving him little in reserve for the final two furlongs, which were run much more slowly than the previous two. Sectional timings must be considered in the light of how a race is run, but always add a fascinating dimension to form.

the standard time for the same distance was 1 minute dead. The time of the winning horse will be given in relation to standard, 'above' meaning slower than standard, 'below' faster.

The great advantage of time is that it supplies a completely objective body of evidence which can be used to compare the abilities of horses who have never raced against each other, and many famous professional backers consider the study of race times one of the most significant weapons in their armoury for the battle against the bookmakers. But the evidence of the clock must be tempered by evidence about the running of that race: was it run at a proper pace, was it run at the end of a day when heavy rain throughout the programme would have transformed the ground, was the horse pushed out to the line or was it easing up? Most of the racing papers have time experts who take much of the mathematical burden away from the punter by compiling ratings based on time: the *Sporting Life*, for instance, has Speed Ratings, and the *Racing Post* has Topspeed.

Course

As we saw in the chapter on racecourses (page 37), the notion of 'horses for courses' is a central one when trying to pick a winner, especially on the more quirky tracks such as Chester or Epsom. A previous course victory by any horse in a race demands attention, for it shows that the horse in question can act effectively on that track. The exact degree of importance which should be attached to such evidence depends on both horse and course, but remember that although all British racecourses are different, many are alike in some ways, and it pays to know something of the nature of each track: is it right-handed or left-handed, is it flat or undulating, galloping or tight? Brighton and Lingfield are often good testing-grounds for Epsom, as both are switchback left-handed tracks: Cacoethes ran at Brighton and Lingfield before running third in the Derby in 1989, and Aliysa, first past the post in the same year's Oaks, had advertised her Classic claims with a brilliant victory at Lingfield.

Trainer and Jockey

The racing press gives detailed statistics about which trainers and jockeys are in good form, and about which are notably successful at a particular racecourse. This can be invaluable information, especially with regard to trainers, for when a stable hits a winning streak it pays to follow it. Jockeys too have purple patches, but in any case note who has ridden a horse in previous races: if for the current race Carson or Eddery or another top jockey is taking the ride on a horse usually partnered by an apprentice or a lesser-known rider, that could be significant. Pay attention also if a top jockey has gone to an obscure meeting to ride for an unfashionable stable: he would not have done so simply for the scenic drive . . .

Draw

Although at most courses the draw (the order in which the runners in a Flat race line up at the start) is of little import in races over more than a mile, in shorter races it is of vital importance – again, more so at some courses than at others. Always note the effect of the draw in races which are building up the form picture, for the draw will have a bearing on how you interpret the face value of the result.

Betting

The racing press will give a brief account of the betting movements of each horse in a race, and this can be highly revealing, for a horse whose odds shorten is being backed, while one whose odds lengthen is attracting less money. The *Racing Post*'s brief description of the variations from Nashwan's starting price of 5–4 for the 1989 Ever Ready Derby read 'op 11–8 tchd 6–4 in places' – that is, the horse's price was 11–8 when racecourse betting on the race opened, and it was momentarily 6–4, though only with some bookmakers ('in places'). His main market rival Cacoethes started at 3–1, and 'op 11–4 tchd 7–2'. What would you make of this terse shorthand if, some time later, you wished to assess the performance of one of those horses in the 1989 Derby? Put simply, the betting moves showed that there was confidence behind Nashwan – he started at a shorter price than he opened and scarcely went longer than that opening price – and little confidence behind Cacoethes, who started at longer than he opened as he did not attract enough money to force his price down. So Cacoethes was 'weak in the market', a phenomenon sometimes illustrated by the continual drift of the horse's price: this does not mean that the horse will not win, but it does mean that it is not expected to.

The Running of the Race

A brief description of the manner in which each horse ran in each race is a crucial element of racing form, as it will tell you whether it was running on at the finish (in which case it has no stamina problems, and might need a longer distance), whether it was able to accelerate, whether it made the pace, whether it encountered any problems in running, and so on. From the depressingly straightforward 'always behind, tailed off' or 'never near enough to challenge' to the equally straightforward 'never headed', these comments will tell you much about each individual running. Watch for 'ran on well', the phrase which tells you that a horse, winning or losing, was keeping going to the end of the race. Mostly such comments are bald and factual, though 'easily' will sometimes offer a value judgement on a winning performance. ('Very easily' was the verdict in Aliysa's two victories before the 1989 Oaks, obvious pointers to her favourite's chance in the Classic.) Factual and to the point, these notes should be read in conjunction with all the other pieces of information which constitute the form. But don't expect hyperbole, rapture or cliché. The *Racing Post*'s comments are supplied by the famously dispassionate Raceform, who described Desert Orchid's epic 1989 Cheltenham Gold Cup win thus: 'jumped well, led to 14th, left in lead 3 out, soon headed, quickened and led flat'; and on Nashwan in the Derby, '4th straight, led over 2f out, driven out, ran on well'.

Time since last Race

Form is most valuable when it is fairly recent, and many shrewd punters will not bet on a horse when its form, however good, belongs to a period

WEIGHT-FOR-AGE SCALES (reproduced by permission of the Jockey Club)

Flat

The scale expresses the number of pounds that it is deemed the average horse in each age group falls short of maturity at different dates and distances. This scale was first used in 1990.

Distance	Age	Jan 1–15	Jan 16–31	Feb 1–14	Feb 15–28	Mar 1–15	Mar 16–31	Apr 1–15	Apr 16–30	May 1–15	May 16–31	Jun 1–15	Jun 16–30	Jul 1–15	Jul 16–31	Aug 1–15	Aug 16–31	Sep 1–15	Sep 16–30	Oct 1–15	Oct 16–31	Nov 1–15	Nov 16–30	Dec 1–15	Dec 16–31
5 furlongs	2	–	–	–	–	–	47	44	41	30	36	34	32	30	28	26	24	22	20	19	18	17	17	16	16
	3	15	15	15	15	14	13	12	11	10	9	8	7	6	5	4	3	2	2	1	1	–	–	–	–
6 furlongs	2	–	–	–	–	–	–	–	–	44	41	38	36	33	31	28	26	24	22	21	20	19	18	17	17
	3	16	16	16	16	15	14	13	12	11	10	9	8	7	6	5	4	3	3	2	2	1	1	–	–
7 furlongs	2	–	–	–	–	–	–	–	–	–	–	–	–	38	35	32	30	27	25	23	22	21	20	19	19
	3	18	18	18	18	17	16	15	14	12	11	10	9	8	7	6	5	4	4	3	3	2	2	1	1
One mile	2	–	–	–	–	–	–	–	–	–	–	–	–	37	34	31	28	26	24	23	22	21	20		
	3	20	20	19	19	18	17	16	15	13	12	11	10	9	8	7	6	5	4	4	3	3	2	2	1
	4	1	1	–	–	–	–	–	–	–	–	–	–	–	–	–	–	–	–	–	–	–	–	–	–
1m 1f	3	22	22	21	20	20	19	18	17	15	14	12	11	10	9	8	7	6	5	5	4	4	3	2	2
	4	2	2	1	1	1	–	–	–	–	–	–	–	–	–	–	–	–	–	–	–	–	–	–	–
1m 2f	3	23	23	22	22	21	20	19	18	16	15	13	12	11	10	9	8	7	6	6	5	5	4	4	3
	4	3	3	2	2	1	1	–	–	–	–	–	–	–	–	–	–	–	–	–	–	–	–	–	–
1m 3f	3	–	–	–	–	23	22	21	20	18	17	15	14	12	11	10	9	8	7	7	6	6	5	4	4
	4	4	4	3	3	2	1	1	–	–	–	–	–	–	–	–	–	–	–	–	–	–	–	–	–
1m 4f	3	–	–	–	–	24	23	22	21	19	18	16	15	13	12	11	10	9	8	8	7	7	6	6	5
	4	5	4	4	3	3	2	2	1	–	–	–	–	–	–	–	–	–	–	–	–	–	–	–	–
1m 5f	3	–	–	–	–	25	24	23	22	20	19	17	16	14	13	12	11	10	9	8	8	7	6	6	5
	4	5	4	4	3	3	2	2	1	–	–	–	–	–	–	–	–	–	–	–	–	–	–	–	–
1m 6f	3	–	–	–	–	26	25	24	23	21	20	18	17	15	14	13	12	11	10	9	9	8	7	7	6
	4	6	5	5	4	4	3	3	2	1	–	–	–	–	–	–	–	–	–	–	–	–	–	–	–
1m 7f	3	–	–	–	–	28	27	26	25	23	21	19	18	16	15	14	13	12	11	10	9	9	8	7	6
	4	6	5	5	4	4	3	3	3	2	1	1	–	–	–	–	–	–	–	–	–	–	–	–	–
Two miles	3	–	–	–	–	29	28	27	26	24	22	20	19	17	16	15	14	13	12	11	10	10	9	8	7
	4	7	7	6	6	5	5	4	4	3	2	1	–	–	–	–	–	–	–	–	–	–	–	–	–
2m 2f	3	–	–	–	–	31	30	29	28	26	24	22	21	19	18	17	16	15	14	13	12	11	10	9	8
	4	8	8	7	7	6	6	5	5	4	3	2	1	–	–	–	–	–	–	–	–	–	–	–	–
2m 4f	3	–	–	–	–	33	32	31	30	28	26	24	22	20	19	18	17	16	15	14	13	12	11	10	9
	4	9	9	8	8	7	7	6	6	5	4	3	2	1	–	–	–	–	–	–	–	–	–	–	–

Jumping

The hurdles scale shows the number of pounds three-year-olds should receive from four-year-olds, and four-year-olds from older horses. The steeplechase scale shows the number of pounds four-year-olds should receive from five-year-olds, and five-year-olds from older horses. This scale has been used since 1985.

Distance	Age	Jan	Feb	Mar	Apr	May	Jun	Jul	Aug	Sep	Oct	Nov	Dec
2m hurdle	3	–	–	–	–	–	–	17	17	16	16	16	14
	4	12	10	8	6	5	5	3	3	2	1	–	–
2m 4f hurdle	3	–	–	–	–	–	–	18	18	17	17	17	15
	4	13	11	9	7	6	6	3	3	2	1	–	–
3m hurdle	3	–	–	–	–	–	–	19	19	18	17	17	16
	4	14	12	10	8	7	7	4	4	3	2	1	–
2m chase	4	–	–	–	–	–	–	12	12	12	12	12	11
	5	10	9	8	7	6	6	3	3	2	1	–	–
2m 4f chase	4	–	–	–	–	–	–	12	12	12	12	12	12
	5	11	10	9	8	7	7	4	4	3	2	1	–
3m chase	4	–	–	–	–	–	–	12	12	12	12	12	12
	5	12	11	10	9	8	8	5	5	4	3	2	1

too far removed from the current race. There are of course exceptions, as when Nashwan was backed down to favouritism for the 1989 Two Thousand Guineas on the strength of glowing reports from the home gallops, despite the fact that he had not raced in public for nearly seven months. A feature of the list of runners in most newspapers is a note of the number of days since the horse last ran: a horse that has not run for a very long time could well be rusty and need this race to make it fit.

Weight

Dominating all the other factors of form is the weight which the horse has to carry. However fast it has run, however much it likes the course and the going, in whatever brilliant form its jockey and trainer currently are – all this evidence is meaningless if it appears to have no chance at the weights. In the Classics all horses carry the same weight (except for the allowance to fillies in the races in which they may take on the colts), so weight is not an element in assessing the likely outcome. But in other races – notably, of course, in handicaps – allowance must be made for discrepancies in the weights. The weight-for-age scale shows the officially designated differences for horses of different ages over different distances at different times of the year, and naturally the effect of weight variations will not be the same at all distances: if a horse is beaten a neck in a five-furlong sprint it will theoretically dead-heat with its conqueror next time they meet if it carries one pound less weight; in a three-mile steeplechase a pound will be worth a length. Naturally, handicapping is an inexact activity: more credence can be given to the distances separating the first three or four home in a race than the distances between the stragglers, and often a horse will win easily but not by a very long distance: the handicapper (and alert students of form) will make due allowances.

A simple guide for relating finishing distances to weight is as follows. *Flat:* 5 furlongs to 7 furlongs: 3 pounds per length; 1 mile to 11 furlongs: 2 pounds per length; 1½ to 2 miles: 1½ pounds per length; over 2 miles: 1 pound per length. *National Hunt:* 1 pound per length, though over extreme distances further adjustments must be made.

So form is a mass of fact, and all you have to do is learn how to read, interpret and use those facts – the magic extra ingredient being your own opinion, in the exercising of which you should bear in mind that some horses (especially sprinters) have 'seams' of form lasting for a few closely spaced races. But remember that form is only one part of the puzzle, and must be accompanied by your judgement of the horse's condition and demeanour before the race. And never forget that the same mass of fact is also available to the bookmakers.

But what if a horse has no form – because it has never run – or the entire field has no form? A field of horses who have never run before is not usually a good betting medium for the casual punter, but if you must have a bet watch how the market moves, as in the absence of form *someone* – in or close to the stable – will have information and will be backing that information with cash. In the Johansens Guides Wood Ditton Stakes at Newmarket on 19 April 1989 none of the twenty runners who faced the starter had ever run, but the market proved a reliable guide, with the well-backed 7–4 favourite Sabotage beating the 9–4 second favourite Porter Rhodes; the next horse in the betting was 8–1. The betting market had pointed unmistakably towards the two horses with the best chances, and as the runners returned to unsaddle John McCririck proclaimed to Channel Four viewers: 'It's an easy business, this horse racing, if you've got no form book!'

BETTING

John McCririck, Channel Four Racing's man in the betting ring, himself worked as a course bookmaker and a private handicapper before developing his journalistic career on the *Sporting Life* from 1972 until 1984. He joined the ITV racing coverage after a spell with the BBC and has been with Channel Four Racing since 1983. He has written the At Large column in the *Racing Post* since 1986, and has won two British Press Awards – Specialist Writer of the Year in 1978 and Campaigning Journalist of the Year in 1979.

When that arm-waving fatso on Channel Four Racing burbles, 'It's "tips with the thumb" the favourite, they've done "ear 'ole" and some are calling "levels you devils" . . . They've flip-flopped now and the original "jolly" is out to "bottle" from "up the arm"' – that could be the final clue to the jigsaw of picking winners.

After the race it all becomes obvious. But beforehand you have the best chance of putting the pieces together correctly if you ensure you have them all to hand in the first place. That means hard work and – when possible – delaying your bet until the runners are down at the start.

Ideally, like our form-book guru, Timeform's Jim McGrath, you should be your own private handicapper, for only by rating horses every day can you expect to master the most reliable racing guide – form.

If you aren't fortunate enough to be able to go racing, settle back and watch us on the box – always having a telephone at the ready. For self-discipline open deposit accounts with several bookmakers. Then you can bet only within pre-set financial limits; very different from the temptations of credit, where zeros can be easier to add on than reef up.

Watch and listen carefully. That early 'tissue' (the bookmakers' guide to the first show) can be the key to where value may come from. And don't ever let your first ideas of the outcome remain inflexible in the face of contrary evidence. Note Channel Four's pre-race 'windows' – interviews with jockeys, trainers, owners or lads – for additional guidance. Snippets from presenter Brough Scott and roving reporter 'Thommo' – Derek Thompson – can prove invaluable.

Judge the condition of the horses in the paddock and going down to the start, taking in the shrewd comments of the 'Noble Lord' John Oaksey and the 'Greatest Jockey' John Francome. And watch out for those last critical clues from the betting ring. Remember: that a horse's odds shorten doesn't mean it is bound to win. But who is backing it, and why? And drifters don't always lose: you want to know who is laying it, and why. Channel Four tries to pass all this on. Sometimes our interpretations are awry, but at least we try. (I'm still pleading with the BBC to let their own man loose in the ring: he could only be an improvement on what viewers are lumbered with now!)

In that frenetic jungle of the betting ring you can often latch on to something highly significant quite late. As the horses are going behind the stalls, or getting into line for a jump race, make your final decision and back your judgement.

And may G.G. – our hawk-eyed race-reader Graham Goode – call your beast in front where it matters . . . at 'double carpet'!

Previous pages:
Bookmakers at Salisbury.

'Betting, particularly on racehorses, is a great force for good,' wrote Woodrow Wyatt: 'For millions placing a bet is the only democratic decision they make regularly on their own responsibility. In the factory or the office their routine tasks are allotted to them to be performed with little personal initiative or discretion ... Dehumanizing fetters constrict the mind and lower the spirit of the average wage-earner. Placing a bet restores his independence and stimulates his brain.' So much for the moral complexion of betting; let us turn to its practicalities.

In Britain the punter has the choice of placing a bet at the odds offered by a bookmaker on or the Tote, the key difference being that a bookmaker will provide odds based on his assessment of the chances of the horses in the race, while the Tote (in full, the Horserace Totalisator Board) operates on a pool system where the backers all put their money in and the winners share the payout. The bookmaker's odds will lengthen (offering a higher return) or shorten (offering a lower one) according to how money is being wagered, but the odds you strike your bet at remain valid for that transaction whatever happens subsequently, unless you bet at starting price; whereas on the Tote, you will not know the return on your stake until after the race.

BETTING WITH THE BOOKIES

To many people the principles and mathematics of betting with a bookmaker – to say nothing of the jargon and frantic arm-waving which accompany it – are completely impenetrable, and even its most basic features escape some of the uninitiated: one of the commonest misconceptions among those unused to betting is that you do not receive your stake back along with your winnings in the event of a successful bet (but if this were so why would anyone ever bet at odds on?). Informed or not, the majority of the population have a bet with a bookie at least once a year, even if it is just a one-off on the Grand National, on which some £80 million was supposedly staked in 1990. The principle of betting with a bookmaker is simple: he offers odds at which you may pitch your money against his. The practice and the maths, however, can be less clear.

For betting to be effective, its practice should be accompanied by an appreciation of the mathematical factors governing the betting market: you may not think that this matters, but the bookmaker certainly will, and every punter should be aware of how a book works and what factors may affect the prices so that he can take advantage of market moves and identify that most sought-after of betting commodities – value.

Odds

Odds are a way of expressing the perceived probability of a horse winning. So evens (1–1) means that there is an equal (50 per cent) chance of the horse winning and losing. At 2–1 against there is a 33.33

ODDS

Some people are baffled by what the odds actually mean: 2–1 may be obvious enough, but what is 13–8? Here are a few of the most common odds quoted for horse racing expressed in more familiar fractions:

evens	1 to 1
11–10	$1\frac{1}{10}$ to 1
6–5	$1\frac{1}{5}$ to 1
5–4	$1\frac{1}{4}$ to 1
11–8	$1\frac{3}{8}$ to 1
6–4	$1\frac{1}{2}$ to 1
13–8	$1\frac{5}{8}$ to 1
7–4	$1\frac{3}{4}$ to 1
15–8	$1\frac{7}{8}$ to 1
85–40	$2\frac{1}{8}$ to 1
9–4	$2\frac{1}{4}$ to 1
5–2	$2\frac{1}{2}$ to 1
11–4	$2\frac{3}{4}$ to 1
100–30	$3\frac{1}{3}$ to 1
7–2	$3\frac{1}{2}$ to 1
9–2	$4\frac{1}{2}$ to 1
11–2	$5\frac{1}{2}$ to 1
13–2	$6\frac{1}{2}$ to 1
15–2	$7\frac{1}{2}$ to 1
17–2	$8\frac{1}{2}$ to 1

ODDS PERCENTAGES

Odds on	PRICE	Odds against
50.00	Evens	50.00
52.38	11–10	47.62
54.55	6–5	45.45
55.56	5–4	44.44
57.89	11–8	42.11
60.00	6–4	40.00
61.90	13–8	38.10
63.64	7–4	36.36
65.22	15–8	34.78
66.67	2–1	33.33
68.00	85–40	32.00
69.23	9–4	30.77
71.43	5–2	28.57
73.33	11–4	26.67
75.00	3–1	25.00
76.92	10–3	23.08
77.78	7–2	22.22
80.00	4–1	20.00
81.82	9–2	18.18
83.33	5–1	16.67
84.62	11–2	15.38
85.71	6–1	14.29
86.67	13–2	13.33
87.50	7–1	12.50
88.24	15–2	11.76
88.89	8–1	11.11
89.47	17–2	10.53
90.00	9–1	10.00
90.91	10–1	9.09
91.67	11–1	8.33
92.31	12–1	7.69
92.86	13–1	7.14
93.33	14–1	6.67
93.75	15–1	6.25
94.12	16–1	5.88
95.24	20–1	4.76
95.65	22–1	4.35
96.15	25–1	3.85
97.06	33–1	2.94
97.56	40–1	2.44
98.04	50–1	1.96
98.51	66–1	1.49
98.77	80–1	1.23
99.01	100–1	0.99
99.60	250–1	0.40
99.80	500–1	0.20

per cent chance of its winning and a 66.67 per cent chance of its losing (that is, two out of every three chances – 2 plus 1 equals 3 – are against its winning). At 2–1 on (the *on* indicating that the odds are reversed, '2–1 on' being the common way of expressing 1–2) there is a 66.67 per cent chance of its winning and a 33.33 per cent chance of its losing. So any horse at 'odds on' is deemed by the bookmakers to be more likely to win than lose. (A useful way of thinking about odds is that with odds against the first number expressed is the multiple of your stake that you will win, the second number the amount that the bookie will keep if you lose – or, if you like, your stake unit. Thus at 6–1 against you put down one to win six.)

The key to intelligent betting is to compare your own opinion of the probability of the horse's winning with the bookmaker's and to back your fancy if the bookies are offering odds longer than you think properly reflect the chance of that horse: such a bet represents 'value', the 'bargain' which every regular punter seeks. Thus when Mtoto's odds went to 4–1 before the King George VI and Queen Elizabeth Diamond Stakes at Ascot in 1988 such a price represented to many backers wonderful value, as he was clearly the best horse in the race on form and his price had lengthened purely on account of the ground being softer than he was thought to like; so if you believed that he could overcome any aversion to such going, 4–1 was great value – and so it proved, as he swept past Unfuwain in the final furlong to reward those who had kept faith with him. (Value usually becomes apparent *after* the race, of course.)

How a Book Works

If betting is often characterized as a mugs' game, this is because in the long run the intelligent and efficient bookmaker is bound to win over the average punter, for the bookmaker is controlling the maths and constructs the odds (or the 'book') for each race in such a way that, in the long term, he will make a profit. He does this by dictating that the total of the percentage probability chances for each race exceed 100 per cent. (Mathematically the chances must come to exactly 100 per cent if all the true probabilities are added up.) To illustrate this we can examine the returned (official) starting prices for the 1990 Gold Seal Oaks and express the odds in percentages:

Horse	S.P.	%
Salsabil	2–1	33.33
In The Groove	85–40	32.00
Kartajana	7–2	22.22
Gharam	12–1	7.69
Ahead	16–1	5.88
Knight's Baroness	16–1	5.88
Cameo Performance	25–1	3.85
Game Plan	50–1	1.96
TOTAL		112.81%

evens
('levels')

11–10
('tips' – with the thumb)

5–4
('wrist')

6–4
('ear 'ole')

2–1
('bottle')

9–4
('top of the head')

3–1
('carpet')
– or possibly 'Burlington Bertie',
100–30

33–1
('double carpet')

'I've got it right for once!'

McCRIRICK'S GUIDE TO TIC-TAC

The language in which bookmakers conduct their business adds to the mystery of betting. Slang terms are used to describe odds, amounts of money, horses and other aspects of the betting operation: for some words and phrases the derivation is reasonably obvious, others are more obscure. Among the commonly used terms, some of which are explained in the main part of this chapter, are:

Bar: if a betting show is concluded '20–1 bar' it means that the horses not listed stand at 20–1 or longer

Bottle: 2–1

Burlington Bertie: 100–30 (rhyming slang)

Carpet: 3–1

Century: £100

Double carpet: 33–1

Ear 'ole: 6–4 (from the tic-tac signal)

Grand: £1,000

Jolly: the favourite (the 'jolly old favourite')

Levels: evens

Monkey: £500

Nap: a newspaper tipster's best bet of the day

On the shoulder: 7–4 (tic-tac)

Pony: £25

Rag: an outsider – a horse with apparently no chance

Rouf: 4–1 ('four' backwards)

Steamer: a horse gambled on significantly on the morning of the race

Tips: 11–10 (tic-tac)

Tissue: the course bookmakers' forecast of how the betting will open

Top of the head: 9–4 (tic-tac)

Up the arm: 11–8 (tic-tac)

With the thumb: the price is being taken and won't last long (tic-tac)

Wrist: 5–4 (tic-tac)

A book in which the probability chances add up to over 100 per cent is described as 'over-round', and in this case the book is over-round by 12.81 per cent, which means that the bookmaker expects to have to pay out £100 for every £112.81 that he takes in bets, leaving him £12.81 profit. When a book is over-round the punter cannot back every runner and be *guaranteed* a return, and as every efficient bookmaker will be betting over-round the notion that you can back every horse in a race and win is clearly nonsense. (Very occasionally the punter can beat the bookies by choosing the best price for each horse from a variety of bookmakers whose prices vary considerably, but this takes great alertness and remarkable powers of mental arithmetic.) Bookmakers do not of course win on every race, but by maintaining the over-roundness of the book they are ensuring that in the long term they will come out on top, for favourites win only around two out of every five races, and in each race the bookmaker will try to contrive the odds so that he has to pay out less than he takes in.

So how does a book work? For big races the betting will begin weeks or even months in advance; for the other key races at the main meetings the major bookmakers will advertise prices on the morning of the race and punters may back at these prices – subject to fluctuations dictated by weight of money – until the proper book is formed before the race itself. (A 'steamer' is a horse which has been heavily backed off-course before the actual pre-race market has been formed.) A form expert in the bookmakers' employ constructs the 'tissue', a forecast of how the betting on the race will open on the course, and initially the course bookmakers (whose activities dictate the officially returned starting price) will probably bet to these prices. Thereafter each course bookmaker will adjust his prices according to public demand and to how he sees the probable outcome of the race: if he takes a lot of money for one horse he will shorten its price in order to dissuade other punters from backing it, which would increase his liability in the event of its winning; if (for whatever reason) he thinks that a horse will not win he will lengthen its price in order to encourage punters to back it and swell his coffers. But throughout all these transactions he will be aware of his own liabilities, and if his potential payout on one horse is more than he can comfortably cover from losing bets on the other horses he may decide to 'lay off' by passing all or some of the money he has taken on that horse on to other bookmakers – that is, by himself betting on that horse. Course bookies communicate such bets among themselves by means of the sign language of 'tic-tac', now so familiar to Channel Four viewers through the prestidigitations of John McCririck.

As the on-course betting market determines the returned starting prices, it is important that money wagered off course in betting shops and through credit accounts with the large bookmakers can be transferred to the course in order for that weight of money to be reflected in the betting market. Representatives of the off-course bookmakers will bet on the course to lodge their off-course money into the market, and will send bets through by means of the 'blower', a telephone service which relays money to the course bookmakers. The largest bookmaker in Britain is Ladbrokes: the 'magic sign' is the tic-tac signal (somewhat like drawing a halo over the head) which indicates Ladbrokes money being brought into the market.

THE TOTE

The principle of Tote betting is simple. All the money bet on all the horses in a race forms a pool which following the race is shared out among those who have won, after a deduction has been made from the pool for running costs, which include contributions to racecourses and to the Betting Levy. There are separate pools for the different sorts of bet – explained in the panel – and each pool is subjected to a different level of deduction: in the 1989–90 financial year the deductions were 16 per cent from the Win pool, 24 per cent from the Place, 29 per cent from the Dual Forecast, and 26 per cent each from the Jackpot and Placepot.

The working of the Tote can be seen in a simple example. Say the Win pool for a race consists of £10,000, of which one thousand £1 bets have been staked on the horse which wins:

pool	£10,000
deduction	£ 1,600
payout	£ 8,400 – dividend £ 8.40 per £1 ticket

The dividend (or the 'Tote return') is declared to a £1 unit and includes the stake, so the actual winnings in the above example are £7.40.

Although on a racecourse you will see displayed approximate Tote odds as the betting takes place before a race, you cannot know exactly what the dividend will be until after the race, and this is the crucial difference between betting with the Tote and with a bookmaker: with a bookmaker you bet either at starting price or at the price which he quotes you or has displayed, and your bet remains at that price; with the Tote you will not know when you make the bet precisely what the odds are.

Because they operate on different principles Tote odds and bookmakers' odds will usually differ. The Tote return on Quest For Fame's victory in the 1990 Derby was £7.50: so the winnings from a £1 bet were £6.50 – odds of 13–2 as against his starting price of 7–1, which offered better value by half a point. But if at the Cheltenham National Hunt Festival earlier in 1990 you had preferred the starting price of Topsham Bay, winner of the National Hunt Chase, you would have done far worse than backing the horse on the Tote, where the return of £64.20 meant odds of over 63–1 – more than half as much again; and Suprise Envoy, winner of a Ripon nursery on August Bank Holiday Monday 1990, paid £64.00 on the Tote – nearly four times the SP of 16–1. In the year to the end of March 1990 the starting price bettered the Tote return for 50 per cent of the races run, the Tote came out on top for 47 per cent, and for the rest (3 per cent) the two were equal.

All the other pools operate in the same way, but it is not possible for the television viewer to know how the Tote odds are looking just before the race, and some off-course betting shops do not bet at Tote odds.

The Tote is an important feature of British racing, with a total betting turnover of over £200 million in the financial year 1989–90 and a major programme of race sponsorship – notably of the Cheltenham Gold Cup, the Ebor Handicap, the Cesarewitch and the Tote Gold Trophy.

TOTE BETTING

Win

You bet on one horse to come first. (The record win dividend was £341. 2s. 6d. to a two-shilling stake on Coolie at Haydock Park on 30 November 1929: the Tote odds of over 3,410–1 compared with a starting price of 100–8: just over 12–1.)

Place

You bet on a horse to be placed:
first or second in races of five, six or seven runners;
first, second or third in races of eight runners or more;
first, second, third or fourth in handicaps of sixteen runners or more.

Dual Forecast

In races of three or more runners, you pick two horses: you win if they finish first and second (in either order).

Jackpot

You pick the winners of the first six races at the designated Jackpot meeting. If there is no winner the pool is carried forward to the next Jackpot meeting. (On 18 June 1966 at Ascot the Jackpot paid £63,114 6s. to a five-shilling stake.)

Placepot

You pick horses to be placed in the first six races (or to win any race with less than five runners). The Placepot operates at all meetings. (The record Placepot dividend was declared at Cheltenham on 14 March 1990: £22,203.20 to a £1 stake.)

THE BETTING BUSINESS

The Course Bookmaker

Among individual on-course bets struck on Nashwan during his glorious summer campaign in 1989 were £80,000 to win £40,000 (2–1 on) in the Coral–Eclipse Stakes and £90,000 to win £20,000 (9–2 on) in the King George VI and Queen Elizabeth Diamond Stakes.

The principal betting ring at most racecourses is in the Tattersalls enclosure, named after the famous company which in 1866 drew up the first rules on betting transactions. (The Tattersalls Committee is still the authority recognized by the Jockey Club for settling all matters of dispute relating to bets, and has the power to 'warn off' – that is, ban from racecourses – an individual for non-payment.) Betting is not allowed in the Members' Enclosure, so the larger companies have representatives who take up a position by the rail separating Members from Tatts, and take bets – mostly in credit – from the members. (These are known as 'rails bookmakers'.) In the main betting ring bookmakers are allotted pitches according to seniority, and they set up shop with a clerk (who records the bets on a large ledger – one column per horse so that the liability on any horse can be rapidly assessed if need be) and other assistants and tic-tac men. The bookmaker himself will handle the money, shovelling it into (and occasionally out of) a large bag suspended from his stand. Dozens of bookmakers all shouting the odds provide a British racecourse with its unique sound. When a bookmaker shouts 'five to four the field' (which usually sounds like 'fidah vaudeville') he is indicating that 5–4 is the shortest price he has on offer; 'I'll take six to four' means he is offering 6–4 on, while 'I'll lay six

A course bookmaker.

to four' means 6–4 against; 'sixes bar one' means that he is is offering all the horses in the race except one at 6–1 or longer. All the while he will be on the look-out for 'faces' – people with inside information whose bets will be highly significant.

Having started betting from the 'tissue', the course bookmaker adjusts the odds according to the flow of money until the race is started, at which point a reporter from the *Sporting Life* and another from the Press Association agree on what is to be the officially returned starting price.

In 1949 a book entitled *How The Other Man Lives*, describing the nature of various occupations, said of course bookmakers: 'Only men of strong constitution and iron nerve can stand the tenseness and excitement of bookmaking for any length of time.' And that was before the representative of Channel Four Racing was watching their every move . . .

Betting Shops

The first betting shops in Great Britain were opened on 1 May 1961. Before then betting on horses could legally take place only on a racecourse or through a credit account; illegal betting, though, was rife, with 'bookies' runners' operating in pubs and clubs, and it was in an attempt to end this rash of illicit activity that Home Secretary R. A. Butler brought in the legislation – the Betting and Gaming Act – which made betting shops possible. Butler noted in his memoirs that 'the House of Commons was so intent on making "betting shops" as sad as possible, in order not to deprave the young, that they ended up more like undertakers' premises.' Indeed, the general ambience of betting shops was deliberately kept seedy and inhospitable for decades (they were not allowed to show races live on television or offer light refreshments to their clients), but in 1986 new legislation allowed a general brightening up and, most significantly, the transmission of races live on television to shops which took the service from SIS (see panel). Even coffee machines appeared, and the notion of a betting shop as an establishment into which no respectable person should ever stray unless he absolutely had to, in which case the experience should be as shaming and uncomfortable as possible, had at last disappeared.

There are now some 10,000 betting shops in Britain, responsible for a large proportion of the £5,000 million bet off-course every year. Since to many people betting shops still have the fascinating but forbidden aura of the bordello, it may help would-be clients overcome their shyness about entering such a place by explaining how you have a bet. It is very simple. Around the walls are displayed a large array of newspapers and television screens giving all sorts of information on the day's sport. When you have decided what you want to back, you take a carbon-backed slip from the dispenser – different sorts of bet require different slips – and write on the details of your bet. It is essential that you fill in this slip accurately: if you got confused and had a fiver on 'Salsagroove' for the Oaks you would have no right to feel aggrieved if the bookmaker called the bet void, and all sorts of disputes arise from wrongly or ambiguously filled-in slips, or slips placing some highly elaborate combination bet when the amount staked does not cover the

SATELLITE INFORMATION SERVICES

Satellite Information Services (SIS) made its first live transmission of racing action on 5 May 1987, and now offers a nationwide service to betting shops in Great Britain and Ireland (and to Austria, the Channel Islands, the Netherlands and West Germany). It provides live coverage of the action from most race meetings (the pictures and commentary supplied by Racecourse Technical Services) and of greyhound racing, as well as comprehensive betting information, previews, interviews and sporting news. SIS covers at least two meetings a day, receiving the RTS pictures (via the British Telecom Tower in London) in its headquarters in Hackney. Here the pictures are integrated with sound and text as appropriate and are sent via the British Telecom transmitter in Docklands to the Intelsat V satellite some 23,000 miles above the equator, from where they are beamed into betting shops. Scheduling the constant flow of pictures and information from several venues is a delicate operation, and SIS has the unusual privilege of being able to delay the start of a greyhound race by two or three minutes if a horse race is late off and a clash seems likely. Apart from betting shops, the SIS service is also supplied to private subscribers, among them the Maktoums and several top trainers.

There is no such thing in racing as a certainty. In the Chepstow Stakes at Chepstow on 28 June 1947 Glendower, ridden by Gordon Richards, started at 20–1 *on* to beat his solitary opponent, Markwell. This was, of course, in the days before starting stalls, and as the tapes of the old-style starting gate went up Glendower whipped round and unseated the great jockey, leaving Markwell to win unopposed. Gordon Richards recalled this embarrassing incident in his autobiography, adding: 'I heard afterwards that a certain gentleman was in the habit of picking out my best ride of the day, and then ringing up his bookmaker and backing it to win one thousand pounds. On that day he selected Glendower, but he did not anticipate that I would start at twenty to one on. That race cost him twenty thousand pounds.'

bets involved. The slip itself is not very difficult. For a win bet you would just need to enter the name of the horse, the time and venue of the race, and the amount you wish to stake. (You also have the option to have the bet 'tax paid', which means that you pay the betting tax on the stake, rather than have the tax – usually 10 per cent – taken off your returns.) You give the slip and your money to the assistant behind the counter, who will time-stamp the slip in a machine and return the bottom copy to you. You then hang around affecting nonchalance as your horse sweeps to victory, and when the 'weighed-in' signal is given saunter to the payout end of the counter to collect your winnings.

Remember that if you have not bet 'tax paid' 10 per cent will be taken off your returns – that is, your winnings and your returned stake. The imposition of betting tax has made a great difference to betting, as it means that at shorter odds the actual winnings are very much reduced. Say you wanted to have £10 on a horse which starts at even money. When it wins your actual profit on the bet will be only £8, as your return will be £20 (£10 winnings plus £10 stake) less 10 per cent tax (£2) taken off the returns. Betting tax does not now apply to bets struck with a bookmaker on the racecourse.

Accounts

To use the wisdom of the Channel Four Racing team to the full for betting purposes you would do well to have an account with a bookmaker so that you can bet by telephone at the very last minute, rather than having to keep scuttling down to the betting shop during the adverts or placing all your bets in advance of the afternoon's transmission. It is easy to open an account: all the major credit firms advertise in the *Sporting Life* and the *Racing Post* and give details of how to apply. You should appreciate the difference between a deposit account – whereby you deposit a sum of money with the bookmaker (probably not less than £100 with the big firms) and can bet until that amount is used up – and a credit account – where you are allowed credit up to an agreed limit. You will be sent a statement regularly, and very occasionally this will be accompanied by a cheque! (You can of course use your credit account with these firms' representatives at race meetings: Tote Credit, with 50,000 clients, has a special office on all courses.) Apart from the big companies there are many small local credit bookmakers, who often provide a more homely service than the large firms.

Ante-Post Betting

Ante-post betting is betting on an event well in advance of its taking place. For several very big races – the first four Classics, the Grand National, the Cheltenham Gold Cup, the Champion Hurdle and the Daily Express Triumph Hurdle – bets are struck months before, while most of the big handicaps (such as the Lincoln, the Cambridgeshire and the Cesarewitch) attract lively markets for several weeks before.

You can even bet years before, if the bookmaker will take the bet. On 9 May 1986 a punter in the West Country asked in a betting shop for a price on a then unnamed four-month-old foal by Mill Reef out of All Along winning the Derby in 1989. He was quoted 500–1 and staked

£300. This was beginning to look like an inspired piece of investment when Along All – as the foal had been named – became one of the best two-year-olds in France in 1988, but the story has no happy ending for the far-sighted backer, as the horse did not run in the Derby.

More successful long-term bets were landed by two owners. In 1967 the famous bookmaker William Hill laid owner Raymond Guest £50,000 to £500 (100–1) against an as yet unraced two-year-old winning the Derby the following year (and, for good measure, £12,500 to £500 the place): the horse was Sir Ivor, who won the Derby easily in 1968 at 5–4 on. And in 1961 advertising man Bill Gollings took such a fancy to the big horse he had bought as a potential chaser that he backed him to win the 1963 Cheltenham Gold Cup: £50 each way at 200–1 with the commission agent Ralph Freeman, and £50 each way at 100–1 with Ladbrokes. (He also backed him to repeat the feat in 1964.) His horse – Mill House – duly won the 1963 Gold Cup, and was second to Arkle in the famous 1964 race.

The great advantage of ante-post betting is of course that you can get very much better odds than the horse will start at (though this is not guaranteed – the horse's odds may lengthen). During the winter of 1988–89 Nashwan was as long as 40–1 for the 1989 Derby; he had shortened to around 6–1 just before his victory in the Two Thousand Guineas, was offered at 3–1 immediately after and shortened to as low as evens with some bookmakers before money for Cacoethes in the week before the race eased Nashwan out a little. A canny punter with a 40–1 ante-post voucher could have 'hedged' by offering some of his bet back to the bookmaker at the shorter odds, thereby reducing the bookie's liability but covering himself in the event of the horse's being beaten. By clever manipulation of his bets the ante-post backer can manoeuvre himself into the enviable position of making a profit whether the horse wins or loses.

But the great disadvantage of ante-post betting is that you lose your money if the horse is withdrawn before the race. The record of the winter favourites for the first four Classics actually taking part in the races for which they have been backed is woeful, and even a month before the 1990 Derby the leading twenty horses in the ante-post market included fourteen who did not run. (If your horse is withdrawn but the race is abandoned you should get your money back, for you cannot lose on an event which does not happen.) Sometimes bookmakers will offer ante-post odds 'with a run' – that is, if the horse does not take part your money is returned. Some clever observers of the ante-post market for the 1989 Cheltenham Gold Cup placed bets on Desert Orchid 'with a run' at 4–1 and 7–2 two months before the race: there was doubt about his participation, but these punters reasoned that at such odds he was a marvellous bet, for if he ran he would certainly start at a shorter price, and the 'with a run' proviso protected them from losing out should he not be in the line-up. They were proved right. Less satisfactory is when you back a horse at long odds well in advance of a big race and it thanks you for your support by turning in a couple of preliminary performances so wretched that its odds for the big race drift: when the race comes a little bit of you is hoping that it will lose so that you are spared the anguish of seeing it come in at a much bigger price than that at which you backed it.

There could be no better illustration of the perils of ante-post betting than the succession of Derby favourites who came and went between the beginning of the 1990 Flat season and the race itself:

Be My Chief: winner of the 1989 Racing Post Trophy, but then in the spring word emerged from Henry Cecil's yard that all was not well . . .

Mukddaam: Nashwan's half-brother won his first race of the term but injured a foot in the Craven Stakes . . .

Bleu De France: the French-trained colt was backed from 66–1 to 10–1, but was then hammered at Longchamp . . .

Belmez: he won the Chester Vase impressively when beating Quest For Fame, but shortly afterwards was injured . . .

Sasaki: Michael Stoute's colt was a real talking horse, and his price was talked down from 66–1 despite the fact that he'd never run. Then he spoiled things by taking part in a race, and was well beaten at Ascot . . .

Digression: won the Royal Lodge Stakes in 1989 and attracted much support through the winter. As other fancied horses passed by the wayside he came in to 7–2 before he had had a run in 1990, but that seasonal reappearance at Goodwood proved a deep disappointment. Still, at least he ran in the Derby – starting at 14–1 . . .

Rock Hopper: won the Lingfield Derby Trial but pulled a muscle in his quarters and withdrew . . .

Razeen: won the Predominate Stakes at Goodwood and thus became an uneasy favourite for the Derby, a position which he maintained on the day of the race, starting at 9–2. He finished fourteenth.

Ante-post betting can be a frustrating and irritating business, but not as irritating as looking through past copies of the *Sporting Life* or the *Racing Post* and seeing those adverts offering 40–1 Nashwan . . .

Frustrating, irritating and depressing – but also fascinating, stimulating and, above all, exciting, betting is an emotional activity. Why else would an apparently sane person in a betting shop shout advice at a horse 100 miles away, or a television viewer scream instructions to a jockey riding his fancy on another continent? It is a commonplace of the philosophy of betting that if punters were as worried about backing losers as they are about missing winners, they would have a much more profitable time. The regular punter gets used to backing losers, and takes it in his stride, for the next bet will surely win: but the hurt of deciding to back a horse, then deciding not to back it, and then seeing it scoot home without your support, takes an age to get over. Yes, the successful professional backers will wait and wait for the right bet, and yes, it's the mug punter who wants to bet on every race who fills the bookie's satchel, and yes, the bookies are bound to win in the long term for they control the odds. The backer is always at a disadvantage, but so what? For the racing enthusiast, life can offer very few better sensations than that moment when you *know* your horse is going to win. And anyway, we can hardly disagree with Damon Runyon's character Sam the Gonoph, who so memorably affirmed: 'I long ago come to the conclusion that all life is six to five against.'

When Serious Trouble won the two-runner Ruddles Best Bitter Stakes at Brighton on 15 May 1990 his starting price of 33–1 on was the shortest SP returned since the abolition of on-course betting tax in April 1987.

Tote counters at Cheltenham.

TYPES OF BET

There are many different types of bet, some of them involving procedures and combinations of baffling complexity. Combination bets are attractive to small punters as they offer the promise of big returns for modest outlay – and naturally they are difficult to pull off. The most usual types of bet are listed here, with sample calculations which exclude any allowance for tax.

Win

Betting on the horse to come first. The return on a £5 win bet at 10–1 is £55: £5 stake plus £50 winnings.

Each Way

Betting on the horse both to win and to be placed (that is, to finish in the first two in races of five, six or seven runners, the first three in races of eight or more runners, or the first four in handicaps with sixteen or more runners: these stipulations can alter from one bookmaker to another). The odds for a place are normally one quarter or one fifth the odds for a win, depending on the nature of the race and the number of runners: the bookmaker will advertise the fraction. An each-way bet is in fact two bets – one for the win and one for the place – and consequently the stake will be twice the unit of the bet: thus a bet of £5 each way costs £10. A bet of £5 each way (with the place odds one quarter of the win odds) on a horse which wins at 10–1 returns winnings of £62.50 (£50 win plus £12.50 place, as the winning horse is also placed) plus your stake of £10 – total return £72.50. If the horse is second you win £12.50 and have your stake on the place bet returned, but lose your £5 win bet: so your return on the £10 invested is £17.50. Obviously it is not worth backing a horse each way if its odds are much less than 5–1, as the amount you will make on the place bet if it is placed but does not win will not cover your loss on the win bet: the niceties of such calculations for off-course bets are distorted by the need to allow for tax, but it should be clear that an on-course each-way bet at 4–1 one quarter the odds a place will yield no gain and no loss if the horse is placed but does not win – but if you tried to bet each way with a course bookmaker at 4–1 you might hear some unusual language . . .

Place

Few bookmakers will bet for place only, though the Tote runs a Place pool on every race with five or more runners.

SYSTEMS

There is an infinite variety of systems with which you can try to beat the bookies, but none is guaranteed to bring you success, and most will confine your betting within so tight a straitjacket as to remove much of the fun. Systems can involve deliberations and calculations of enormous complexity, or can be very simple. To back the favourite in every race might seem a sound system, but only around two out of every five favourites win, and in the long term you will lose. Another popular habit is to back the outsider in a field of three. You might come out on top if you follow the selection of a particular newspaper pundit throughout a season, though few of them consistently show a profit on their nap choices. To follow a jockey or a trainer through a season might work, but not necessarily: if you had placed a £1 win bet on each of Pat Eddery's 838 rides during the 1989 Flat (turf) season you would have backed 171 winners but lost £148.00. Following runner-up Steve Cauthen would have brought a mere 163 winners but a much more satisfactory £47.49 profit. Cauthen was the only one of the top *thirty-three* jockeys to show a profit in this way. Blind allegiance to runners sent out by the leading trainer Michael Stoute over the same period would have lost £66.49, though following Henry Cecil's runners would have brought a gain of £50.43.

Bookmakers like backers to follow systems. Enough said.

Combination Bets

These are individual bets which combine two or more horses in a single wager: if one horse loses the whole bet is lost. They can be win or each way, and include:

Double

Combining two horses in different races. If the first wins, the winnings and stake go on to the second. A simple way of calculating the winnings on a double is to add one to each of the odds, multiply them, and subtract one from the total. A £5 double on horses which both win at 2–1 yields a return of £45: £40 winnings plus £5 stake, as the first win gives a return of £15, which then goes on the second horse at 2–1 and brings £30 winnings plus £15 stake: £45. (A bookmaker will not accept a double bet calculated in this way on two events where the first result has a direct bearing on the second. The weekend before the 1989 Two Thousand Guineas the price for Nashwan for the Guineas was around 6–1, and he stood at a similar price for the Derby. But the price for the double was around 20–1, as victory in the first race would obviously have a very direct influence on his chance in the second.)

Treble

Combining three horses in different races. Again, add one to each of the winning odds, multiply them, and subtract one from the total to find the winnings. So a £5 treble on three horses which each win at 2–1 yields a return of £135: winnings of £130 plus the £5 stake.

Accumulator

Combining any number of horses to win different races, calculating the winnings in the same way as for a double or a treble. The old ITV Seven was a seven-horse accumulator: had your seven choices in a £5 accumulator all obliged at 2–1 you would have relieved your bookmaker of £10,930 in winnings.

Multiple Bets

These are ways of combining several horses in different sorts of bet. The names under which such bets go are simply a shorthand for a recognized menu of individual bets, so success does not depend on each horse winning. Multiple bets can be win or each way.

Patent

A wager combining three different horses in different races in seven separate bets – three singles, three doubles, and one treble. Thus if the horses are A, B and C, the Patent consists of:

singles: A
                B
                C

doubles: A with B
           A with C
           B with C

treble: A with B with C

A £1 win Patent will cost you £7; a £1 each-way Patent costs £14. Say you have a £1 win Patent on A, B and C and they all win at 2–1: your winnings are £6 (three £1 singles each winning at 2–1) plus £24 (three £1 doubles with each horse winning at 2–1) plus £26 (a £1 treble with each horse winning at 2–1): total winnings of £56. But if two of the horses win at 2–1 while the third horse loses, you would still make a profit. You win £4 (two £1 singles each winning at 2–1) plus £8 (one £1 double with each horse winning at 2–1): total winnings £12. But of your seven bets four (one single, two doubles, one treble) have lost, so your profit is £12 less £4: £8.

Yankee

A bet combining four different horses in different races in eleven bets (so a £1 win Yankee costs £11). The horses are connected in six doubles, four trebles and one four-horse accumulator. (A Lucky 15 is a fifteen-bet wager adding four singles to the eleven bets of the Yankee.)

Super Yankee

A bet combining five selections in ten doubles, ten trebles, five fourfolds and one five-horse accumulator – twenty-six bets. (Also known as a Canadian.)

Heinz

A bet combining six selections in fifty-seven bets: fifteen doubles, twenty trebles, fifteen fourfolds, six fivefolds and one six-horse accumulator.

Speciality Bets

These apply to just one race and include:

Forecast

The Tote Dual Forecast involves giving the first and second horses in either order. The Computer Straight Forecast is a betting shop wager which involves predicting the first two in correct order (so called because the dividend is calculated by computer).

Tricast

In handicaps of eight or more declared runners and no fewer than six actual runners, the punter must select the first three in correct order. Again, a computer declares the dividend.

Betting Coups

Lord George Bentinck pulled off a clever coup in the 1836 St Leger with Elis. In those days racehorses travelled to meetings on foot, and when Elis was known to be still in Goodwood – fifteen days' walk from Doncaster – a few days before the race, bookmakers pushed his price out. But Bentinck transported the horse to Yorkshire in only three days in a specially constructed horse box pulled by six post horses; Elis did his bit, winning by two lengths and landing a huge gamble for Bentinck.

Coups are very carefully contrived bets which involve a great deal of planning by the connections of the horse and others in the know, and can be divided broadly into two categories – the successful and the unsuccessful. The unsuccessful divide again into two further categories – the legal and the fraudulent. For it is rarely the case that a successful coup will turn out to have been brought about by illegal means: the success of a coup occurs when its perpetrators are paid out by the bookies, and at any sniff of illegality most bookmakers will withhold payment.

Usually a coup will be brought about by the horse being carefully prepared for a race in such a way that the bookmakers have a less accurate idea of its chance than those who are backing it, and will consequently let it be backed at an over-generous price. The history of the Turf is peppered with occasions when a massive amount of money had caused a dramatic reduction in the odds of a horse, such as Dorothy Paget's mediocre Tuppence in the 1933 Derby (see page 89). More successful bets in the Classics were on Talma II, who was backed down from 100–6 to 7–1 on the day of the 1951 St Leger, which he won by ten lengths, and on Tulyar, backed on the day of the 1952 Derby from 100–6 to 11–2 favourite: ridden by Charlie Smirke, he won by three quarters of a length from Gay Time. Two spectacular losing gambles in the Derby since the war involved Tudor Minstrel, backed as if defeat were out of the question to 7–4 on in 1947 (he finished fourth, as described on page 131), and Dancing Brave, who just failed to get to Shahrastani in 1986. But big bets are sometimes easier to land in smaller races: the famed professional punter Alex Bird landed one of the biggest bets of his career with Signification in a small race at Liverpool on Grand National Day, 1952: the horse won at 7–2, having opened in the betting at 100–6.

Certainly the coup which pushes against – and sometimes through – the bounds of legality is easier to pull off in a small race which will attract little attention, and the most sensational frauds of the post-war era have taken place in minor events. A horse named Francasal won a selling race at Bath on 16 July 1953 at 10–1, but investigations revealed that he had been switched for a 'ringer' – a horse of very similar appearance but markedly different ability, in this case a much faster animal named Santa Amaro. The main perpetrators of the affair were convicted and jailed. When Flockton Grey won a two-year-old maiden race at Leicester in March 1982 at 10–1 suspicions were aroused, not least because of the ease of his twenty-length victory: the horse turned out to be the three-year-old Good Hand. Again those who had masterminded the coup ended up in court, and Flockton Grey himself spent years in police custody: he was subsequently co-owned by Michael Aspel.

But perhaps the most ingenious coup attempted in recent years was the affair of Gay Future, who won the Ulverston Novices' Hurdle at Cartmel on 26 August 1974, Bank Holiday Monday. The essence of this intricate story is that an unnamed horse had been sent by the planners of the coup, based in Ireland, to the stables of trainer Anthony Collins at Troon in Scotland. Collins had entered a horse called Gay Future and another horse, Racionzer, in the race at Cartmel, and two other horses – Opera Cloak and Ankerwyke – in races at other courses on the same day and both starting within half an hour of the Cartmel race. On that Bank Holiday morning members of the syndicate who were staging the coup placed bets in a variety of betting shops in London on doubles connecting Gay Future with Opera Cloak or with Ankerwyke: doubles are deemed by bookmakers to be 'mugs' bets', and betting in small amounts in this manner would not have aroused suspicion. Meanwhile the 'real' Gay Future, who had been prepared for his race in Ireland, had been brought over the Irish Sea, swapped for the horse in Collins's charge, and sent off to Cartmel for the race. Neither Ankerwyke nor Opera Cloak reached the courses where they were supposed to be running (it transpired that they had never left their trainer's stable). When one leg of a double is a non-runner the bet becomes a single on the remaining horse, so a large amount of money was then running on Gay Future; but the 'blower' system which transmits off-course money to the course betting market was not operating to Cartmel that very busy Bank Holiday Monday (as the planners of the coup had cleverly been aware), and by the time the bookmakers realized what was afoot they could get his price down only by dispatching a representative to the course to bet on him there. But the bookies' man did not arrive in time. Before he had entered the paddock at Cartmel Gay Future's flanks had had soap flakes rubbed into them to give the impression that he was sweating freely and so put off on-course punters. The horse played his own part in the coup by strolling home fifteen lengths in front of his rivals at 10–1. Most of the betting shops who had taken the bets withheld payment, though some later regarded the matter as a legitimate coup and paid out. (The conspirators stood to win around £300,000.) The police launched a prosecution, and Collins and William Murphy, the Irish building contractor who was the main brain behind the coup, were convicted of conspiracy to defraud the bookmakers, and fined. Conflicting views were aired about whether the matter should have been brought to court; whatever the legality or illegality of the episode, the Gay Future affair was a coup of remarkable cunning and ingenuity.

Not a coup, but a nice little earner none the less. Mrs Kate Horgan shows her appreciation to her husband John's colt Tirol, who has just won the General Accident Two Thousand Guineas at Newmarket in May 1990 to land the family some substantial bets. 'We've got a lot of dough from this race,' said owner Horgan: 'It could be into six figures.'

THE RACE

Graham Goode has commentated on horse racing for two decades, both on television and through racecourse commentaries for Racecourse Technical Services. He has called his own colours to victory in a flat race, a hurdle and a steeplechase.

The essence of racing is the race itself – the horses being urged on by their jockeys, stretching for the winning post at thirty to forty miles per hour. The race commentator's job is to describe this, the sharp end of the action.

The commentator leads a lonely existence, perched in a commentary box on top of the grandstand (though at Sandown Park the position is actually in the stand, high at the back). My only method of contact with Channel Four colleagues is the umbilical cord of sound which goes from my headset to the scanner van from where the programme is directed. The good point about being the commentator is that I am invariably at the very best vantage point from which to describe the action.

In order to be able to recognize individual runners at a distance and at speed I have to do my homework. I write down on a large sketch pad the names of the horses, and underneath the names of their jockeys; I then draw in with a felt pen the colours of the owners. In the Flat season I get through a lot of maroon and blue pens, for these are the prevailing colours of Sheikh Mohammed and his brothers Hamdan Al-Maktoum and Maktoum Al-Maktoum: it is very rare indeed for an afternoon to go by without at least one runner going to post in those colours, and it would be an easy job if I could just say 'Maktoum' instead of Algaihabane or Ghatanfar or Almadaniyah or Elmajarrah.

Each horse's name clearly means something to someone. I seem to recall an English owner some while ago whose naming of his horses indicated his growing frustration with the pursuit. The first, called Kind Hearted, was of little account. The owner then forked out for a well-bred horse he named Tender Hearted, but this raced without distinction, so the third was named Half Hearted. Again no success, and the owner's disillusionment was expressed when naming his fourth undistinguished purchase: Hoof Hearted.

During the running of the race I alternate between looking at a monitor and looking through my binoculars (a pair of hand-held West German Zeiss Dialyt 8 × 56 – purchased after El Gran Senor's victory in the General Accident Two Thousand Guineas in 1984), as I have to watch all aspects of the race, and not just the action on the screen. The other great tool of my trade is the form book, which I consult to find out who are the front runners and who might come with a late flourish, for I have to anticipate what could happen, and expect the unexpected.

It can be very pleasant in summer, up in my isolated perch on the roof. But there are also problems. On Newmarket's July Course the beautiful beech trees which make the situation so very attractive are sprayed so that the insects don't fall into the Pimms: but they are only sprayed to a certain level, and the little bugs crawl above this line and make for the commentary box. So if you go to the July Meeting you can always spot the commentator: he's the one who in the height of summer is dressed for winter and is carrying two cans of flyspray along with his binoculars!

Graham Goode

Previous pages:
Tattenham Corner, Epsom.

Before the Race

On arrival at the course the runners are taken into the racecourse stables. Each horse has a passport which identifies it very precisely by its markings (in order to avoid substitution of a 'ringer' – a horse of similar appearance but dissimilar ability) and certifies that it has received all the required vaccinations: without this passport the horse may not enter the course, and even with it may be subjected to examination by a vet to check that it is who the passport says it is. After its morning feed the horse will not eat again until after the race, and will not be allowed to drink from about four hours before the race.

The stable lad settles the horse in its box and gives it a final grooming – often with an eye to the award for the best turned-out horse which is judged on appearance in the parade ring for some races. About half an hour before the race it is taken into the pre-parade ring, where it will be led round to await being saddled by the trainer.

Meanwhile the jockey has arrived in the changing room, where he will change into the colours of the owner (which are kept by the trainer). The jockey's valet will have brought along the saddle (or saddles) which he will be using for that afternoon's racing, and to ensure that the jockey and saddle are at the correct weight for the race will, if necessary, put lead weights into the pockets of the weight-cloth which the horse will carry underneath the saddle. The jockey will check on the changing-room scales that he is at the required weight, and then, when signalled by a weighing room official, reports to the Clerk of the Scales to be weighed out for the race, by sitting with his equipment on the scales for confirmation by the Clerk that he is at the correct weight. Included in the rider's weight when weighing out (and later when weighing in) are everything that the horse is to carry except the jockey's skull cap (which is exempt from the weighing in order to remove the temptation to wear a dangerously light helmet), whip, bridle, and anything to be worn on the horse's legs: so what is weighed out is the jockey, his clothing (though an allowance is made for a jump jockey's back protector), saddle and number-cloth and weight-cloth, and (if applicable) the horse's breast-girth (the strap or straps which go round the front of the horse to keep the saddle in place) and blinkers. If the correct weight is registered, the saddle with its related equipment is then passed to the trainer (or his representative) who will go off to saddle the horse.

The trainer saddles the horse in a box by the pre-parade ring, finishing off with a sponge round its eyes and in its mouth, and then the lad leads it off to the parade ring proper.

The jockeys' changing room: Peter Scudamore pulls his riding silks on over his back protector at Devon and Exeter racecourse. On the left is master valet John Buckingham, who had his own moment of glory as a jockey, taking Foinavon through the bedlam at the twenty-third fence to win the 1967 Grand National at 100–1.

In the Paddock, and Going Down

The parade ring, or paddock, is where the horse is formally displayed to the spectators before the race. In contrast to practice in many other

The jockey's valet is one of the most important backroom boys of racing. He transports from meeting to meeting most of the equipment belonging to the jockeys who hire him (and who will pay him around 10 per cent of their riding fees for that meeting): boots, breeches, saddles, weight-cloths, and so on. He prepares this equipment (supplemented by the owner's colours, which are brought to the racecourse by the trainer) in the changing room before each race, bearing in mind what equipment each jockey will require for each race (what size saddle, for instance) and how much weight will need to be put into the weight-cloth. He will assist the jockeys in dressing, making running repairs, supplying extra equipment which a young or forgetful jockey might not have, and generally ensuring that events in the jockeys' changing room – a scene of sometimes manic activity into which even trainers may not venture – run smoothly. Most top jockeys leave all their equipment with their valet, keeping with them only their own helmets and back protectors; at the end of the day's racing the valet is responsible for cleaning it. The next day, whether at the same course or at some other venue, it will be all ready and waiting for them when they arrive in the changing room.

countries – notably the USA – horses spend a good deal of time in the parade ring at British courses, and paddock inspection is one of the key ways of assessing the condition of a runner.

Although to an extent equine beauty, as with human, is in the eye of the beholder, it helps to be aware of the paddock characteristics of some horses, lest their demeanour before the race prove off-putting. That superb hurdler and chaser Night Nurse, for instance, always seemed half asleep as he walked round the paddock, though he would wake up soon enough in the race; with the 1990 Grand National and Whitbread hero Mr Frisk, well known to be a nervous individual, punters would worry were he not in a lather of sweat. Generally jumpers become much more familiar to racegoers and television viewers than Flat horses, and paddock observers will know what to expect from the appearance of these old campaigners. With less well known horses it is useful to know what to look for.

What takes the fancy in a horse will always contain an element of the indefinable, and its fitness and well-being in the paddock must be judged on an overall impression. There are several key elements to a good conformation in a horse. Look for an intelligent and alert demeanour, with a bold eye, big ears pointing slightly inwards (though 'lop ears' that flop forwards are often a sign of stamina and genuineness); the carriage of the head should be high, and the neck in good proportion to body size and length. The shoulder should be well sloped back to drive the forelegs to maximum effect, and the chest and girth area deep and wide to provide plenty of room for a big heart and good lungs. The back should be short and strong, and the quarters, which drive the hind legs and provide the real power, should be well-muscled and rounded. It can pay, too, to look for a few more specific signs.

Sweating Up

Sweating up before a race is not necessarily a bad sign; it depends on the nature of the sweat. (It also depends, of course, on the nature of the weather, as a horse is much more likely to sweat when it is hot.) Sweating around the ears or eyes is not a good sign, as it suggests agitated nervousness. Nor is 'frothy' sweating. But sweating on the neck can augur well, often indicating keen anticipation.

The Walk

A horse which walks well will gallop well, and the horse striding out round the paddock will probably stride out well in the race. A sign of a good walker is 'tracking up': when the hind foot overlaps or falls in front of the hoofprint left by the front foot. Such niceties are not easy to spot on television, but it is simple enough to see whether a horse moves easily and loosely at the walk, rather than taking short, mincing strides. Many horses in the paddock bob up and down as they are led round: this is usually a sign of general keenness. The horse that will not be led quietly round is showing signs of irritation. Horses in the paddock tend to be silent, but unraced or inexperienced two-year-olds may well whinny to each other in alarm at their strange surroundings.

EQUIPMENT

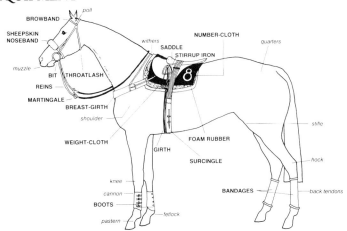

The equipment which a horse carries in a race varies according to a number of factors, including the preferences of its trainer, the physique and temperament of the horse and the weight it is set to carry. The drawing above (on which a few of the most commonly mentioned points of the horse are given in italic type) illustrates the basic equipment. The **bridle** is normally made of leather, though the part of the reins which the jockey will hold is usually coated in rubber to improve grip. In theory the **sheepskin noseband** will encourage a horse to look further ahead, stretch out its feet and keep its head down, but in practice it is used primarily on account of stable custom. (Another common variation on the standard bridle is the fitting of the Australian cheeker, the rubber strip which runs down the horse's nose and is attached to the bit to keep it high in the mouth.) The **martingale** in this case consists of two metal rings connected by a leather strap: it keeps the reins in place and prevents them from going over the horse's head. On the horse's back will be placed: a sheet of **foam rubber** (or sometimes a piece of chamois leather); the **weight-cloth** (if needed), a pad incorporating pockets into which are inserted metal strips which bring the weight of the jockey and equipment up to the required level; the **number-cloth**; and the **saddle** itself. Most jockeys have several saddles, choosing for each ride one appropriate to the weight to be carried: a modern racing saddle can weigh as little as one pound, though a jockey with no weight problem will probably ride on one weighing four or six pounds. (Saddles are usually made of leather – sometimes with a sheepskin-covered seat – but very light saddles may be made of felt.) The saddle is secured in place on the horse's back by the **girth**, which is buckled under the flaps each side of the saddle, and by the **surcingle**, the extra strap which goes right round the horse's belly and over the top of the saddle. Further security is afforded by a **breast-girth** (illustrated in the drawing) or a **breastplate** (straps attached to each side of the saddle which are joined to the girth by another strap passing between the forelegs). Leather **boots** are common with jumpers, as they afford protection from knocks and cuts when taking the obstacles. **Bandages** offer some protection but are mainly used as support (like the strapping on an athlete's knee).

Blinkers are fitted to a horse to help it concentrate during a race, as they reduce its range of vision from 180 degrees to around 30 degrees and thus demand that it look straight ahead. They are sometimes known as the 'rogue's badge' on account of the untrustworthiness which their use implies, but plenty of perfectly genuine horses have run regularly in blinkers. By helping the horse to keep its mind on the job they can bring about a remarkable transformation in performance, and it is often worth taking notice of any horse running in blinkers for the first time.

A **visor** is a pair of blinkers with a slit cut in each of the shields: this allows for a small amount of lateral vision, so that the horse can see other horses alongside.

A **hood** leaves the eyes clear but covers the ears: some horses are affected by noise. (A horse with no or very defective vision in one eye may wear an **eyeshield**, similar to a pair of blinkers but with one eye completely covered over. Some very good racehorses have had only one eye, among them The Dancer, third to Bireme in the 1980 Oaks.)

All racecourses impose limits on the number of horses which can safely be accommodated on that course for races over each distance. (On the Flat these are often dictated by the width of the course at the start: obviously a narrow course can accommodate fewer runners in starting stalls than a wide one.) If the number of declared runners exceeds the safety limit there are three possible courses of action:

Eliminations: in handicaps, horses are eliminated from the lowest weight up until the maximum number of runners is left; in Pattern races, elimination starts with the horse lowest in the Jockey Club ratings.

Ballots: for a wide range of races the field is thinned by balloting out the required number of runners, though exemptions are usually allowed for certain horses (such as previous winners).

Division: the race is divided into two (or more) races.

┌─WALKOVER──────────

A walkover is a race with only one runner. The jockey must weigh out and weigh in, following the standard procedures, but does not have to cover the entire distance of the race: the horse simply has to be ridden past the Judge's box. (The point-to-pointer Rossa Prince has the unusual distinction of failing to win a walkover: at Tweseldown in May 1990 he bolted while being saddled for his solitary effort and could not be retrieved by the time he was due in the parade ring, so was disqualified.)

Condition

A fit horse will give off the same air of muscularity and power as a human athlete. A shiny, well-groomed coat advertises its general health, and it is in the horse's quarters that fitness is most apparent. A useful check is to watch a horse from behind: if it is well muscled up around the tail it will display 'hard marks' – grooves either side of the muscle. An unfit horse will appear much flabbier. Irregular twitching of the ears and swishing of the tail tend to be signs of an over-tense horse, while dull eyes, listless carriage of the neck and tired ears suggest that it is not tense enough. A tubby horse will not be fit, and a horse which appears 'tucked up' or 'run up light' (lean and ribby) behind the saddle may have 'gone over the top'.

'Over the top' is where a horse is deemed to have gone when it has had too much racing for the season, and although this can sometimes be diagnosed before a race through paddock symptoms of edginess or listlessness, more often it only becomes apparent after the horse has failed to show its true form in the race. How to interpret paddock appearance depends a great deal on the time of the year and the stage of the season. A horse grows a winter coat, so cannot be expected to be a picture of gleaming health on a cold day in February. The condition of early runners on the Flat in the spring will depend on the nature of the previous winter, as most horses (especially fillies and mares) will not thrive until they have felt the sun on their backs. Towards the end of the Flat season certain horses will obviously be starting to 'train off' – they lose their form and are in need of a break. During the closing weeks of the Flat season a horse will start to 'go in its coat' – grow its winter coat – and although fillies tend to lose form as their coats change it rarely makes a difference to colts.

The prologue to most big races is the parade, when the field is led past the stands to give those who are not able to get to the paddock the opportunity to study the horses. Whether there is a parade or not, the horses will canter past the stands to the start, and this is the chance to supplement paddock inspection with a close-up of the horse in action. Much can be learned from the way the horse goes down. If it strides out well on the way to post – 'pokes its toe' – it is at ease on the ground. But a horse who moves scratchingly ('goes down short') is clearly not enjoying the going – and is going to enjoy it much less when galloping at racing speed. It is folly, though, to assume that any horse moving slowly to the start is feeling the ground: another explanation might be that the animal is a hard puller, and the jockey is taking him down gently to avoid his running away. Sometimes a horse is so highly strung that the Stewards of the meeting give permission for it to be taken down all by itself in advance of the other runners: Michael Stoute's decision to have Shadeed break away from the parade of the 1985 Two Thousand Guineas – without permission – incurred the wrath of the Newmarket Stewards, who fined him for transgressing the rules, but it minimized the nervous strain on the horse by abbreviating the preliminaries, and Shadeed duly repaid Stoute's thoughtfulness in beating Bairn by a head. Where races of that magnitude can be won and lost by such minute distances anything which helps keep the horse on good terms with itself and therefore ready to give of its best must be considered. The parade for a race such as the Derby puts a great strain on the young and inexperienced horses who take part, but adds immeasurably to the sense of occasion for the racegoers and viewers.

At the Start

Once arrived at the start, the runners come under the jurisdiction of the Starter, who checks them against the list of runners and riders which he has obtained from the Clerk of the Scales, and calls the roll to remind each rider (in a Flat race) of his draw. The horses will then walk round for a few minutes to settle after the canter to the start and to have their girths adjusted: a horse will usually blow itself out when its saddle is being put on, and by the time it has reached the start the jockey will need to see that the girths are tightened.

All Flat races must start from stalls or, if for some reason stalls are not possible or not practical, by the Starter dropping a flag. (Flag starts are often used for long-distance races, where the importance of all the runners starting evenly is less acute than in shorter races.) National Hunt races are started by a starting gate – normally the type in which an elastic tape is drawn across the course and released upwards by a lever controlled by the Starter – or flag. For a Flat race the horses are loaded into the stalls, odd numbers first, then even; horses which are known to dislike a prolonged wait in the stalls may be put in last, at the discretion of the Starter, but once a horse has been loaded in it cannot be released until the front gates are opened by the Starter. No horse may be held in the stalls nor started from outside the stalls, but it is now allowed for a horse of exceptional length not to have the rear gate of the stall shut behind him but to make use instead of a specially designed strap which clips round the open rear gates, thus allowing the horse to stand comfortably in the stalls. Outsize horses owe this modification to the protests of a very big and long three-year-old named Scallywag, who could not be persuaded to enter the stalls for the 1976 King Edward VII Stakes at Royal Ascot; his trainer Bruce Hobbs devised the strap to replace the rear doors, and Scallywag ran third to Crow in the St Leger.

The teams of stalls handlers are supplied by Racecourse Technical Services and undertake their uniquely awkward job with skill and sympathy. If a horse is reluctant to enter its stall they will try various ways of persuading it – including enticing it with a handful of fresh sweet grass – before resorting to the strong-arm tactics of getting a strap round the horse's backside and heaving it in. If the horse will still not co-operate they will try blindfolding it and walking it round to disorientate it so that it will not realize that it is being led up to the stalls. A horse which steadfastly refuses to enter the stalls is reported to the Stewards, and must take a stalls test before being allowed to race again. A horse which simply will not enter is left, and does not come under Starter's orders.

The condition of 'under Starter's orders', signalled by the raising of a white flag by the start, takes effect as soon as the Starter is satisfied that the field is ready to go – so that in the case of a stalls start the horses are normally under orders for no more than a couple of seconds before

┌─ **THE STARTER** ─────────

In the days before starting stalls, the Starter was able to ruin a race by letting the field go before all the horses were in a line, or allowing an enterprising jockey to steal a flying start. That can still happen in jump racing (the starts of which are often accompanied by a vociferous debate between jockeys and Starter about whether the field is ready to go), but the use of stalls for flat races should ensure a level start for all. The Starter, who is employed by the Jockey Club, makes sure that all the horses are at the start, that they start (if appropriate) from the correct draw, and that the starting process goes as smoothly as possible. He can order the exclusion from the race of an unruly horse, and can report any rider guilty of misconduct at the start to the Stewards of the meeting. In between races he will return to the weighing room to witness the weighing out.

Any race which is started before its advertised time is void.

Under Starter's orders: Michael Sayers about to send the field on its way at Sandown Park in April 1989.

Although every horse in a race must run on its merits, it is perfectly legitimate for the connections of a horse to run another horse (usually but not necessarily in the same ownership) as a pacemaker, to ensure that the race is run at a true and sensible pace which will suit the connections' major contender. Some horses advertise latent ability through the pacemaking role: Osborne nearly caused the ultimate embarrassment at Hurst Park in 1954 when the previous year's St Leger winner Premonition, for whom Osborne had been setting the gallop, only just got by him to win by a short head in a controversial finish which saw the pacemaker bumped and squeezed and certainly the moral victor. Riboson, ridden by Jimmy Lindley, was the pacemaker for Bustino in the 1974 St Leger and did his job so well that not only did Bustino win the Classic but Riboson stayed on to take third place in his own right; and the following year Bustino nearly benefited again in spectacular style from the use of pacemakers when Highest and Kinglet successively maintained a blistering gallop for him in his King George VI and Queen Elizabeth Diamond Stakes struggle with Grundy. The primary role for Deploy in the Budweiser Irish Derby in 1990 was to act as a pacemaker for his stable companion Quest For Fame. But the Derby winner ran below his best and Deploy kept going wonderfully well all the way up the straight, headed only by Salsabil in the closing stages to be beaten three quarters of a length.

they are released. In a flag- or gate-started race a horse may become unruly after the field is under orders and cause a delay – a nerve-racking time for punters, as all bets stand as soon as the field is under orders, whereas backers of a horse which is withdrawn before coming under orders have their money returned. (Many people, including John McCririck, feel that the rule whereby bets stand as soon as the field is under orders is unfair, pointing to the injustice suffered by backers of that infuriating steeplechaser Vodkatini who lost their money on the occasions when he whipped round as the race started and took no part.)

Some 100 yards down the course from the start stands a man with a red flag. His role is to wave the runners down should the Starter signal to him that the start was false – say because a fault in the stalls mechanism caused some of the stalls not to open. It is not easy to pull up a racehorse in full flight and false starts can cause confusion and pandemonium. At the start of the 1986 Portland Handicap at Doncaster the stalls were damaged and the race had to be started by flag. It is one thing to start a field of sedate jumpers or stayers by flag, quite another to dispatch by this method twenty-three sprinters all keyed up to hurtle five and a half furlongs up the Doncaster straight. Two false starts ensued – after the first of which five runners completed the entire course and had to be withdrawn: the Starter's anguished cry as the field swept off was well picked up by the Channel Four microphones: 'Come back, you buggers!'

Reading the Race

There are three main ways of watching a race. One is simply to enjoy the spectacle, with its colour, noise and excitement. The second is to concentrate all your attention on the horse you've backed, which is fine if your choice is involved in the finish and even finer if it wins, but can distract you from the great events taking shape at the head of the field. The third is to try to 'read' the race, to interpret what happens during the race in order correctly to use the information gained on some future occasion. Race-reading is a difficult art, and the level of difficulty varies according to the nature of the race, the number of runners, the course, the pace, and various other factors, but it is a skill which can be very profitably – and very enjoyably – deployed.

The most obvious way of turning race-reading to good use is in spotting one of the beaten horses running a particularly encouraging race, thus suggesting that its performance will improve (this would be 'one for the notebook'). So a horse in a race over one mile might appear to have difficulty in keeping up with the pace in the early stages and fail to get into a challenging position, but sustain his pace in the closing stages ('run on'). This suggests that a longer distance will be to his liking, and he may be worth supporting next time out if the race is over one and a quarter miles or further. The point is that not everybody might have noticed his performance in the earlier race, and you may be able to back the horse at good odds.

There are several factors to take into account in forming your analysis of the action:

Pace

A 'truly run' race is one in which the runners maintain a good speed from the start, depending on the distance of the race and the going. Sprint races are almost invariably truly run, for what is the point of dawdling in a sprint? But even big races can be run at a false pace: the runners in the 1989 General Accident One Thousand Guineas set off at a very slow rate for a mile race at Newmarket, because none of the seven jockeys in the race wanted to make the pace (each in the belief that his horse needed to come from behind). Walter Swinburn on Musical Bliss took the initiative by sending his mount into the lead and it paid off, but a false pace is often the excuse for a beaten horse. Whatever the distance, a race which starts off at a crawl can develop into a sprint, and thus the form may be suspect. Similarly, a race can be run at a suicidally fast pace: the 1987 King George VI Rank Chase at Kempton Park saw Desert Orchid and Beau Ranger set off at a scorching gallop: it may have been exciting to watch, but they both ran out of puff long before the straight, leaving Nupsala to come through and take the race.

Distances

It is generally felt that a race where all the runners finish very close to one another is unlikely to be a very good race in terms of the quality of its contestants – they can't *all* be brilliant, so they're probably all mediocre. (This does not, of course, apply to handicaps, which are specifically aimed at bringing about a bunched finish.) But a false pace naturally can distort the meaning of the finishing distances, as a race run at a dawdle gives less opportunity for the field to get strung out: the last horse in the 1989 One Thousand Guineas was only a little over four lengths behind the winner.

Style of Running

Horses run races in different ways, and have preferences for certain sorts of going, for left-hand or right-hand tracks, for front-running or being held up. A knowledge of the preferences of the horses in a race will help you deduce whether that race is being run to suit a particular horse. And you can tell if a horse is unhappy on the going – most obviously when the ground is too firm, when it will seem unwilling to stride out properly (and is said to be 'feeling the ground'), and may be hanging its head to one side or keeping it high. Such a horse may 'change its legs' – that is, adjust its galloping action. A horse will 'lead' with one of its forelegs, the last of its legs to strike the ground during the cycle of the stride. On a left-hand track the horse should lead with its near foreleg (that is, its left front leg), and if it is uneasy on the ground it will change to leading with the other leg, especially when under pressure towards the end of the race. A horse with a 'round' action lifts its knees high during the stride and is usually better suited by soft ground. Desert Orchid notwithstanding, most horses are happier running left-handed: from early days they are led on the left, saddled from the left, lunged to the left, and so build up an inclination to go to the left. (Significantly, almost all racetracks in the USA are left-handed.)

A horse which is 'green' shows signs of inexperience. Horses race on

---

THE JUDGE

The Judge, who is employed by the Stewards of the Jockey Club, must occupy the Judge's box (situated in a raised position well back from the winning line) at the time the horses pass the winning post. (The winner is determined according to which horse gets any part of its head – excluding the ears – past the post first.) The Judge must announce his decision immediately – or after consulting the evidence of the photo-finish camera – and his decision is final unless an objection is lodged or a Stewards' Enquiry called and the placings are subsequently altered. If a mistake does occur, it can be corrected by the Judge up to five days after the race, or by the Stewards of the Jockey Club within fourteen days.

The Judge's other main responsibility is to declare the distances between the horses who finish the race. He bases these on the evidence of the photo-finish strip, and in Britain is confined to the following: dead heat; short head; head; neck; half a length; three quarters of a length; one length; one and a half lengths; two, two and a half, three, three and a half lengths; four, five, six, eight, ten, twelve, fifteen, twenty, twenty-five and thirty lengths. Anything over thirty lengths is a 'distance'.

Between races the Judge will familiarize himself with the jockeys' colours in the next race by watching the weighing out and by studying the runners in the paddock.

The greatest ever number of runners in a Flat race was fifty-eight, in the Lincolnshire Handicap at Lincoln on 13 March 1948.

Most falls are caused by the horse misjudging when to take off: too soon and it may not be able to clear the jump cleanly, too late and it will not have time to get enough spring into its leap. Either way it will clout the obstacle. Another common cause of falls is overjumping: the horse jumps too extravagantly and slithers onto its belly on landing. (A horse whose nose touches the ground as it attempts to balance itself on clearing a jump is said to have 'pecked on landing'.) Should a jockey part company with his horse he may remount (and be assisted in so doing) as long as he gets on again at the place where contact was severed: the last remounted horse to have been placed in the Grand National was Loving Words in 1982 (jockey Richard Hoare had been dislodged at the fourth last).

the Flat very early in their lives – well before they are mature – and it is not surprising that some of them, however well trained, do not immediately realize what is required of them on the racecourse. The most common form of greenness is an inability to run straight and true to the line: the green horse may be distracted by the crowd and generally bewildered by what is happening around him, and wander off a straight course. This is why a jockey will often keep an inexperienced horse at full throttle even though he is winning his race easily, for the race is an education for the horse and he will benefit from being shown how to stretch out and gallop home.

A word about the whip. The use of the whip has become a controversial issue, and the Jockey Club lays down guidelines for jockeys and Stewards to prevent its excessive use. In the hands of a good jockey the whip is an essential tool, necessary for keeping the horse running straight, and for driving it to an extra effort in a tight finish. Most horses will veer away from the whip, so if in a finish the horse is drifting to the left the jockey will use it on his left side to correct the wandering: the ability to pull the whip through from one hand to the other in a split second is a vital component of jockeyship. Usually the jockey will give the horse a couple of smacks with the whip to get it to its maximum pace and will then wave the whip – without hitting the horse – to keep encouraging it to the line. Some horses resent its application and will not run on (swishing the tail is a common sign of disagreement with the rider's method), and many horses simply give their best without the rider having any recourse to it at all: Bustino's heroic effort in the 1975 King George VI and Queen Elizabeth Diamond Stakes finish against Grundy was a fine example of a horse running as fast as he possibly could under a wise jockey (Joe Mercer) who knew that the whip would not make the slightest difference. To use the whip during such an effort could distract and unbalance the horse: better to stick with 'hands and heels' to keep the horse going.

Taking the Jumps

A jump race adds an extra dimension to race-reading, as the decisions which jockeys have to make when putting their horses at the obstacles will affect the outcome dramatically. If two horses are going together into the final fence a good jump can win the race, but an inexperienced jumper may not be able to take off well before the fence in order to gain the advantage, and his jockey may allow him to 'fiddle' it and then ride a finish once the fence has been safely negotiated. But if he is well in the lead at the last the jockey may just ask the horse to 'pop' the fence in order to ensure his safe arrival on the other side. The key to clean jumping is for the jockey to be able to 'see a stride' well before the fence and adjust his horse at the approach so that he will jump it efficiently.

No two races are alike, and often arguments can be made that had the race been run differently the outcome would have been different. But however the race is run, the moment of truth is always the winning post – or rather, the invisible line stretching across the course from the winning post, presided over by the Judge, who has the invaluable aid of the photo-finish camera (see page 42).

RIDING OFFENCES

As amended in March 1990, the controversial Rule 153(i) in the Jockey Club Rules of Racing states:

When a horse or its rider has caused interference

(a) by accident in any part of a Flat race or a National Hunt Flat Race or after the penultimate obstacle in a Steeple Chase or Hurdle race the horse shall, on an objection under Rule 170(iv) [the rule concerning disputes and objections] be placed behind the horse or horses with which it has interfered or placed last if the Stewards are satisfied that the interference improved the placing of the horse causing the interference. If they are not so satisfied they shall overrule the objection and order that the placings shall remain unchanged.

(b) by careless riding in any part of the race the horse shall, on an objection under Rule 170(iv), be disqualified or placed behind the horse or horses with which it has interfered or placed last except that the Stewards may order that the placings shall remain unchanged if the Judge has placed the horse behind the horse or horses with which it has interfered.

(c) by reckless riding or intentionally in any part of a race the horse shall, on an objection under Rule 170(iv), be disqualified.

Within the context of this rule, 'reckless' means without regard to the consequences of a riding manoeuvre and 'careless' means failing to take reasonable steps to avoid causing interference, or causing it through misjudgement or inattention. ('Improper' riding covers other misconduct and improper use of the whip.)

The rule is highly controversial because disqualification of a horse whose jockey has been convicted of a riding offence penalizes not only the jockey but its owner and trainer and – of course – those who have backed it. The most hotly debated applications of the rule in recent years have been the 1980 Two Thousand Guineas (see page 183) and the 1988 Ascot Gold Cup, in which Royal Gait, the winner by five lengths, was disqualified after his jockey Cash Asmussen was adjudged guilty of careless riding after an incident as the field entered the straight: El Conquistador, who had set a blistering gallop for a two and a half mile race, was back-pedalling and was bumped by the rapidly improving Royal Gait. El Conquistador's jockey Tony Clark was unseated, and the Stewards suspended Asmussen for seven days for careless riding. Many observers felt that the interference was accidental – in which case Royal Gait should have kept the race. The nub of the controversy is that the rule merges a disciplinary matter (riding) and the equity of the result, and in the opinion of many experts these are separate matters and should be dealt with separately. The issue provoked fierce debate again in July 1990 when Lydia Pearce, having won the Pigot Diamond Ladies' Stakes on If Memory Serves, had her mount placed last after hampering New Mexico (who finished fifth) directly after the start. New Mexico was brought into the money by being placed fourth, and Mrs Pearce suspended for four days.

RUNNING TERMS

Some of the terms regularly used to describe horses in running may require explanation. A horse is **on the bridle** (or **on the bit**) when it is going well within itself and is not being pushed along by its jockey: so a measure of the ease of Sea Bird II's win in the 1965 Derby was that he won without coming off the bit. **Off the bridle** (or **off the bit**) means that the horse is being asked to make an effort: a horse in this situation is sometimes referred to as being **let down**, and it is being **scrubbed along** when the jockey is pushing away in order to encourage it to go faster. Horses' heads move up and down as they run, and a finish deemed to be **on the nod** is one which is so close that the winner will be the horse whose nose happens to be in the right position on the line. (Racecourse and television commentators often employ a variety of phrases from other pursuits – 'flat to the boards', 'coming with a wet sail', 'nip and tuck', and so on.)

The primary duty of the Clerk of the Scales is to weigh out the jockeys before the race – when each jockey presents himself to the Clerk with his equipment, sits on the scales (having declared any overweight) and has confirmed that his horse will be carrying the correct allotted weight – and weigh him back in after the race. Should a rider fail to weigh in or weigh in illegally lighter than he weighed out, it is the duty of the Clerk of the Scales to lodge an objection. But the Clerk's responsibilities go further. He is in overall charge of the racecourse number-board, on which will be displayed the rider of each horse in the race, the draw (in a Flat race), allowances claimed, overweight, the wearing of blinkers or a visor, any change of colours, and other relevant official information regarding that race. At the end of each day's racing he makes a return to the *Racing Calendar* Office giving details of the weights carried in every race, of which horses failed to complete the course, and why, of complaints to and decisions of the Stewards, of all fines inflicted, and of all horses sold or claimed.

After the Race

The runners pull up and are reunited with their stable lads. The placed horses are led into the unsaddling enclosure, while the others are unsaddled away from the main ring, and the post-mortem starts. The jockey Paul Barton has told how he informed a trainer on whose horse he had just finished tailed off in a novices' chase that the horse would be fine when he matured: he needed more time. 'How much time does he need?' asked the trainer: 'he's already eleven.' The reasons for defeat which jockeys give owners and trainers are legion, and some of them are accurate. But the essence of racing is that hope springs eternal, and this hope must be kept alive.

The jockeys dismount and return to the Clerk of the Scales to weigh in. All jockeys who have ridden in a race may be required to weigh in (unless prevented by injury), at the discretion of the Clerk, and the jockeys of all placed horses must do so: a placed horse whose jockey, for whatever reason, fails to weigh in will be disqualified. So will a jockey whose weight at weighing in is different from that at weighing out, though a jockey is allowed to fall one pound below the weighed-out weight to take into account the possible slimming effects of his exertions. A jockey who weighs in at two pounds or more *over* the weighed-out weight is reported to the Stewards. The weight carried by a horse in a race is of crucial importance, and discrepancies between weighing out and weighing in are very serious. In order to prevent any switching of weighable items, the Jockey Club Rules stipulate that 'if a rider touches, except accidentally, any person or thing other than his own equipment before weighing in his horse shall, on an objection under Rule 170(iv), be disqualified, unless he can satisfy the Stewards that he was justified by extraordinary circumstances.' It is for this reason that triumphant jockeys are not in the habit of euphorically embracing the other connections on dismounting.

If a jockey wishes to lodge an objection over some incident in the race, he does so to the Clerk of the Scales on returning to the weighing room.

If all the placed riders weigh in correctly and there is no objection by a jockey nor any Stewards' Enquiry, the announcement 'weighed in' is made, and the result stands. At least, it stands as far as the immediate settlement of bets is concerned. If any prohibited substance is found in the horse's specimen he will be disqualified subsequently.

The horses are led away. The winner will usually have to offer a urine specimen (or, if the horse can't produce one, a blood specimen) for sending off to the Horseracing Forensic Laboratory in Newmarket (other runners may be subjected to a routine sampling on the direction of the Stewards). They are then washed down and returned to their horseboxes for the journey home.

Meanwhile the human element takes in any prize-giving ceremony and moves off, either to prepare for the next race or to slip into the bar for celebration or commiseration. A few, of course, will be subjected to the attentions of Brough Scott or Derek Thompson . . .

EIGHT GREAT RACES

What makes a race linger on in the memory, sending you searching for the video or compelling you to describe it to friends in the bar after a day on the course years after the event? A bravely fought finish, a particularly brilliant or courageous performance by horse or jockey, a controversial result, the exhilaration of landing a gamble or of witnessing a group of really top-class horses battle it out – all or any of these can do it. The Channel Four Racing team have between them witnessed many thousands of races, but each of the eight described here was something special.

Victoria Cup
Hurst Park, 29 April 1961

Nowadays the Victoria Cup is just another good handicap run at Ascot, but in the early 1960s this competitive seven-furlong race was one of the big betting events of the early part of the Flat season. The 1961 contest was the penultimate running to be held at Hurst Park, the popular course by the River Thames near Hampton Court which closed in 1962, and a field of twenty-one went to post. The names of some of the jockeys summon up memories of a bygone era: Peter Robinson, Eddie Cracknell, Harry Carr, Tommy Gosling, Brian Jago, Duncan Keith, Doug Smith, Scobie Breasley, Jimmy Lindley, Eph Smith, Tommy Carter, Ray Reader, Willie Snaith. But Lester Piggott, Joe Mercer, Geoff Lewis and the twenty-year-old Bobby Elliott also had rides: it wasn't so long ago. Favourite at 11–2 was Honeymoor, who had carried 9 stone 1 pound into third place in the Lincolnshire Handicap the previous month. Bass Rock, ridden by Peter Robinson (who died in 1978), was second favourite: his previous race that season had been a victory in the Hylton Handicap at Liverpool (on the day that Nicolaus Silver won the Grand National). Three other horses beaten in the Lincoln sought consolation in the Victoria Cup, but it was Bass Rock, owned by Lord Rosebery and trained by Jack Jarvis at Newmarket, who swept through on the outside in the final furlong to score an easy victory by one and a half lengths over Fulshaw Cross, with Welsh Rake third and joint top-weight Nice Guy running on to take fourth, two necks behind the second. The favourite Honeymoor never reached the front rank and finished well down the field. Then as now the big handicaps took some solving.

One of those sublime races when your horse was always going to win. Coming into view from the dog-leg seven-furlong start the late Peter Robinson had Lord Rosebery's distinctive pink and yellow silks prominent on Bass Rock (backed from 10–1 to 7–1), and they duly cut down Fulshaw Cross inside the last furlong. Sadly Hurst Park closed a year later, and Bass Rock never raced again. Neither will ever be forgotten.

JOHN MCCRIRICK

Grand Steeplechase de Paris
Auteuil, 17 June 1962

I was lucky enough to be at Auteuil the day Fred Winter won the Grand Steeplechase de Paris on Mandarin. The bit broke in Mandarin's mouth after four fences so Fred had neither brakes nor steering for this unfamiliar twisting four-mile marathon, and then Mandarin broke down three fences from home – but, riding as only he could ride, Fred kept him in front to the end. Both horse and rider richly deserved the accolade Napoleon gave to Marshal Ney – the bravest of the brave.

JOHN OAKSEY

By the time the eleven-year-old Mandarin got to Auteuil in June 1962 he was approaching the end of a career which had marked him out as one of the best and toughest chasers of the post-war era. He had won both the Hennessy Gold Cup and the King George VI Chase twice, and in March 1962 had taken the Cheltenham Gold Cup, beating Fortria by a length. But nothing he had achieved matched what was to follow that steamy afternoon in the Bois de Boulogne . . .

Ridden by Fred Winter (who was severely debilitated by a stomach upset), Mandarin was 2–1 favourite for the Grand Steeplechase de Paris, in which he had finished second three years earlier. The race was unlike anything seen in Britain, being run over 6,500 metres of a track of extraordinary complexity – two separate figures-of-eight in different directions, then once round the outside – and negotiating obstacles a far cry from the jumps at Sandown or Cheltenham: a varied assortment including such curiosities as 'Le Bullfinch', a white post-and-rails topping a little bank. At the third fence the rubber bit in Mandarin's mouth snapped, leaving Fred Winter to face the remaining three and a half miles of twists and turns without any means of guiding the horse except pressure from his knees and the swing of his body: he had no contact with Mandarin's mouth, as the bit was dangling uselessly under the horse's neck. Showing the sportsmanship which characterizes steeplechase jockeys whatever their nationality, the French riders, aware of what was going on, helped Mandarin stay in the race by driving up onto his outside going round the bends. Just before the final turn Fred Winter had to wrench the horse away from running out, and at that point the tendons in Mandarin's old forelegs gave: he had broken down. But still he crashed through the last fence in front and set off for the line, relentlessly pursued by the French horse Lumino. They flashed past the post together, but Mandarin had held on, by a head.

Grand National Chase
Liverpool, 31 March 1973

'All around me people were jumping up and down with wild excitement, but I sat there like a sphinx, unable to move, trying to take in what was happening': Noel Le Mare's reaction to owning a Grand National winner sums up for me what was the most incredible race I've ever seen.

DEREK THOMPSON

The record books supply the facts: Red Rum won by three quarters of a length from Crisp, with L'Escargot twenty-five lengths back in third place and Spanish Steps fourth. And yet, a decade and a half later, the result of the 1973 Grand National still seems wrong. When we watch a recording of this famous race, we can hardly believe, at second Bechers or at the last fence or at the Elbow, that Crisp can possibly fail to win. But every time the recording tells the same story: Crisp, after a display of jumping and galloping the like of which had never been seen at Liverpool, was caught two strides from the post by a horse carrying twenty-three pounds less than he. Crisp was not, in a sense, unlucky; but never has a beaten horse so deserved to win.

Australian-bred Crisp was thought to be best at two and a half miles (the Grand National was nearly four and a half), and had won the Two Mile Champion Chase at Cheltenham in 1971 in scorching style. Although there were understandable doubts about his stamina, he was a high-class horse and his jumping was superb, and for the 1973 Grand

National (in which he carried top weight) he started 9–1 joint favourite with Red Rum, a scrapper of a horse who had been through several trainers and was now in the charge of the genial Ginger McCain, who mixed training with selling second-hand cars in Southport, not far from Aintree.

Crisp, ridden by Richard Pitman, was towards the head of affairs in the race practically from the start, and by Bechers Brook (the sixth fence) he had swung into the lead. Already it was an exhilarating sight, and as he increased his advantage going to the Canal Turn his performance was already something very special: Liverpool clearly held no terrors for Crisp, and by the Chair fence in front of the stands at the end of the first circuit he was a good twenty lengths in front of his pursuers. He strode out into the country for the second circuit, jumped brilliantly over the five fences before Bechers, then swept over Bechers itself (see page 106) and after the Canal Turn made towards the grandstand still apparently going well within himself. It was an exhibition round, but one of his rivals was not prepared to keep a respectful distance, and as Crisp crossed the Melling Road before lining up the approach to the second last fence it became apparent that Brian Fletcher on Red Rum was slowly closing the gap. At the second last Crisp still had a very long lead, but his stride was shortening and he was quickly reaching the end of his tether – and all the while Red Rum was scampering closer, full of running. Crisp sent the gorse flying at the last fence and by now it was simply a matter of whether he could last home, for Red Rum was gaining inexorably with every stride. Approaching the Elbow, where the runners veer off the main Grand National course towards the winning post, Crisp appeared to stagger with fatigue. He completely lost his action and had slowed to little more than a trot, but still it seemed he might hang on. Out on his feet, he could not manage it, and Red Rum caught him just before the post.

Red Rum went on to win another two Grand Nationals and become the greatest Liverpool horse of all, but for most people the 1973 race will always be the Crisp Grand National. When the horses next met Crisp enjoyed an easy victory, but that was beside the point. He had put up the most heroic performance ever seen in the National, and had lost. As Peter Bromley said in his radio commentary, 'We will never see another race like that in a hundred years.'

Two Thousand Guineas
Newmarket, 3 May 1980

Few races in recent memory have had quite the sensational impact of the Two Thousand Guineas in 1980, when the French-trained Nureyev won brilliantly, only to be disqualified under the notorious Rule 153 and placed last. He was the first horse in the history of the Two Thousand Guineas to be disqualified after passing the post first and the first disqualified horse in any Classic for over sixty years.

Nureyev was hot favourite for the Two Thousand Guineas after a brilliant trial in the Prix Djebel, but he faced a strong field, including Tyrnavos, who had won the Craven Stakes, Final Straw, winner of the Greenham Stakes, the inexperienced Posse, third in the Greenham, Night Alert, trained by Vincent O'Brien and winner of the Gladness

The 1980 Two Thousand Guineas had the lot – a top-quality field, a thrilling finish, and high drama. The disqualification of Stavros Niarchos's million-dollar colt Nureyev for shoving Posse out of the way over two furlongs out offered proof once again of the old adage: 'All men are equal on the Turf and under it.'

JOHN TYRREL

Stakes, and Known Fact, winner the previous season of the Middle Park Stakes and a promising fourth in the Greenham. Nureyev was clearly the best horse in the race on the day, but his jockey Philippe Paquet, riding initially with blithe confidence, suddenly found himself behind a wall of horses just over two furlongs out and barged his way through, stopping Posse (ridden by Pat Eddery) in his tracks and very nearly bringing him down. Once through, Nureyev had a stirring tussle with Known Fact (Willie Carson) before prevailing by a neck, with the luckless Posse only three quarters of a length further behind. The Stewards deliberated for nearly an hour before disqualifying the French-trained horse and suspending Paquet for reckless riding. Known Fact was awarded the race, with Posse second and Night Alert third. As is often the case with disqualifications under Rule 153, the race sparked off much discussion, though few disagreed with the view that, given the current state of the Rule, the Stewards at Newmarket had to act as they did.

The rules are different in France, but apparently neither Nureyev's owner Stavros Niarchos nor his trainer François Boutin bore any grudge against the English authorities, as they intended to run the horse in the Derby. But he caught a viral chill which prevented his taking part and he never ran again. He was clearly a top-class racehorse and clearly the best horse in the field for the 1980 Two Thousand Guineas; Known Fact, though, turned out to be a very high-class performer in his own right, winning Goodwood's Waterford Crystal Mile and beating Kris in the Queen Elizabeth II Stakes at Ascot.

The finish of the Two Thousand Guineas in 1980: Nureyev is first past the post, with Known Fact (rails) second and Posse third.

Whitbread Gold Cup
Sandown Park, 28 April 1984

The 1984 Whitbread Gold Cup produced what was probably the finest – and certainly the closest – finish to any major steeplechase in the history of the sport. Yet even before the race started it promised to be something special, for on its outcome rested several possibilities: should Ashley House or Lettoch win, Michael Dickinson would be champion trainer for the 1983–84 season, while victory by Plundering would give Fred Winter the title; Diamond Edge, a fine chaser who had won the race in 1979 and 1981, was aiming to score a unique treble and consolidate a remarkable comeback from injury at the age of thirteen, and moreover was giving Fulke Walwyn's jockey Bill Smith his last ride; Special Cargo, who had also returned from a long period of leg injury, was looking to provide the Queen Mother with her most valuable and prestigious triumph; and a win for either Diamond Edge or Special Cargo would give trainer Fulke Walwyn a seventh victory in the race.

Diamond Edge jumping at Sandown Park was always an uplifting sight, and he made much of the running. But three fences out Lettoch and Plundering joined him to dispute the lead; Kevin Mooney on Special Cargo was back in sixth and apparently beaten. Approaching the last fence Lettoch and Plundering were fighting it out, with Diamond Edge hanging on grimly a little behind and, almost unnoticed, Special Cargo beginning to rally (see page 107). This is how Graham Goode called the remarkable closing stages for television viewers:

> They've got one to jump in the Whitbread! And there's nothing to choose between Plundering and Lettoch – very little to choose between the two, Plundering on the near side, Lettoch on the far side. At the last – they took it

When I kick the bucket, the 1984 Whitbread is the one race I want to be remembered for having called.

GRAHAM GOODE

The photo finish for the 1984 Whitbread Gold Cup: Special Cargo (far side) beats Lettoch by a short head, with Diamond Edge the same distance away third. Plundering is fourth.

together, landed together – with Diamond Edge racing in between these horses again! It's Plundering, Lettoch, Diamond Edge rallying, Special Cargo coming with a run – and Diamond Edge is coming through – Diamond Edge just coming through to shade Lettoch – Special Cargo finishing well – a three-way photo in the Whitbread!! What a fantastic finish – Diamond Edge, Special Cargo and Lettoch, these three in a photo. And Kevin Mooney thinks that he's won on Special Cargo, giving a victory salute. . . . You'd have to travel a million miles to see a better race . . .

Kevin Mooney was right. Special Cargo had got up on the line to pip Lettoch by a short head, with Diamond Edge another short head away in third and Plundering a length and a half back in fourth. John Oaksey, commenting on the television replay, gave the verdict of everyone who saw the race: 'I honestly have never seen a finish as exciting as this.'

Tote Cheltenham Gold Cup
Cheltenham, 13 March 1986

Dawn Run, Wayward Lad, Forgive 'N Forget and Run And Skip. What a race! I can still recall its finish vividly and I still remember trembling in its glorious aftermath.

JIM MCGRATH

Few occasions in racing history have matched the day when Dawn Run became the first horse to add triumph in the Cheltenham Gold Cup to victory in the Champion Hurdle. This grand Irish mare had taken the hurdling crown at 5–4 on in 1984, but she had not found the transition to the larger obstacles easy, and the Gold Cup was only her fifth race over steeplechase fences. Her last outing before the race had been a disaster: she unshipped Tony Mullins at the final open ditch of a chase at Cheltenham in January. Jonjo O'Neill (who had won the Champion Hurdle on her) replaced Mullins in the Gold Cup, for which she started 15–8 favourite. Her main rivals were the 1985 winner Forgive 'N Forget, Combs Ditch, the front-running Run And Skip, and Wayward Lad, who had won the King George VI Chase at Kempton Park three times and was the third of Michael Dickinson's first five home in the 1983 Gold Cup.

Of the five principals only Combs Ditch was not in contention as they swept down the hill towards the third last fence, but the fast pace which Dawn Run had set in the earlier part of the race looked like taking its toll as she was joined by the more experienced Wayward Lad, Run And Skip and Forgive 'N Forget. Rounding the final turn all four had a chance, and O'Neill conjured a tremendous jump out of the mare at the second last. Run And Skip lost his place and at the last (see page 108) it seemed to be between Wayward Lad and Forgive 'N Forget, but halfway up the run-in Dawn Run started to rally. As she went past Forgive 'N Forget, Wayward Lad was still three lengths up but, dead tired, he started to wander to the left. Spotting this chink of hope, Jonjo O'Neill asked Dawn Run for one final effort, and she slogged on courageously to beat Wayward Lad by a length, with Forgive 'N Forget two and a half lengths further back in third. The scenes which followed are as famous as the race itself, with horse, jockey and connections being mobbed by a delirious crowd as they made their way back to the unsaddling enclosure.

Less than four months after the joyful bedlam of Gold Cup day Dawn Run was dead, killed instantly with a broken neck in the Grande Course de Haies d'Auteuil in Paris on 27 June.

Trusthouse Forte Prix de l'Arc de Triomphe
Longchamp, 5 October 1986

Dancing Brave's sprint up the Longchamp straight to grab the 1986 Arc was one of the most inspiring sights which the British racing fan has had in the last two decades. For not since Mill Reef in 1971 had a British horse delivered such a performance against the cream of the rest of Europe in the continent's most prestigious race. By winning in the manner he did, Dancing Brave announced himself one of the great horses of the age.

Fifteen runners went to post for the Arc, with the usual huge British contingent at Longchamp backing Dancing Brave down to 11–10 favourite. Second favourite was Bering, who had won the Prix du Jockey-Club Lancia (French Derby), and among the other runners were the German Derby winner Acatenango, who had won his previous twelve races, the 'Iron Lady' Triptych, fresh from a close third in the Phoenix Champion Stakes, and the Aga Khan's Shardari, winner of the Matchmaker International at York. There was also Shahrastani, with whom Dancing Brave had clashed twice earlier that season – in the Derby, when Dancing Brave's ultra-late surge failed by half a length to pin back Shahrastani and Walter Swinburn, and in the King George VI and Queen Elizabeth Diamond Stakes, where Dancing Brave had taken emphatic revenge. He had also won the Two Thousand Guineas and the Eclipse Stakes. This was some season: the Arc would put him into the super-league.

And he was not found wanting. As usual there was a fierce early pace, but Pat Eddery on Dancing Brave was in no hurry. At the turn into the straight he was four from the back, and two furlongs out Shardari took the lead, only to be challenged by a rapidly accelerating Bering. Then Dancing Brave appeared on the outside (see pages 104–5), surging past his rivals with an electrifying burst of speed to win going away from Bering, with Triptych running on to take third, a short head in front of Shahrastani. The official verdict of one and a half lengths seriously undervalued the distance by which Dancing Brave beat Bering, but measurement apart it was an extraordinary effort at the end of such a testing race, and will linger in the memory long after the horse's subsequent disappointment in the Breeders' Cup Turf has been forgiven and forgotten.

Pat Eddery's ride on Dancing Brave was the most daring and most brilliant closing manoeuvre ever filmed. Turning into the Longchamp straight Pat had five Classic winners in front of him queueing up to sprint. With quite incredible nerve Pat let them commit themselves and then devastatingly trumped all their aces by getting Dancing Brave to put in the fastest finish in the whole Arc story.

BROUGH SCOTT

Three Chimneys Dewhurst Stakes
Newmarket, 14 October 1988

The Dewhurst Stakes, run over seven furlongs on the Friday of the big Newmarket meeting which features the Cesarewitch and the Champion Stakes on the Saturday, has long been the most significant two-year-old race of the Flat season. It rarely attracts a large field, and in 1988 only six runners went to post. Favourite at 6–4 was Prince Of Dance, trained by Major Dick Hern and ridden by Willie Carson. The first offspring of the 1983 Oaks winner Sun Princess, he had been an impressive winner of his previous three races (though he had had one victory removed from him when he was found not to have met the qualifications for

Two very good, very tough horses battling out the finish of the top two-year-old race of the season and proving inseparable: neither deserved to lose and neither did – a very good result.

JOHN FRANCOME

entry). The outsider of the six was Scenic, trained by Barry Hills for Sheikh Mohammed and ridden by Hills's son Michael. Scenic had won two of his previous three races but started in the Dewhurst the rank outsider at 33–1 (he had even touched 50–1). Samoan led until the final two furlongs, when Scenic took up the running as Prince Of Dance began to challenge. As they entered the final furlong Prince Of Dance took a narrow lead, but Scenic would not give up, and though he drifted to his left under extreme pressure and seemed to push Prince Of Dance out of his rhythm, he battled on resolutely and refused to give

DOPING

With techniques for the detection of proscribed drugs in a racehorse's system becoming ever more sophisticated, the likelihood of a horse being deliberately doped – either to win or to lose – is becoming increasingly remote: in 1989 just sixteen tests carried out on horses in Britain proved positive. Most horses (but not all) that win a race in Britain are subjected to routine tests (usually of urine) in the course sampling unit, and the specimens are sent to the Horseracing Forensic Laboratory in Newmarket for analysis: not until a horse's specimen has been cleared will the prize money for the race be released to the connections. In addition, the course Stewards may order a dope test to be carried out on any other horse in a race, often one which runs inexplicably badly. A notable example was Playschool, who ran dismally when favourite for the 1988 Cheltenham Gold Cup: many people suspected that he had been 'got at' or 'nobbled', but the dope test proved negative.

Two decades have passed since Alloway Lad was proved to have been doped to lose the Egmont Handicap at Epsom in 1969, and since then there has been no proven case of doping to lose. Normally in such cases suspicion will fall not on those closely connected with the horse (after all, the trainer or lad can ensure that it does not win by much simpler methods than drugs – a bucket of water shortly before the race would stop it quite well): doping to lose is far more likely to come from someone involved in the betting on a race.

Doping to win, or to improve the horse's performance, is a different matter. Highly elaborate monitoring of the specimens ensures that a trainer who allows his charge to be given that little extra something is likely to be found out, though chemistry can be one step ahead of analysis. The Jockey Club Rules state unambiguously that the trainer is responsible for whatever is administered to his horses, and if the proscribed substance finds its way into the horse through a contaminated foodstuff the trainer is nevertheless responsible. Some drugs may be used while a horse is in training – as controlled medication to preserve race fitness – but must not be present in the horse's system when it is racing.

Such drugs include antibiotics and anabolic steroids, and it was the steroid 19 Nortestosterone that was detected in samples taken best to his rival. But Prince Of Dance fought back and at the line they could not be separated (see page 111). Saratogan ran on to be third, half a length behind the dead-heaters. Although the immediate reaction from some quarters was that the form of the race could not be too hot, and Scenic's drifting on to Prince Of Dance had made the latter seem unlucky not to have won outright, it was a superb race: two brave colts battling it out to the line, and neither having to be declared the loser. But the race had a sad postscript: Prince Of Dance was put down in June 1989 after he was found to have cancer of the spine.

from the chaser Cavvies Clown after three races which he won in January 1988. Trainer David Elsworth revealed that he had administered the drug – of great therapeutic use on account of its body-building effects – the previous November on veterinary advice. That is allowable, but it is not allowable for the horse to race when such drugs are present in its system, so Cavvies Clown was disqualified from the three races, and Elsworth was saddled with a hefty fine of £17,500. The horse will almost always be disqualified if a prohibited substance – a list of them is under constant review and is published in the *Racing Calendar* – is found in its system. There have been many famous cases over the last few years: French-trained Trepan lost the Prince of Wales Stakes at Royal Ascot and the Eclipse Stakes at Sandown Park in 1976 after traces of a stimulant were found, and Tied Cottage lost the 1980 Cheltenham Gold Cup after theobromine (one of the stimulants in Trepan) was discovered in his urine; his trainer was exonerated but none the less the horse had to forfeit the race. More recently, the specimen taken from Aliysa after she had won the 1989 Gold Seal Oaks was tested positive: trainer Michael Stoute revealed that the substance detected had been a derivative of camphor, commonly used in the treatment of respiratory infections, sprains and strains, but a prohibited substance nevertheless.

The Aga Khan, owner of Aliysa, also owned Vayrann, whose specimen after he had won the Champion Stakes in 1981 contained traces of a banned steroid. But the Jockey Club was unable to prove that the substance had been *administered* to the horse, and veterinary experts concluded that entires are capable of producing an amount of their own steroids naturally. Vayrann kept the race, and in 1986 the Jockey Club introduced the notion of 'threshold levels', whereby some substances are allowed up to a specified level.

Rules on drugs differ from country to country, and discrepancies are particularly keenly felt when British horses go to race in the USA, where some states allow the use of drugs which are banned in Britain: Butazolidin ('bute'), for instance, which reduces the pain of lameness or arthritis, and Furosemide (Lasix), an anti-coagulant drug used to combat the bursting of blood vessels.

DERBY
DAY

WITH
CHANNEL
FOUR

The brown wire goes to live, the blue to neutral. . . . Part of the eighteen miles of cable needed to send Derby Day around the world.

In the Portakabin, Brough Scott gets last-minute information . . .

. . . while John Oaksey finishes off his colouring . . .

Previous pages:
Derek Thompson interviews Roger Charlton (left) and Khalid Abdullah after Quest For Fame's Derby victory.

'Hey, big fella – how ya doing?' Derek Thompson genially pats the noble head – not of some steaming equine hero in the winner's enclosure but of John Oaksey, huddled against the cold and the rain in the commentary position overlooking the paddock at Epsom. Thommo, the indefatigable roving reporter of the Channel Four Racing team, has been perched on the roof of the commentary position to introduce preview pieces which form part of the build-up to the greatest Flat race in the world, and now pauses to greet Oaksey before hurrying back across to the grandstand to see which celebrities can be wheeled out of the Ever Ready tent for an interview. Back in the paddock commentary box John Oaksey puts the finishing touches to his form notes on the big-race runners. His partner on paddock duty, John Francome, has disappeared momentarily but now reappears, clutching two toasted sandwiches purchased from a booth near the parade ring. Oaksey gratefully accepts one, eager for sustenance to combat the awful weather. Here is the full glamour of being a Channel Four Racing presenter! It is cold, it is wet, it is windy, and the rudimentary scaffolding-and-steel construction from which Oaksey and Francome cast their expert eyes over the runners in the big race offers little comfort against the elements. On any other day their situation would be miserable, but not today. For whatever the weather, this is a very special occasion. It's Derby Day.

Planning the Channel Four Racing coverage of the biggest occasion in the programme's year has been going on for many months, not only to construct the content of the three hours of transmission but to make that transmission technically possible. Some ten weeks before the big day, turf on the racecourse lawns is lifted to allow the installation of some of the eighteen miles of cable needed to produce the sound and pictures which will be carried to sixty-eight countries around the globe. The Derby attracts Channel Four Racing's biggest domestic viewing of the year – between four and five million – and a worldwide audience said to be a hundred times that figure: two million people in Japan will watch the 1990 race live by satellite, as will racegoers at Happy Valley in Hong Kong – as the last event of their evening's entertainment. The figures for the 1989 running included a million in Denmark, 375,000 in Mauritius, 102,000 in Zimbabwe and 54,000 in Canada. In Dubai the reported number of viewers was 276,000, not bad for a country whose official population at the last count (1985) was under 420,000: let's hope they all had a patriotic few *dirham* on Nashwan, owned by Dubai's Minister of Finance, Sheikh Hamdan Al-Maktoum.

In order to bring the race to this huge audience a dozen technical vehicles lumber on to Epsom racecourse the weekend before the big day. They include scanner vans, the mobile control vehicles from which the transmission is directed; the VTR van, where video recordings to be used during the programme are stored and each lined up on one of ten video machines for transfer to the screen at the

```
            B.S. intros

            VT (SOT) FORM GUIDE (Jim McGrath v/o added a.m.)

            MAC

            ROYAL PARTY EN ROUTE TO PADDOCK

            JOCKEYS LEAVING WEIGHING ROOM (on radio camera)
            ─────────────────────────────────
            RADIO CAMERA TO PRESS STAND
            ─────────────────────────────────
            RACE PRELIMS   20" average per horse)

            To include VT (v/o) ENDOSCOPIC SHOTS WHEN ON RAZEEN

            NO VT ARCHIVE CLIPS NOR WINDOWS

            BETTING/MAC

            B.S. (out of vision) intros (sripted)

            PARADE + GRAMS + CAPGEN CRAWL DERBY FACTS

            RAZEEN + TBA CANTER BACK PAST STANDS - J.O. + J.F. v/o

            MAC (window)

            B.S. (out of vision) throws (scripted)

            COMMERCIAL BREAK  3.40 (retain vision + f/x for overseas viewers)

            VT HORSES CROSSING ROAD - B.S. v/o

            BETTING - J.T.

            HORSES AT START

            Inc. VT (SOT) WINDOW MONTAGE

15.45.00    EVER READY DERBY (1m 4f)

            Repaly(s), etc.
            ───────────────────────────────────
            RADIO CAMERA ALONGSIDE WINNER'S CIRCLE THEN LEDGE
            ─  ─  ─  ─────────────────────────────
            S.P.

            B.S. + WINNING JOCKEY

            D.T. + WINNING TRAINER
```

A page of the running order, which choreographs each slot in the programme. Brough Scott provides the introduction to Jim McGrath's form guide: this is on videotape, and Jim's voice-over will have been added that morning. Then to John McCririck for betting news, then to views of the Royal party on the way to the paddock; then the radio camera covers the jockeys leaving the weighing room, after which that camera must move to the press stand for its next shots. The parade for the race will be accompanied by music (provided on 'grams') with a running scroll of Derby facts 'crawling' along the foot of the screen. 'Windows' are the cameo appearances of a presenter or an interviewee in the corner of the screen while the main picture continues to be shown. Brough Scott 'throws' to the commercial break with a scripted (as opposed to an impromptu) few words.

appropriate moment; links vans, housing the technical equipment which brings together all the different elements and which then sends the signal via the Millbank Tower near Westminster to the Central London Switching Centre in British Telecom Tower, from where it is broadcast to domestic television sets and sent by satellite around the world; the 'CapGen' vehicle, the caption tender where the graphics for the programme are compiled; and vans meeting other essential needs: generators, a mobile canteen, and a lavatory block. Once this wagon train has made camp – the majority of the vans huddled together at the back of the temporary stand beyond the Epsom winning post, five others nestled in a hollow of the Downs over towards the Derby start – an army of technicians starts to fit it all together.

. . . and John McCririck searches out the Derby stats, as production assistant Jane Garrod makes final amendments to the day's schedule.

John Francome and Jim McGrath
discuss the Derby form.

In the CapGen van Sue Nicolle (left)
and Dinah Quinnen check through the
running order . . .

. . . and John Tyrrel chronicles the
betting moves.

In the VTR van Jane Garrod and
associate producer Mark Jackson
confirm the list of recordings to be
used through the afternoon.

It takes nearly 150 people on the course to bring viewers the Derby coverage. Twelve production staff are headed by executive producer Andrew Franklin, who will command the transmission from the main scanner van; seven presenters are on duty; and there are some 130 technical staff – two floor managers, vision mixers, cameramen, sound-men, riggers, drivers – supplied by Thames Television. (Channel Four Racing is based in the South Bank Television Centre in London, but the production crew for each meeting comes from the local region: so Thames covers Epsom, London Weekend Television a Saturday at Kempton, Yorkshire Television covers Doncaster, and so on.)

On Tuesday afternoon, the day before the Derby, the whole team gets together to confirm that everything is in place: presenters check their positions, technicians ensure that all connections between the different elements of this highly complex operation are working smoothly, cameramen go to their positions to show the programme's senior director Bob Gardam, snug in his scanner van, the range and direction of the pictures he will be receiving. Twenty-one cameras will be used, including one on a 150-foot crane and two remotely-controlled mini-cameras situated on top of the starting stalls. The Derby start is a key element of the excitement of the race, and the other director Doug Hammond controls detailed coverage of the start from the scanner van over on the Downs. As the technical run-through proceeds, the commentators continue their own preparations: Graham Goode arrives to check out his booth, perched precariously on top of the stand, John Oaksey records voice-overs, John Tyrrel masterminds the compilation of the captions, Brough Scott finalizes the script for his links.

At ten o'clock that evening Channel Four is to broadcast a Derby preview, and Brough goes out to the one-and-a-half-mile start to record the opening shots. Technical hitches demand several takes, but eventually the slot is recorded, and off go Brough and floor manager Russell Norman to record another at Tattenham Corner, where the wind is beginning to get up, causing other technical niggles. John McCririck, who will also appear on the preview programme, likewise has to record his piece a couple of times, not for technical reasons but because it is felt that his rousing call to punters to make the bookies bleed might be a little strong. 'Tone it down, John!' He does, and the piece is safely in the can.

By the end of Tuesday afternoon everything is deemed to be in order. The presenters have finished their preparations and departed, the technical equipment has passed muster and the vans are locked for the night. Meanwhile, a member of the racecourse staff is putting the finishing touch to Epsom's preparations for its greatest day by removing the signs offering free racecards. They'll cost a quid tomorrow!

Derby Day itself dawns dull but dry, though the forecast suggests that the weather will have deteriorated significantly by the time of the big race. Throughout the morning, during which the Channel Four Racing team provides live inserts on the build-up to the big race for

Channel Four Daily, TV-am and the ITV network, the cramped Portakabin which constitutes the presenters' base is a hive of activity. John McCririck, resplendent in his morning suit and a brocade waistcoat the design of which would not look out of place in a rococo Italian church, sits in one corner compiling his statistical nuggets while the Noble Lord continues to enter the colours of each runner on to his racecard – an essential task for any commentator. John Oaksey uses printed stickers which he colours in, but Graham Goode prefers to lock the colours into his memory by drawing them freehand on large sheets of paper: his Derby card is reproduced on page 110. Although he will spend the whole afternoon in his booth on top of the stand, Graham too wears morning dress, for his route there leads through the Club Enclosure, and this is Derby Day. The same sartorial requirement extends to the floor managers who will accompany presenters Brough Scott and Derek Thompson at their different positions around the course.

On more normal Channel Four Racing days the transmission is preceded by a conference at which Andrew Franklin takes the team through the running order for that day's programme, but for Derby Day the sequence has been decided well in advance and each presenter will know exactly what is required of him, and when.

As transmission time approaches the presenters move off to their respective positions: Graham Goode to his booth on the roof, where college student Chris Jones will assist him by providing an additional set of eyes and ears; John Oaksey and John Francome to their metal box overlooking the paddock; Brough Scott and Derek Thompson to the positions from which they will introduce different segments of the programme and conduct interviews; John McCririck to the betting ring; and John Tyrrel to the CapGen van, from where he gives out results and betting shows. It's crowded in there: at one end of the van sits Jo James, who through one ear receives details of betting and results both from Epsom and from the day's other meeting at Yarmouth, and through the other gets immediate information from John McCririck in the ring, and alongside him are ranged CapGen operators Teresa Wadeson, Sue Nicolle and Dinah Quinnen, preparing the captions which will be shown on the screen. Any sympathy for those spending Derby Day afternoon stuck away inside rather than outside savouring the occasion's unique atmosphere could be spared in 1990, for as the time approaches when the programme will go on the air the weather is rapidly becoming a real killjoy, threatening to put a distinct (and literal) dampener on the traditional notion of Derby Day as a popular celebration. But never mind, this *is* Derby Day, and that extra flow of adrenalin sets all nerves a little more on edge than usual as Bob Gardam's assistant Jane Garrod counts down to the start of transmission. Five, four, three, two, one . . .

Cue Brough. 'Two hundred and ten years since Lord Derby's name was first put to a horse race at Epsom, that one word – Derby – has become part of the dictionary.' The programme is under way, and soon page upon page of the running order is folded back as the time of the big race approaches. Bob Gardam in the scanner van is directing coverage of more than just a horse race, though: he must convey the essence of the event, and he sprays instructions at the cameramen

'Cue Brough!' Bob Gardam (nearest camera) calls the shots in the scanner van. The large screen directly in front of him shows what is actually being transmitted, while the wall of other smaller screens display the pictures coming through from each of the twenty-one cameras situated around the course, as well as material previously recorded or set up as captions. From this gallery of pictures he constructs the programme according to the running order but making due allowance for the unexpected.

In the paddock commentary position, John Oaksey and John Francome fight the elements . . .

. . . and are joined by Jim McGrath (or is it Dick Tracy?) taking shelter from the storm.

TELEVISING RACING

In 1927 the Grand National and the Derby were first broadcast on radio, and in 1931 John Logie Baird experimented with televising the Derby, which the following year was broadcast to an audience in the Metropole cinema in Victoria, London. Live televising of races to domestic receivers first began in 1946, though regular transmissions were only established some time later. In January 1948 the BBC televised three National Hunt races from Sandown Park, and soon afterwards struck deals with Kempton Park and Ascot for regular coverage. When the independent television network was introduced in 1955 television coverage of racing increased, culminating in the 'ITV Seven' in which seven races from two courses were shown each Saturday afternoon.

The ITV mid-week coverage shifted to Channel Four in 1984, and all racing on the independent network has been on Channel Four since late 1985. Channel Four Racing was scheduled in 1990 to show something over eighty days' racing from Britain, and in addition many of the big overseas occasions.

('steady, twelve, where's those helicopters? – five: I want people, five!') and presenters ('stand by, Derek . . . cue Graham . . .'). Brough Scott, Derek Thompson and John McCririck, who speak to camera (without the benefit of autocue), receive Bob's exhortations through discreet earpieces and speak to him through small microphones attached to their jackets; the others are connected to the scanner van through microphone and earphone sets, through which a babel of sound passes for the entire duration of the programme, even to the extent of a presenter receiving urgent instructions while on the air. The Derby Day transmission is not very old before Graham Goode has experience of this, for the running order, however meticulously constructed, cannot take account of the unexpected and dramatic happenings which any race meeting can throw up. The first race on Derby Day 1990 produces drama in the shape of a dog who gleefully gambols along the straight near the winning post while the runners are down at the start. The dog seems to have disappeared by the time the race begins, but as Graham is calling the horses round Tattenham Corner and into the straight it is picked up by another camera – not on air – as it hurtles towards the oncoming runners, courting a horrific accident. This is instantly conveyed along Graham's earphones, and with scarcely a break in his honeyed phrasing he alerts the viewers to the situation even as Bob Gardam brings in a different camera angle to show the impostor hammering up the straight towards the runners. Happily the dog swerves off and disaster is avoided, but the incident has served to show just what the Channel Four Racing team has to be alert to.

As the afternoon progresses the weather gets worse. The rain starts to sweep in horizontally, bringing in the basic but highly irritating technical problem of raindrops on the camera lenses. Brough Scott's hairstyle fights a losing battle with the wind, and Derek Thompson is reduced to getting Roger Moore to hold the umbrella while he conducts the traditional Derby Day interview with Moore and George Hamilton on the lawn outside the hospitality tent of sponsors Ever Ready. John McCririck has The Booby on hand to hold the umbrella over him while he lays into the punters for their lack of serious betting on the big race: 'This is a terrible Derby – there's no money. Why don't *you*' – he pleads to the watching millions – 'come racing, with your pockets laden with readies, to give it to the bookmakers? They're not taking anything here. These miserable punters – nobody's having a bet!' There's the odd minor lapse: Brough provides a short but ringing introduction to the parade, and before the parade sequence with its music starts viewers at home hear, 'Is that the best you can do?', followed by raucous laughter. But John Francome has picked Quest For Fame as the pick of the paddock, and the race itself rises above the muddle of a confused betting market over the last few weeks to produce a rousing performance from Khalid Abdullah's colt. Graham Goode, his box buffeted by the wind, commentates on the Derby partly from what he sees on his monitor and partly from what he sees through his binoculars. After the race winning jockey Pat Eddery is debriefed by Brough Scott, and Derek Thompson has a word with trainer Roger Charlton and a rare interview with owner Abdullah.

As the weather continues to go downhill, so does the behaviour of McCririck. The faithful Booby is still sheltering him with the umbrella as he completes his round-up of the Derby betting and looks forward to Saturday's Oaks, and he turns to embrace her: 'She's absolutely frozen, and she doesn't back horses; she's sensible – she loves her boy!' Over to Brough, who has the appropriate comment: 'Pass the sick-bag, Norman.' But Brough has a problem. The rain is now slanting in at such an awkward angle that within seconds of starting his slot his good looks are blurred out of all recognition. Cue Tyrrel. A reprise of the Derby result and the run-down of winners from the day's two meetings, then back to Brough: the lens has been wiped and his features restored to clarity. Meanwhile Derek Thompson is still acting the stage-door groupie on the lawn outside the Ever Ready tent where the celebrities are whooping it up. Some hardy souls are persuaded to brave the elements and have a few words with him – Babs and Robert Powell (who backed the big winner) and George Cole: looking with wistful envy at the toffs swigging champagne inside the pavilion, Thommo asks Arthur Daley, 'What's it like inside there?'

'Let's take a look at the head-on.' Brough Scott and floor manager Russell Norman study the monitor.

It's better than out here, that's for sure, as John Francome, who has nipped off to the racecourse stables to interview the winning lad Marcus Cleary, would agree. While the soggy tens of thousands on the Downs gather around the spluttering barbecues or shelter in the beer tents, the Channel Four team presents the last race of their coverage, and Derek Thompson announces the result of the special Derby Day picture puzzle: the horse whose name is depicted in Paul Hardman's cartoon is – of course! – Quest For Fame. Brough offers a brief look forward to the next day's Coronation Cup programme and signs off. Run the roller credits over film of the Derby finish, and reach the final item on the running order, timed to the last second: '16.54.45: OUT'. Channel Four Racing is off the air.

But the day's work is not over yet. As the technical staff regroup around the vans for a drink – well deserved after delivering the programme in such foul conditions – some of the presenters have other tasks to complete. Back in the Portakabin, John McCririck is compiling his betting report for the next morning's *Racing Post*. Brough Scott bashes out his own notes on his portable word processor, pausing every now and again to blow the circulation back into frozen fingers.

Wet, windswept and weary revellers squeeze one last taste from Derby Day before making their way to the crush of the train home or the tedium of the traffic jam, but the Channel Four Racing circus is in town for four days, and tomorrow the team will be back.

COME RACING!

'Come racing!'

John McCririck's call alerts television viewers to the betting advantages to be had from being on the course, but there are many other reasons why a trip to the races is such a popular day out, and why racecourse attendances are showing such a marked increase. If you have never been racing or if you go only rarely, these hints might help you plan and enjoy your day.

With the Flat season running from March to November (excluding all-weather racing), and the National Hunt season from late July or early August to the beginning of June (or late May), racing takes place in England most days of the year except Sundays, Good Friday and Christmas Day. Certain Bank Holidays – Easter Monday, August Bank Holiday Monday and Boxing Day – feature a very large number of meetings. The coming week's fixtures are listed in most Sunday newspapers, and complete fixture lists for the year appear regularly in the *Sporting Life* and the *Racing Post*. Or you can phone the course you want to visit. All the national daily papers and most of the major regional papers carry programmes for each meeting, except on the very busy days, when they may omit the lesser cards.

It is often a good idea to take advice from a friend in the know about what sort of meeting you might want to attend. Cheltenham on Gold Cup day could put you off the sport altogether if you dislike huge crowds, queueing for a drink (with very little hope of actually getting to the bar), cold, wind, rain, sleet and other climatic extremities, traffic jams, losing money, and Irish priests. On the other hand, your spirits might soar at the heroics from horse and rider which the day invariably produces, you might thrill to the experience of being among 50,000 devotees – and you might back a few winners. Race meetings are different in predictable ways: at Newmarket you will hardly be able to make anything of the race until the runners enter the final quarter mile, as there is no round course, whereas at Fontwell Park the horses are never very far away. And they are also different in unpredictable ways: fine weather can make all the difference to your enjoyment, and so can backing winners, but neither can be guaranteed.

Your day will certainly be enriched by attending your first meeting in the company of someone who knows about the sport. He or she will be able to explain what is going on and may prevent your making embarrassing pronouncements in public: for instance, the lady whose horrified 'Oh my God, there's a man on the course!' amused a corner of the Members' stand at Cheltenham as the field for one of the big hurdle races at the 1989 Festival meeting lined up had not realized that a course official with a red flag stands a hundred yards or so in front of the runners at the start of every race to wave the field down in the event of a false start. And to have a winning day while your clued-up friend comes out losing could be exquisitely satisfying.

In any case, try to find out what are the attractions of a particular day

Previous pages:
The July Course at Newmarket.

or a particular course, and choose one to suit what you are after – on a scale from being present at a great sporting occasion to having the leisure to see quietly and at close quarters how a race meeting works. Each course has its own ambience: at Ascot and at Newmarket you will not make friends by displaying your tattoos in the Members' Enclosure, while at the smaller meetings the clientele is usually more local and easy-going. Remember that great races – and in particular great horses – attract very big crowds and are not always the ideal introduction, however exciting they may be.

Most racecourses are waking up to the fact that in order to provide a family day out they have to offer some entertainment for the children, and several courses have adventure playgrounds and similar distractions. You can take usually take small children into the enclosures, but bear in mind that it might be difficult to keep a three-year-old happy for several hours simply on the prospect of seeing Salsabil.

Facilities for the disabled are at last being improved, too, with special viewing areas for those confined to wheelchairs now becoming a familiar feature of many enclosures.

You meet the nicest people at the races: Mark Cranham's photograph captures a brief encounter in the unsaddling enclosure after the 1987 Cheltenham Gold Cup.

What to Wear and What to Take (and What to Leave Behind)

Nowadays morning dress is compulsory only in the Royal Enclosure at Royal Ascot and in the Club Enclosure at Epsom on Derby Day. At several courses a man is required to wear a jacket and tie (or jacket and polo-neck jersey) in the Members' Enclosure – though the rules are not always rigorously enforced – and the wearing of jeans (on either male or female legs) might not be popular with gatemen in such enclosures. If in doubt, phone the course before you get dressed. It is very important to dress comfortably and sensibly, as a day's racing can be an energetic affair, and it would be a shame not to watch a steeplechase at Kempton Park from the last fence because you're worried about getting mud – an occupational hazard at most courses – on your best shoes. Contrary to popular opinion the most important part of the racegoer's apparel is not the hat – brown trilby for a man, model of Sydney Opera House for a woman – but the footwear: you will probably be on your feet for several hours and your shoes may suffer a variety of depredations. Galoshes are a good idea for those muddy jumping days in mid-winter.

The key to comfortable dressing for racing is to have enough room in your garb to house the few essentials for a satisfactory day: a pencil or pen; a racing paper; your official racecard (available at the course for a small charge or free); a notebook; binoculars (which can be hired at the course); cash. Bear in mind that at many courses cameras are not permitted in other than the cheap enclosures, and that if you do take a camera on a gloomy day you must disarm the flash, as flash photography will upset horses.

You will not normally be able to take alcohol into the course unless you are stocking the bar in a private box. You might also wish to leave behind any misconceptions about a day at the races being an excuse for an afternoon's binge *al fresco*, and the equally commonly held error that racing is no fun without betting. Certainly it adds spice, but you can have a perfectly enjoyable day without betting at all.

Getting There and Getting In

Aim to arrive at the course at least half an hour before the first race, in order to familiarize yourself with the geography of the enclosures. (If you arrive very early, walk round the course – this is usually allowed – to appreciate its contours and the skill of the jockeys who will be riding on it. To walk the course before a big race can add wonderfully to the build-up of atmosphere and tension.) For big days there are often special race trains, sometimes combining entrance to the course with the train fare in an attractive deal. On very popular days race traffic can be appalling, so allow extra time, and then double the time you've allowed: better to arrive too early and have a leisurely drink while you study the form than seethe in a traffic jam two miles from the course while your fancy in the first race is trotting up. (Parking at many courses is not as plentiful or as efficient as it might be – especially in soggy conditions – and it can pay to park locally and walk a little extra distance: you will also find it easier to get away after the races.)

Never buy a racecard from a wandering seller in the car park: he will have 'marked your card' and will expect payment for his advice. Buy your racecard only from the clearly marked official selling points.

Most racecourses are divided into several enclosures. Top of the range is the Members' Enclosure, for the use of annual members of the course but normally also available to non-members for a daily charge. This charge varies hugely, depending on the course and on the day. To get into the Members' Enclosure at Sandown Park on Whitbread Gold Cup day in 1990 cost £20, while on an ordinary day at Sandown it would cost about half that. (For really major events – such as the Whitbread – courses are now adopting an all-ticket policy in some enclosures in order to prevent overcrowding. Tickets can be booked in advance and none or very few are available on the day. The course will supply details on request.) If you go into Members' you will be given a small cardboard badge which you will need to display each time you return to the enclosure having been away from it. (During the ultra-hot summer of 1976 a man was spotted in the Members' Enclosure at Bath racecourse with his badge attached to the sweaty hairs on his bare chest.) The Members' Enclosure will have the best facilities (though no bookmakers – you'll have to leave the enclosure to frequent them) and the best view of the racing, and often will have exclusive use of good vantage points for parade ring and unsaddling enclosure.

The next enclosure down is normally Tattersalls ('Tatts'), which has access to parade ring and unsaddling enclosure but tends to be further from the winning post than Members'. This is where the main betting ring will be situated, and the entrance charge will be between a half and two thirds of that for a day badge to Members'. Below Tatts comes the Silver Ring (so called because most of the betting in the enclosure used to be in silver rather than in notes), which normally would command no view of parade ring or unsaddling enclosure but which would be correspondingly cheap to get into. There is often a 'course' enclosure where the facilities are somewhat rudimentary and the view very restricted, though there will be a small number of bookmakers betting there. All enclosures normally have Tote facilities. (Note that different courses have a different combination of enclosures: Sandown Park has no Silver Ring, for example.)

Whichever enclosure you opt for, do not watch every race from the same position: try to find different vantage points for different races, and certainly go right down to the rails for at least one race to experience the thrill of the action close up. Watch a race from the main betting ring, and hear how the bookies bet 'in running', altering the odds as the race unfolds. At jump meetings, desert the stands for a race or two and position yourself by a fence or hurdle to get the real flavour of the sport: it is the immediacy of standing by a jump as a field of chasers streams over, birch flying, jockeys urging, hooves pounding, which cannot be properly transmitted by television. The true speed, colour and noise of racing can be appreciated only in the flesh.

Betting

Do not feel you have to bet, any more than you have to quaff champagne or bawl 'Come on, my son!' as the runners swing into the straight. But if you do want to bet, bear in mind that there is no betting tax on bets struck with an on-course bookmaker, whereas an off-course bookmaker would have to tax you 9 or (more probably) 10 per cent on stakes ('tax paid') or on returns. (If you used the on-course betting shop a tax of 6 per cent would be levied, however.)

The bookmaker will display the amount of the minimum stake he will accept (usually £2 or more) and, on a board, the odds he currently offers for each horse in the next race. When you strike a bet with him the odds displayed apply to that bet irrespective of whether they subsequently lengthen or shorten, and he will announce the bet to his clerk as it is made with you. Thus if you wish to have £5 on Nashwan to win and he is displaying Nashwan at 3–1 you should approach him with your fiver and say '£5 to win, Nashwan'; he will announce '£15 to £5 Nashwan' to his clerk, to whom he will also announce the number printed on a coloured card which he will give you. (If he has rubbed off the '3' against Nashwan's name on his board by the time you get to him you will not be able to bet at that price.) The card is your record of the bet, and it is wise to make a note on the card of the transaction (in case you find yourself at the end of the afternoon with several cards and you can't remember which is a winning one). When Nashwan wins you return to the bookmaker (after 'weighed in' has been announced, though most bookmakers will settle sooner if the result is obviously clear cut), and give him the card; he announces the number to his clerk, who tells him what the bet was. He then gives you £20 (your winnings plus your stake). In case of any dispute arising an official visits the ring after each race to arbitrate.

Among the boons of being on course among the bookmakers is that you can bet 'in running' – that is, a bookmaker will not stop taking bets after the race has started but will continue to offer odds based on his reading of what is happening in the race. Many course bookmakers will also offer odds on the outcome of a photo finish or a Stewards' Enquiry. But the great joy of betting on course (beyond the absence of tax) is that by watching carefully how the betting market is moving you can 'beat the book' by taking a price longer that that at which the horse will start. (For more details, see the chapter on betting.)

Never mind the freebie comforts of the hospitality tent – get in the thick of it to enjoy a day's racing to the full – even if tic-tac goes over your head. Hardy racegoers at Cheltenham in November 1989.

A modern racecard. The card for the Guardian Classic Trial at Sandown Park on 28 April 1990 shows how far the information provided in the racecards at the top courses has improved in recent years, especially in the provision of a brief form guide to each horse, highly useful to the non-specialist student of form. The card gives the conditions of the race (and indicates the part of the course over which it will be run), the number of entries and the prize money (for an explanation of how this is calculated, see page 64); 'A' and 'E' at the end of the conditions are abbreviations used in the Jockey Club's programme book, 'A' indicating that apprentice allowances may not be claimed in this race and 'E' that entries for horses trained in Belgium, Germany, Denmark, Norway, France, Italy and Sweden may be made to the respective Turf authorities in those countries; 'SS' indicates that the race will be started from starting stalls. For each horse is given: the number it will carry; its name, trainer, weight it is set to carry, draw, breeding, owner, colours, jockey, breeder and form summary; the form figures and abbreviations to the left of each horse's listing are explained on page 142. After the list of runners follow the standard time, a guide to the starting prices, details of last year's result and a reminder about retaining all betting tickets: if in doubt about the wisdom of this advice, see pages 41-2.

Many first-time racegoers are nervous of encountering the mysteries of wagering with bookmakers and prefer the more anonymous experience of betting with the Tote, 'the Machine' which operates on a pool basis (see page 157). To lay a Tote bet you simply go to one of the many counters situated all over the course and state the nature of your bet, your stake and the number (not name) of the horse – or numbers of the horses. You will be given a ticket which, if successful, you take back to the same or any other Tote counter to exchange for your winnings (plus stake). Tote dividends are declared after each race to a £1 unit and include the stake. Remember that the big difference between a Tote bet and a bet with a bookmaker is that with the former you will not know the exact odds of your horse until the dividend is declared, though screens by the counters will give you the approximate odds at any time, and you can thus work out whether you are likely to do better or worse than bookmakers' prices by betting with the Tote. (Incidentally, if you are celebrating so vigorously that you forget to collect by the end of the day, don't throw away your ticket: you can send it in to the Tote and they will send you your winnings by post.)

It is wise to decide in advance how much you are prepared to lose – and not to exceed your limit. The best attitude to take towards betting on a racecourse is simply that it is part of the cost of your fun: so winnings are a bonus and losses just a part of the overall cost of the day. Resist the temptation to chase losses and plunge in the 'Getting Out Stakes' – the last race on the card when embattled punters try to recoup their losses. There is always another day, always another good thing to bet on.

Making the Most of it

A day at the races can be an absorbing experience, and to get the most out of it you should be prepared to move around a good deal and witness every aspect of the sport at as close quarters as is practical and permissible. Go to the pre-parade ring, where the horses walk round before being saddled: you will pick up valuable clues to the well-being and temperament of the runners. Watch them being saddled, in boxes by the pre-parade ring, and see how they become keyed up as the saddle is put on. Then to the parade ring, to study the runners in more detail and assess whether your fancy looks the part: watch it canter down to the start, then nip off to have your bet, and then find a good place in the stand. After the race you rush off to witness the return of the victorious horse to the unsaddling enclosure – the most emotional moment of all the events surrounding the race itself, and marvellous to be part of if welcoming Desert Orchid after winning the Whitbread in 1988 or Nashwan after his Guineas. Watch the condition not only of the winner but of the placed horses: have they had an easy or a hard race? And the demeanour of the connections of beaten horses can be instructive: are they annoyed at not winning, or pleased with a performance which promises greater things next time out? (Reach for that notebook.) This is the time to keep your ears open: try to catch what the jockeys of beaten horses – including those being unsaddled outside the enclosure for the placed horses – are telling the connections, and pick up hints for the future. This is all part of the fascination of racing, and can only be properly experienced on the racecourse itself.

Allow yourself leisure later in the afternoon for a little reflection over a drink and a sandwich (but remember that racecourse food is notoriously expensive). Should your reflection lead to the realization that you have no money left, many courses have banks – or the Secretary will probably cash you a cheque.

Getting out of the racecourse can be no less problematic than getting out on your betting, for several thousand years of human development have failed to find a solution to the problem of how to clear racecourse car parks on even a mildly popular day. Those who try to 'get away quick' from Sandown on Whitbread or Eclipse day might just manage it if they leave before the main event, but often you just have to accept that hundreds of cars all approaching one exit at about the same time are likely to cause a blockage. Time was when you could linger in the bar, watch a re-run of the day's racing on television and indulge in that pleasurably painful activity which ends most days at the races – the exercise of hindsight. By the time you had realized where you'd gone wrong the traffic would have cleared. Nowadays the bars tend to close half an hour after the starting time of the last race.

A day's racing is a busy day, and there is much more to do and to see than many people realize. Even the most ordinary day is a refreshing experience, and occasionally it will turn into one of those very special sporting occasions when you are simply grateful to be able to say, 'I was there.'

Come racing!

INDEX

This index includes all the main subjects and terms covered in the book and the principal horses and people mentioned. Page numbers in bold type refer to definitions or main descriptive entries; numbers in italic refer to illustrations.